A YEAR OF

The Story of Hull Kingston Rovers
2022 Season

Dan Crowther

Copyright © Dan Crowther 2022
All rights reserved

The moral right of the author has been asserted

Photography has been reproduced with the kind permission of Hull KR

The cover and illustrations were designed by Joshua Cameron Firth

Acknowledgements

Thank you to Craig Franklin, Jodie Cunningham, Joshua Cameron Firth, Lesley McNicol, Michael Carter, Nick Halafihi, Paul Lakin, Phil Caplan, Roger Pugh and Trevor Tutu.

INTRODUCTION

When I decided to publish a book about Hull Kingston Rovers during 2021, my pure intention was to document the club's history above anything else. History itself is so important – it's one of my favourite subjects. Without it, we can't learn how cultures, governments, society, technology and so many other things have evolved, plus why and how we can learn from all of it.

In the case of Hull KR, its evolution has to be one of the most fascinating that the sport of rugby league has ever seen. From roving the Victorian streets of 19th century Hull in search of a home, to finding and settling into one before then being kicked out due to a certain other Hull team offering more rent than what Rovers could afford. The story could have ended there. Quite frankly, if it did, then 'Hull Kingston Rovers' would have been a footnote in history; as of 2022, a tale from well over 125 years ago, in a city which would be supporting one rugby team – Hull FC – in this hypothetical scenario. Instead, the 'Robin Redbreasts' inhabited the less industrial and populated East Hull area, refusing to die. They made the eastern side their own, fostering a community spirit and cultivating an institution. They didn't just tackle their bitter, local rivals, but they also became one of the greatest club sides to hail from the British Isles less than a century later.

Through their heroism, 15 men immortalised themselves into the history of this famed club on 3 May 1980, when they defeated the 'old enemy' in front of over 95,000 spectators at one of the most famous stadiums in the whole world, Wembley. Given the history between the two clubs and the fact that the match was contested for what was then the sport's biggest prize, the romanticism was, and still is, unrivalled in a sporting sense. Yet that day was just one proud chapter in a book that kept on growing.

The club knew hard times. In fact, for most of its history, it was faced with adversity. It barely even made the 21st century. If there was one thing that was an ever-present, it was the unbreakable bond between the supporters and the club itself. When Rovers first moved to East Hull, it was largely a downtrodden community seeking hope. They gave it life through the means of purpose and something to look forward to, and by 2000, some of the same community's descendants returned the favour by sticking with Rovers through their hard times. In the end, it paid off and the club eventually found itself in a better place.

It was a good job that Rovers managed to stick around because to date, the 2020s have marked one of the most interesting periods in the history of Hull KR. Since their heady days of the 1980s, the sport had changed. The 1996 advent of Super League led to dominance between a select number of clubs; only four had won the competition's Grand Final since its first staging in 1998. Rovers had returned to the top-flight in 2007 and even briefly dazzled before stagnating on and off the field.

Things eventually fell into place towards the end of 2020 when Paul Lakin returned to Craven Park as the club's chief executive. Lakin was returning with experience from association football, having worked in key commercial roles at Stoke City and Wolverhampton Wanderers. He was inheriting a Rovers on-field department that was headed up by Tony Smith, an Australian whose record as a head coach was very hard to beat in the modern day. In the first season of the Lakin-Smith power structure, Rovers improved to a sixth-place finish; making their first play-off appearance since 2013. It didn't feel like a 'one-off'. Rovers' team was brimming with young talent, most of which had been tied down to long-term contracts. At long last, the club appeared to be heading somewhere.

And that's how this new story starts.

Sporting achievements are never truly appreciated without context, and history also helps to provide context. Unless a person understood the perennial underachievement that Rovers suffered through, then the achievements of those involved at Hull KR in 2021 would be filed under 'unappreciated'. My latest book intends to be another historical resource, providing a contemporary, detailed view on the events that unfolded throughout 2022. It's not just for the enjoyment of the reader in the present, but also for future generations to come.

I would like to thank many people. Firstly, yourself, the reader. A good number of people supported my first book, *The Robin Sings*

Again. It's fantastic to have you on board. I'd like to thank Phil Caplan, whose kindness and will to help me has never gone unappreciated.

I have maintained a direct line of communication with Paul Lakin throughout the time period of writing the book. I have had the pleasure of speaking with Paul about the club's direction on the field, and his confident nature was awe-inspiring to somebody like myself who has long wished for the Robins to be successful again. Craig Franklin is another figure at Hull KR that I have had the pleasure of speaking with. Craig is passionate about storing the Robins' history and is often coming up with fresh ideas to do so. He has also been a tremendous help to myself and this latest entry, and I appreciate that very much.

I want to thank Jodie Cunningham and Trevor Tutu for their contributions to this chronicle. Jodie has been one of the modern-day superstars of women's rugby league during some of its most important years and she greatly enriched this publication. Trevor also enriched it by sharing some anecdotes surrounding his father, Desmond, who turned out to be one of the unlikeliest, yet most famous Rovers fans in history.

Lesley McNicol, who is one of many unsung heroes throughout the club's storied history, was happy to provide a very interesting tale from the late 1960s and I thank her for that. Likewise, another unsung hero and ex-chief executive Nick Halafihi was happy to provide the readers with the inside story on expanding Rovers' business during a time they truly needed it. Thank you, Nick.

I want to thank Michael Carter and club historian Roger Pugh for their assistance. Both have been happy to assist me whenever possible, and it's greatly appreciated. Mike can also be credited with the statistics that you will find in the back matter.

Last but certainly not least, I want to show my appreciation for Joshua Cameron Firth, who has designed the book cover for the second year running. Josh is a very talented artist, and with his improvement rate, the sky is the limit.

I hope you enjoy the book.

Dan Crowther
Hull, East Yorkshire
September 2022

PRE-SEASON	1
FEBRUARY	27
MARCH	43
A WOMEN'S REVOLUTION	69
APRIL	81
MAY	121
THE REBRAND	141
JUNE	155
JULY	171
AUGUST	201
SEPTEMBER	227
EPILOGUE	233

PRE-SEASON

The first major news of pre-season came in the form of assistant coach Danny McGuire committing his future to the club by signing a contract extension on 9 October. McGuire had moved into the role just under a year earlier, aiding head coach Tony Smith alongside David Hodgson and Stanley Gene during the Robins' 2021 campaign. The 38-year-old also held the title of 'Head of Recruitment', combining the role with his job as assistant. Upon the news of his contract extension, it was also announced that McGuire would be relinquishing the recruitment role, effectively fully handing his former responsibilities over to Smith and CEO Paul Lakin. After his retirement in 2019, one could get the feeling that McGuire was on a personal mission to outdo the great Colin Hutton from the point of view of serving the Robins in multiple roles. After all, McGuire up until this point had served as a player, an assistant coach, the Head of Recruitment, a half-backs coach, working with the academy and also had been part of the club's commercial department. The final key role that McGuire could one day fill would be the head coach position. Given his ties with his hometown club Leeds Rhinos, a seed of doubt would always be planted into the supporter base about such a possibility, despite McGuire himself continually talking the Robins up as a club very close to his heart in the time he had spent with them.

The Robins' progressive 2021 season saw the likes of Jordan Abdull and Mikey Lewis come to the fore in terms of their performances and it didn't go unnoticed further afield. On 15 and 16 October, Lewis and Abdull earned their first caps for England and England Knights respectively. Lewis was up first, starting in the halves alongside Huddersfield's Will Pryce in a comprehensive 56-4 victory over Jamaica in Castleford. After showing some early signs of apprehension and nerves, he settled into the game and quickly made his mark by producing all of the qualities that saw him earn a reputation as being one of the country's biggest rising stars. His most notable moment was scoring a try which was similar to the one he scored against Warrington during the 19-0 play-off victory at the back end of 2021. Despite occasional errors that crept into his game, Lewis had a debut to remember and vindicated coach Paul Anderson's choice in rewarding the 20-year-old with his first cap.

On the following day it was Abdull's turn to debut for his country, this time at senior level. Stade Gilbert Brutus was the place where Rovers' Grand Final dream was shattered on 1 October, but just three weeks later, Abdull was back in Perpignan again - this time representing England against France. He started alongside St Helens' Jonny Lomax and was also on kicking duties. It seemed like England were to be in for a comfortable afternoon in part thanks to Abdull's creativity and kicking game as they raced into an early 20-0 lead, but the French outfit got themselves back into the contest after stemming the English tide. In the end, England were 30-10 victors. After the game, Abdull spoke to the local press about his aspirations of being involved in the 2022 World Cup. Describing the experience of his debut as "a bit surreal", he told the *Hull Daily Mail*: 'Whether I get a dig at the World Cup, that's up to him (coach Shaun Wane) but I'd like to say I've given myself every opportunity to finish this year as a potential World Cup player. It just depends on how I can start next season and my form.'

To a certain degree, injuries were a hallmark of the Robins' 2021 season; and as injuries racked up from August onwards, they were one of the key issues in why Rovers couldn't lift the Super League trophy at the back end of the campaign. Those injury issues were still very much prevalent during the winter of 2021; seven players (Ben Crooks, Dean Hadley, Ethan Ryan, Lachlan Coote, Matt Parcell, Matty Storton and Will Dagger) had all undergone surgery after the season's end, and Coote, Crooks and Dagger were touch-and-go in terms of being available for the first competitive game of 2022. One player who was very unlikely to feature was Ethan Ryan, who was set to undergo another wrist operation in mid-November. The 25-year-old, now luckless by nature, had been plagued by wrist issues since he joined the club. He had been a try-scorer supreme at Bradford, bagging 89 tries in 99 appearances, but Ryan had only made 11 appearances in two years after swapping Odsal for Craven Park in late 2019. Still, he had shown Tony Smith enough to reward him with a two-year extension halfway through the previous season.

Away from the field, and thankfully, the operating table, news filtered through on 21 October that star forward George King had penned a four-year contract extension with Hull KR in what was a tremendous piece of business for the club. King was initially doubted by sections of the fans when he first arrived at Rovers at the back end of the 2020 season, but he proved all of his doubters wrong with numerous stellar showings throughout 2021. He had firmly established himself as one of, if not the most influential members of the pack throughout the previous year. With a new season ahead, plus a World Cup at the end of the campaign, 2022 had potential to be the 26-year-old's biggest year in the sport to date.

With rumours swirling around that the club would be sponsored by a 'national' company ahead of 2022, some were disappointed when Connexin - a Hull-based internet provider - was announced as the club's new principal sponsor on 26 October. The disappointment of some was not entirely a reflection on Connexin as a company, but more the fact that some had expected a bigger name, with gambling company Bet365 being touted due to Paul Lakin's connections at his former employers Stoke City.

With the internet now an integral part of everyday life, the city of Hull was unique in Britain as the only place to have just one telecom provider in KCOM. Rovers' new partners, Connexin, first established in 2006, had steadily grown over 15 years and aimed to break the long-lasting KCOM monopoly. Their sponsorship of the Robins was seen as a progressive leap for the company, with CEO and founder Furqan Alamgir describing the club as a 'community institution'.

Just three days later, Rovers' supporters saw even more of the Connexin brand as the club's 2022 home shirt was officially launched. 2022 marked 140 years since the club was founded, and in celebrating their anniversary, Rovers released a jersey that featured a predominant red colour for the second year in succession, but most notably it featured a low blue band, with two white bands on either side of it. It was very similar to the club's 2018 home jersey effort minus the band placement and lack of paint splashing gimmick, which itself was modelled on the original 1883 jersey and its 1983 reincarnation.

A YEAR OF CHANGE

The overall reaction from fans swayed towards the negative side. For some, their goodwill was already tainted by the club's rebrand, and the new shirt only annoyed them further. Others felt that Rovers were failing to establish an identity with their branding due to the chopping and changing of designs over the years. Some even pointed to the likes of Leeds Rhinos and Warrington Wolves as the way to go; those two clubs invariably had very similar looking shirts year-on-year, and these supporters wished that the Robins would stick to their 'traditional' white shirt with a red band look. For many, the aforementioned design was the definitive look for Hull Kingston Rovers. After all, they had played most of their history in that kit and also achieved their most famous day in history up until this point when they conquered Hull FC 10-5 at Wembley in the 1980 Challenge Cup final while wearing the same design. However, when the club first formed, they wore a red shirt with a blue band; the club's 'Robins' nickname emanated from it, too. Their legendary Championship and Premiership double-winning season of 1983-84 was written into the history books while donning the red and blue, as was their subsequent Championship success in 1985. The majority of the supporter base and the wider sporting world associated Hull KR with the white shirt and red band look, classing it as tradition. Yet the red and blue band was equally etched into the memories of many fans of a certain generation too, considering it was ubiquitous during the pinnacle of the club's second golden era.

Weeks after the shirt was released, the club invited a cross section of its fans to provide initial feedback on their 2023 retail merchandise. To qualify, fans would've had to have purchased official merchandise once a season and they would also have to sign a non-disclosure agreement ahead of the process. The process itself would involve the chosen individuals delivering feedback on design packs – which themselves would contain hundreds of ideas. The timing of the invitation was very close to the criticism that Rovers had received over the design of the home shirt, which suggested it was a direct response in terms of avoiding a similar situation in the future.

The 2022 pre-season friendlies would see the Robins travel to Championship outfit Dewsbury Rams, before facing fellow Super League side Huddersfield Giants at Craven Park. Having two pre-season games was definitely an improvement on the previous season considering that they only played one - Castleford to be precise - in Adam Milner's testimonial. The prospect of two fixtures could have served as a platform for Tony Smith to rotate his squad and bed in his new recruits easier, which was a luxury that he didn't have in 2021. The Milner testimonial match accentuated Rovers' defensive weaknesses and they had no time to improve on it in actual matches before being thrown into the proverbial lion's den against Catalans in the first competitive game of that season. It took Smith and his team many weeks to solve their defensive woes.

For the southern hemisphere boys among the Rovers ranks, the build to the pre-season games would feel like home from home as the club announced on 10 November that their pre-season training camp would be taking place in Tenerife. It was the first time that Rovers' pre-season camp would be taking place overseas since January 2018, when the club had just been promoted back to the top-flight after a year in the Championship. A trip abroad didn't materialise during the winter of 2019, while COVID-19 thwarted any chance of one taking place towards the end of 2020. Nevertheless, 2021 itself was a year of positive change and the holiday camp could have been viewed as a reward.

Christmas came early for the Robins' fanbase on 12 November when it was unveiled by the club that Mikey Lewis had signed a new four-year deal. He had only signed a four-year deal as recently as 2019, but if anything, 2021 showed the club how much of a promising talent they had on their hands, as Lewis starred in many eye-catching performances after returning from multiple loan spells in the Championship at York. Speaking to the club's official website, Lewis reflected on 2021 and then looked ahead to 2022: 'It was a rollercoaster all right, to play at one of the greatest stadiums in the world (Wembley with York) was a fantastic feeling and then going 80 minutes close to a Grand Final was a great achievement. But Tony (Smith) has kept me level-headed every step of the way to make sure I'm doing my job to the best I could. I'm very excited for 2022. We've seen a few glimpses of what we can do as a team. With the recruitment we've done, the team we've got, and the injured boys coming back like Elliot (Minchella). It's very exciting, we think we can go that one step further this year and it starts with this pre-season.'

The club broke new ground on 14 November when it revealed that Paula Cullen had become the Robins' first-ever dedicated player welfare officer for the academy and scholarship players. It was a 'first' for a Super League club, and Rovers rightfully pointed out that the appointment came at a crucial time in relation to bedding their youth set-up back into normality after they had spent two years in limbo due to the Coronavirus. They also thanked the Rovers Supporters Group (RSG) for aiding them with the financial package required to create the job role. Speaking on her appointment, Cullen told the club's official website: 'I'm really excited to start the role. It's really important after our younger players have been stuck inside for 18 months away from their rugby with the COVID-19 pandemic. The most important thing is to get these young people back on the pitch supported with a clear 360 welfare profile, identifying what they need from us to thrive. It's a first of its kind in Super League and I'm really excited about it. I've already spoken to some of the lads earlier this week about identifying mental health champions in the teams to build those networks and get players talking if they need to.'

Cullen had an extensive background in mental health, having been a councillor for over 20 years by this point. Based in Beverley, she had spent a large amount of her career dealing with post-traumatic stress disorder in the military, working with sufferers and their families. As well as that, she had worked at family mediation and women's centres, dealing with many mental issues that plagued people in their lives. The move was a commendable new step made by Rovers and had the potential to serve as a catalyst for other Super League clubs to follow suit.

There was to be some player outgoings during mid-November. Three days after the Cullen appointment, young forward Tom Whur rejoined League 1 outfit Rochdale Hornets on a season-long loan. He was dropping into League 1 alongside under-18s player Liam Carr, who left the club to join Hunslet just five days earlier. The third exit was that of Anesu Mudoti, who was released from his contract on 19 November. Mudoti had joined Rovers ahead of the 2020 season alongside four others that were signed directly from Bradford Bulls. The 20-year-old prop struggled with injuries throughout his time at

Craven Park, and it didn't help that the reserves league was cancelled due to the Coronavirus. He subsequently dropped into the third tier, linking up with Keighley Cougars on a two-year deal.

On the same day as Mudoti's release, Hull Kingston Rovers announced that they would be renewing their dual-registration partnership with Dewsbury Rams for 2022. The two sides had already previously agreed to face one another in a pre-season friendly, and the relations between the two clubs were only strengthened by this news. Tony Smith, who revealed that he had a developed a great relationship with Rams coach Lee Greenwood, explained that the arrangement would see Dewsbury players join the Robins' reserve side for game time, while the Rovers players that happened to be on the fringes would drop into the Championship and represent Dewsbury in their bid to break into the Robins' first-team.

21 November saw the official unveiling of the club's new away kit. The shirt itself was predominantly yellow, complimented by a wavey blue band in the central area. But by far the most striking element of the new release was its inner detail. Marketed as 'Icons of Hull', the shirt featured representations of the Humber Bridge, River Hull, Spurn Point Lighthouse, the three coronets of Hull and the BHS Ship Mural (which spelt Hull). At the time of the unveiling, Paul Lakin told the official club website: 'we've said from the start that in our 140th anniversary year we want to use this as an opportunity to look forward and evolve just as much as we want to celebrate the past. From the launch of our new crest, to unveiling 2022 designs that provide modern interpretations of classic designs, to this which celebrates our 140-year link with the city. It allows us to use some new colours not seen before on our away shirt and showcase the area we are proud to call home. It's a fantastic opportunity to promote our city and region, and we know that we are an icon of the city that provides a great platform for our area to a national and worldwide TV audience. So, for our supporters to not only wear our badge on their chest, but have it placed alongside the best of what we have to offer as a region, will be a proud moment, I'm sure.'
The shirt earned much more acclaim than the home shirt ever did, with many supporters praising the design and the marketing campaign. The campaign itself had a lot of dedication and thought put into it; three

players (Dean Hadley, Jordan Abdull and Will Tate) modelled the shirt outside of The Deep, the Humber Bridge and inside Hull Minster respectively. While the shirt typically wouldn't please everybody, the reaction was certainly more positive than the one Rovers received after the unveiling of the home strip.

On the following day, Hull Kingston Rovers received heart-breaking news that former player Asuquo "Zook" Ema had been diagnosed with leukaemia. The 58-year-old made his debut in 1983-84, and went on to make 233 appearances and scored 18 tries; predominantly playing as a prop-forward between 1983 and 1992. To others, he was known as a member of the fire service, given that he had served the local area for three decades.

In response to the saddening news, the club donated Mikey Lewis' playing shirt from his debut season in 2019 to support Ema and his family. In a raffle format, the entrants could pay £5 per number (in which there was a total of 400). By the time the raffle had been finalised, everybody involved had raised a sum of over £1,800. That figure was just a drop in the ocean in terms of how much money was raised for Ema. Over a period of time, various events were set up in and around the city in the hope of raising funds to support a much-loved figure. As ever, the local community could be called upon when one of its own needed help.

Upon the release of the 2022 fixture list, the most notable pieces of news were that Rovers would have to face Hull FC on 15 April and then travel to France to take on newly-promoted Toulouse Olympique just three days later in what felt like a harsh punishment from the rugby league gods. The topic of a Hull derby would be brought up again, as it was revealed that the Robins would be facing Hull at the annual Magic Weekend event at Newcastle United's St James' Park. The Rugby Football League had stuck to their formula of placing the first versus third, second versus fourth, and so on, from the previous season when formatting the fixtures for the event. It would be the first time that the sides would face each other in Newcastle since 2018 - Hull had emerged victorious with a 34-22 win on that occasion.

The club announced the signing of Castleford Tigers' Adam Rusling on a reserve contract for 2022. Rusling, 18, was actually born in Hull but found himself in West Yorkshire before joining the Robins. A half-back by trade, he made his Super League debut halfway through 2021, providing an assist in a game against Salford, but he played the vast majority of his rugby in Castleford's U19s set up throughout the year. Head of Player Development Jason Netherton was pleased about the signing, telling the club's official website: 'Once we found out Adam was available from Castleford, there were conversations from the off on him signing him up. I got him in as soon as I could. I spoke to Paul (Lakin) and we've put Adam on a reserve contract the same as the other six we've signed up already. He's keen to show what he can do. He's going to spend as much time as he possibly can training with the first team and hope to impress the staff and earn himself a full-time contract.'

In yet another unique off-field appointment, Rovers announced on 26 November that PhD researcher Brianna Mulhern had joined the club. The 23-year-old Northern Irish woman was travelling from her home country to undertake the role, while still being part of Ulster University's School of Sport as a PhD researcher in concussion biomechanics. In short, her purpose at Rovers was to begin research which would contribute to improving the safety of the players in the future, as well as the ability to see 'exactly' what they were putting their bodies through during games. For example, the hope for the future would be that if Mulhern was at a game, then she could detect in real time – through the means of data – how and where an impact had occurred as well as its magnitude. It would then give the physio team an opportunity to protect the player by taking them off if need be.

Throughout pre-season, speculation was mounting from within the fanbase that forward Korbin Sims would not be returning to the club. The Australian had flown back to his home country to visit his son, who he hadn't seen since his arrival in England in late 2020. As part of the club's mental health awareness campaign in mid-2021, Sims expressed his anguish at not seeing his boy, and the club granted him a few weeks' leave upon the climax of the season, thus giving birth to speculation that he might not return.

A YEAR OF CHANGE

The rumour and innuendo had also been fuelled by a new rumour that towering NRL forward Dylan Napa had been offered a contract by the club, despite Rovers having no quota spots available at the time. On 4 December, Sims revealed his journey back to Hull through the means of Instagram, when he photographed an aeroplane that he would be boarding on. The news of Sims' imminent journey quelled the immediate speculation, but since he was entering the final year of his two-year contract, it wouldn't be too long until speculation on his future would once again surface.

COVID-19 was a common thread of Hull KR's 2021 season; whether it be game cancellations, financial implications or anything else, the virus ruthlessly conspired against the club as well as many others. On 6 December it reared its ugly head once more, as Rovers' pre-season training camp, based in Tenerife, was deferred due to fears over Coronavirus-related complications. The UK COVID-19 landscape was ever-evolving due to the emergence of variants, and in light of that, plus travelling regulations, the club decided to safeguard their personnel against the possibility of quarantines at such a special time of the year.

The postponement of the planned ten-day trip was the latest addition to Rovers' recent history of pre-season calamities. During the winter of 2018, a floodlight python infamously collapsed onto the Craven Park pitch, just five years after it was first installed at the ground. Luckily nobody was hurt during the incident, but the club's pre-season preparations were heavily impacted. They had to relocate to Hull University for over seven weeks before returning to the stadium. A year later, Rovers had planned to spend three weeks at an RAF station in Lincoln, with Tony Smith hoping for a 'military-style' training regime for his 2020 squad. That fell through due to the club giving the camp too short a notice, and instead they looked to Scarborough as a replacement. In the end, they just spent one night on the North East coast before heading back down to Hull. 2021's pre-season was restrictive game wide due to the pandemic, but the club felt things were going to be different for 2022. Instead, the ghastly virus ensured that it would be another disrupted off-season in terms of preparation.

Rovers replenished their academy numbers further on 7 December when they revealed that Cameron Bellard had successfully earned a contract with the club following a trial. Bellard, 17, drew the attention of club officials after a string of impressive performances while playing for amateur side East Hull. Jason Netherton, who initiated the deal, told the club's website: 'He's been fantastic. We gave Cameron a three-month trial on the back of some great performances for East Hull and he's taken his chance with both hands. He's a real success story for the game, he's not had a scholarship or been in an academy system and we've picked him up. Cam's trained really well, he was the unanimous winner of Trainer of the Month from all of the academy staff which is a first since the academy restarted.'

Danny McGuire added to his ever-growing portfolio of job roles on 13 December when it was announced that he would be becoming the head coach of the club's reserves. The competition had been on a two-year hiatus due to the pandemic and was now returning for the new season. McGuire's selection options would revolve around academy players, fringe first-teamers, reserve part-timers and any Dewsbury players that would pass through what was sure to be a revolving door. McGuire spoke to the club's official website about his new opportunity: 'I'm excited. I suppose it's my first challenge as a coach. It will be really good and I feel there was some missed opportunities for some players last year. It gives lads aged 19-20 the opportunity to play regular rugby league. I've always been a big backer of the academy – I love to see young, local players come through the system and get opportunities. We've got a lot of players putting pressure on some of our senior players and they get a chance to express themselves regularly (with the reserves), it will be a good challenge for them.'

With news relatively quiet ahead of Christmas, it was an interesting time to reflect upon how the bookmakers saw Rovers' chances ahead of 2022. Despite overachieving in 2021, the feeling on the betting floor was that the Robins were due for a mid-table finish in '22. Paddy Power had Rovers down at 25/1 to win the Grand Final, fancying Castleford, Hull FC (both 16/1) and Huddersfield (20/1) with a better chance – despite Tony Smith's men beating all three sides to a play-off berth in the previous season. The club was given an outside chance of repeating their 2021 success of earning a spot in the play-offs, however. Betfred gave them a 7/4 shot; Sky Bet 5/4; Sporting Index

A YEAR OF CHANGE

13/10. The contingent of Castleford, Huddersfield and Hull, as well as the established order, were once again backed for a higher finish.
Even though the bookmakers didn't envisage Rovers in the Old Trafford picture, they didn't foresee a relegation scrap either. Super League's principal sponsors, Betfred, had the Robins down at 12/1 to finish bottom of the pile, with Salford (10/3) and Wakefield (7/2) behind them. Top-flight new boys Toulouse were backed for an instant return to the second tier at 4/5, especially since they hadn't reinvigorated their Championship core with any stand-out signings.

Boxing Day saw the death of famed human rights activist and Nobel Prize winner Desmond Tutu at the age of 90. The news would initially appear to be completely inconsequential from a Rovers perspective, yet in a surprising revelation, Tutu was actually said to be a fan of the club.
His shock Rovers fandom was revealed on Twitter by his son, Trevor. While receiving an outpouring of condolences, one user mentioned that they were from Hull, and in response Trevor said: 'I don't want to worry you, but my dad was a Hull Kingston Rovers supporter. I think he imagined he might get a role as scrumhalf - everybody is allowed their fantasies' Continuing, he said: 'He never even got a trial at Hull KR, but loved the game and the people'
Desmond Tutu previously had history with the city of Hull itself, first visiting in February 1989 when he gave a civic service at Holy Trinity Parish Church. Along with Nelson Mandela, Tutu was a famous anti-apartheid and his service was centred around pressurising the British government to economically sanction South Africa until the country ended the apartheid. His affiliation with Hull had already been set in stone earlier in 1987, when he was awarded the city's Freedom of the City Award; it was given to him in-person during the 1989 visit.
Tutu also drew positive attention to one of Hull's most famous sons, William Wilberforce, a major driving force behind the abolition of slavery during the late 18th century. His second visit to the city in 1999 was even more high-profile: Tutu was rewarded with a Wilberforce Medal – given to individuals who gave a significant contribution to human rights – by Queen Elizabeth II herself at Guildhall.
He visited Hull a further two times. Once in 2005, and the fourth and final time being in 2007 before bowing out from public life in 2010. By that time, he was an official patron for Wilberforce Institute for the

Study of Slavery and Emancipation and once remarked that Wilberforce 'made him proud to be a human' after visiting Wilberforce House.

However, Tutu's association with Hull Kingston Rovers and rugby league itself began during the early 1960s, as his son Trevor explained: 'My father trained as a priest under the tutelage of the monks of the Community of the Resurrection in Rosettenville in Johannesburg, South Africa. They are an order that has its mother house at Mirfield in Yorkshire. When my father first came to the UK in 1962 it was as a student, and for the first couple of weeks when he arrived, the rest of the family was not with him, so he took the opportunity to visit Mirfield. During his stay he must have let out that he had played rugby as a schoolboy, and one of the monks had asked if would he like to go to a match. They must have been talking at cross-purposes, as rugby league is almost unheard of in South Africa, and my father's experience was of playing as a scrum-half in union, but coming from South Africa where if he attended a match, it would have been to sell cold drinks and snacks, the idea of going to a match as a spectator was enticing. The actual experience was even better than its anticipation - nobody threw him out, and they were all so warm and welcoming, so much more outgoing than the people he was going to end up with in the south of England and London. He was completely entranced by what had happened, and ended up supporting Hull KR for the rest of his life even though his actual understanding of some of the rules remained sketchy.'

Although some of league's rules would continue to confuse Tutu at times, his love of the game remained unblemished: 'I think that the experience of seeing his first live game won him over, and the fact that the other supporters welcomed him with open arms played a significant part in his love of the game. The game as it is played, and the commitment to the tackle was also a huge factor. Because he was physically small, he had to commit to the tackle in ways that bigger players do not do in union, so seeing whole teams with that commitment was very attractive to him.'

The days of rugby league's terrestrial television exposure for its club game – which would be making its return in 2022 through the means of a two-year ten game per season deal with Channel 4 – also impacted Tutu's fandom of the sport and illustrated its importance at the same time: 'The biggest part of it was that it was a sport we could share, as the BBC's Grandstand used to show matches in the afternoon on Saturdays, and I could watch with him. At that time, we were not able to watch soccer. Match of the Day came on after my bedtime, so rugby league it was. My suspicion is that Eddie Waring's commentary was also a factor in his affection for the game.'

The legendary Eddie Waring's name evokes memories from British rugby league fans of all backgrounds, but Tutu's too: 'I can remember one match where some forward had been tackled to the ground and had his head rubbed into the mud, and he got up missing his gum-guard, and its lack showed that he had no front teeth at all. The TV cameras took a long slow close-up of him, with mud all over his face, no teeth, and the commentator - I can't swear it was Eddie Waring said, "That's a face only a mother could love." And my father burst into laughter. It became a standing family joke when we saw somebody less good looking than the high standards set by Helen of Troy or Narcissus, to tell each other: "That's a face only a mother could love."'

While Roger Millward would go on to become Tutu's undisputed favourite Rovers player, he also took a shine to a certain Cumbrian forward: 'My father was much taken by one of the forwards, Bill Holliday, whom my father, for obvious reasons, always used to refer to as ''Billy'' Holliday.' Holliday was a no-nonsense forward and Great Britain representative that amassed 145 appearances for the club between 1965 and 1968.

Trevor ended his reflections of his dad's Rovers rugby league memories with a lovely message for the club's fans – present and future: 'I think that he would like the supporters to know, "God loves you", and he would admonish them to "Love one another, so that your love reflects that of God, and allows them to make the world a better place for everyone."' Hull FC fans may have been left hanging in regards to the 'To love one another' admonition, but it's likely that the late Desmond would understand. After all, 'Once a Robin, always a Robin'

With pre-season well underway and the new year welcomed in, everything appeared to be going swimmingly until 3 January when it was announced that star centre Brad Takairangi had been arrested by Humberside Police on suspicion of drink driving. The club's official statement read: 'Hull KR have been made aware by the player and his legal representative of allegations brought against him by Humberside Police. The matter is under review by the club and will be dealt with internally. There will be no further comment at this stage from the club or player.'

It was believed that a number of players had been on a night out, celebrating Korbin Sims' 30th birthday on the night in which the incident occurred. Takairangi, 32, was immediately stood down from training following the news. However, on the following day, Takairangi resumed training. Days later, Tony Smith would publicly address the ordeal, telling the *Hull Daily Mail*: 'Brad has put his hand up about his situation and discussed it openly with the team. He's taken things in the right manner and I've got no problem in terms of people being honest about their actions. He's been very honest and totally up front about everything that happened. We appreciate that. Now it's up to us to pull together and help him. We will. We'll help him in any way we can and he'll help us as well by focusing on his job, his team and his family.'

When referencing the event, *Hull Daily Mail* believed that there was a 'dark cloud hanging over Craven Park', but in the immediate term the biggest dark cloud was an Ormicon-shaped one that was hanging over every stadium in the sport. After a frustrating 2021 for supporters in terms of missing out on attending live games, the possibility of such events repeating itself in 2022 was close to becoming an unwanted reality.

Omicron was the name of a COVID-19 variant that had first surfaced in South Africa in the latter part of the November that had just passed. Throughout August 2021, the COVID case rate in England was diminishing to levels of around 25,000 per day after a late spike at the end of July; the whole time period coincided with the return of live spectators to rugby league matches. However, by late December, cases were spiralling out of control, reaching up to an astonishing 131,698 7-day average basis on 1 January.

The uprise in COVID cases had already ravaged the football calendar in the run-up to the sport's busiest time of the season – Christmas – and there's little doubting that the rugby league authorities would have been looking on with concern that the same might be about to happen to their sport with the new season just over a month away.

Hull Kingston Rovers announced that they would be renewing their kit manufacturing deal with Elite Pro Sports until 2026. The extension, which was announced on 5 January, would see the Doncaster-based firm become the club's second-longest serving manufacturer behind Adidas, who had supplied kits for the Robins between 1976 and 1989.

EPS were originally known as XBlades when they first came on board at the back end of 2016, but changed to their new name in May 2019, and their branding subsequently became 'Oxen' from the 2020 season. Opinions would inevitably be divided on the job that EPS had done in terms of their designs. Their success, however, was undeniable. 2017 was a record-breaking year in terms of merchandise sales for the club, spearheaded by a home shirt that paid homage to the great Roger Millward following his untimely death in the previous year.

In 2019, retail manager Laura George described EPS' time as a 'golden era' for the club from the point of view of shirt designs, as well as the range and quality of the products. Fast forward to 2022, and Paul Lakin had nice words to say about EPS too, telling the club's website: 'We are excited to be working with Oxen for a further four years. The retail industry across all sectors has of course seen massive disruption in recent years and we're grateful to the guidance and support Elite Pro Sports have given us to navigate through this. We are therefore pleased that we are able to announce this extended partnership on the back of both the new home and away shirts outstripping 2021 sales to date. The modernised branding, we launched ahead of 2022, has given the club a big lift across retail, with so much more flexibility and creativity now available to us. We look forward to working with Oxen to see where this can take us to over the coming seasons. The improved terms of the deal will also allow us to combat market inflation and fix prices for supporters as much as possible, whilst maintaining the quality of product that Oxen has consistently delivered on.'

It was announced that Shaun Kenny-Dowall and Elliott Minchella would be retained as captain and vice-captain respectively. The news broke on 13 January and was unsurprising. After all, Kenny-Dowall had enjoyed a storming first season as captain, leading by example on and off the field. Minchella, on the other hand, was unfortunate in 2021 after suffering a season-ending ACL injury in what was only his second game of the competitive season. Throughout 2020 he had demonstrated his capability to play at the highest level, despite coming into a disjointed and losing outfit. It naturally brought higher expectations for 2021, but his injury curtailed that campaign. He and the club hoped that the worst was behind him for 2022 and the fact that Tony Smith retained him as his vice-captain displayed faith in abundance.

On 17 January it was announced that Hull College would be stepping down as the principal sponsors of Craven Park. They would be retaining their support of the club in the way of community-based projects and the college also took its place amongst Rovers' platinum sponsorship partners. A part of Paul Lakin's club statement read: 'We are pleased to continue our relationship with Hull College into 2022 and to retain them as our new West Stand partner. We appreciate priorities and circumstances change, so the mutual decision to evolve the partnership into something different than originally planned has allowed both parties to plan for the upcoming year with clarity.'
Hull College had suffered with concerning financial issues from the 2010s and gained a £54m government bailout package in 2018. Its long-term financial future was still uncertain, which made Lakin's 'circumstances change' wording all the more prominent. The deal was worth £240,000 over a three-year period before Hull College pulled out. The arrangement was signed off in July 2019 – without the college board's consent - when the business itself was still being overseen by regulators and had once again failed to hit its budgeted target income.

A day later, a new principal stadium sponsor stepped forward. East Hull-based multi-disciplined firm Sewell Group were announced, meaning that Rovers' home ground would be known as 'Sewell Group Craven Park'. In a sense it was more useful information for broadcasters and journalists to take note of, since fans of every club would continue to refer to the ground as just 'Craven Park'. What was more important was how much the deal meant to the club after Hull College dropped out. After all, one of Paul Lakin's primary aims when returning to the Robins was to make the club self-sustainable, since Rovers' subsistence relied on Neil Hudgell.

The new arrangement seemed well matched. On the day of the announcement, the club had wasted no time in changing the exterior of the West Stand, changing it from 'Hull College' to 'Sewell Group' Craven Park and one of the signs at the side of the main one read: 'Part of the East Hull community for over 140 years'

Although Sewell's origins lay within Rovers' heartland, company chief Paul Sewell admitted that it had taken 'some time' for Sewell to become involved in the company, but they were finally there. He told the club's website: 'We know the fantastic work Hull KR do in the local area to support and improve the health and wellbeing of the community, through the fantastic schemes they run. We're delighted to be able to support this, and the club, in their journey on the eve of their 140th anniversary.'

Away from the commercial dealings the club would be faced with an injury, as it was announced on the same day that new signing Frankie Halton would be out for a month after sustaining a 2cm tear in his pec muscle during a weightlift session. The setback meant that he would at least be absent for the season opener against Wigan. Regardless of the injury, Halton was still very much on Tony Smith's mind, as he told the Hull Daily Mail: 'As I've said to him, it is going to be a long season. He'll have plenty of opportunities. I'm a bit disappointed for him because he's been one of the really impressive boys and one of our new boys. He wants to make an impression on his start here with us. Unfortunately, that will be a little delayed now.'

The focus would soon shift back onto the club's commercial affairs on 19 January, as Rovers announced an eye-catching deal with American headwear company New Era Cap Company. The agreement would see the firm produce a range of caps, beanie hats and bucket hats, all of which would showcase the club's new crest.

For decades New Era were synonymous with Major League Baseball (MLB), but the early 2010s marked a period in which they began to expand their business. They partnered up with the National Football League (NFL) and the National Basketball Association (NBA) – tying up all three of America's most popular sporting leagues under one portfolio. They ventured a little closer to home in 2015 when they reached an agreement with Manchester United and eventually other football clubs, and then in 2021 they became a merchandise partner for the 2021 Rugby League World Cup before striking a deal with the Robins.

The deal, at least on paper, seemed impressive. After all, New Era were noted across the globe for their quality and designs, creating added quality that the club-designed merchandise couldn't touch. Such high standards would be followed by a high price point, however, with each item priced at £24.99. Regardless, it didn't take long for most of the new products to be cleared off the shelves.

A YEAR OF CHANGE

21/1/2022
Dewsbury Rams vs. Hull Kingston Rovers
Pre-Season Friendly

Dewsbury: Sweeting, Gabriel, Ryder, Greensmith, Graham, Smith, Beharrell, Kidd, Butterworth, Beckett, Walton, Tomlinson, Schofield
Interchanges: Annakin, Peltier, Magrin, Ferguson, Walker, Knowles, Sykes, Turner, Carr

Rovers: Laulu-Togaga'e, Wood, Takairangi, Kenny-Dowall, Hall, Lewis, Abdull, Vete, Litten, Sims, Linnett, Johnson, Storton
Interchanges: Keinhorst, Milnes, Maher, Richards, Garratt, Tate, Cavanaugh, Moore, Okoro, Kirkbright, Wilkinson, Dawson, Rusling

Dewsbury were actually in a better position than Rovers at the start of the 21st century – after all, the Rams had topped the Northern Ford Premiership in 1999 and 2000 after reaping the rewards from top coaching and improved investment. While on the other hand, all the Robins could hope for was a play-off spot back then after coming close to being pushed off the financial precipice at the back end of the 1990s. Now, the situation was completely different: on a clear Friday night, the part-time Dewsbury players would look across the park at their opposite numbers and see a number of internationals – both past and present - as Rovers fielded a strong side for their first pre-season outing. A number of youngsters and new signings would make up the bulk of the bench.

Rustiness was to be expected after 113 days away following their Super League play-off semi-final defeat in Perpignan, but Rovers finally broke Dewsbury's resistance after 15 minutes through Mikey Lewis. After that, the floodgates soon opened: Sam Wood, Albert Vete, Ryan Hall and Jez Litten all went over, but Laulu-Togaga'e's effort just before the hooter was arguably the pick of the bunch. The speedster burnt off the retreating Rams defenders after profiting from a handy Kenny-Dowall offload. Rovers went into the half-time break cruising at 36-0.

The disparity between the two sides would continue into the second half, with Matty Storton, Luis Johnson and Will Tate getting themselves on the scoresheet. At this point, Jordan Abdull had kicked a superb eight out of eight conversions – including some from the sideline. It marked a vast improvement on the goalkicking woes that hindered Rovers throughout 2021.

Dewsbury had their own moments throughout the game, including an excellent 40/20 execution, and they finally got points on the board after back-to-back tries through Schofield and Kidd. By that stage the Rovers side was looking a lot more inexperienced, since Tony Smith handed opportunities to a whole raft of youngsters, giving the experienced pros some respite. A potential arm issue for Korbin Sims in the first half served as a warning sign for potential injuries that could have taken place.

Although Dewsbury had earned themselves a few tries, it would be Rovers who would steal the limelight and have the final say on the proceedings, as Tate scored his second try after galloping over the full length of the pitch to end the game at 60-12 in what was an excellent demonstration of pace and stamina.

There was very little that the coaching staff and squad could grumble about following the test. Despite being without nine first-team players, they produced some of the positive rugby that was integral to their 2021 success; handed opportunity to eight youngsters; and came away largely unscathed apart from Will Maher suffering a fractured eye socket and the Sims scare. At a minimum, Maher was expected to miss the season opener. Laulu-Togaga'e would affectionately be known as 'PLT', a lovely gesture – or a nickname that masked people's inability to pronounce and/or spell Phoenix's real surname on a consistent basis. PLT had one of the strongest showings of the night alongside Sam Wood; both men were the only players to play the full 80 minutes. Wood, 24, was genuinely a strong contender to push for a first-team place for the forthcoming season since Rovers did possess one of the oldest backlines in the entire division, while PLT would have to bide his time since he was behind the likes of Lachlan Coote and Will Dagger at full-back.

Full-Time Score: Dewsbury Rams 12-60 Hull Kingston Rovers
Attendance: 1,822

A YEAR OF CHANGE

30/1/2022
Hull Kingston Rovers vs. Huddersfield Giants
Pre-Season Friendly

Rovers: Dagger, Wood, Takairangi, Kenny-Dowall, Hall, Abdull, Lewis, Vete, Parcell, King, Linnett, Johnson, Storton
Interchanges: Litten, Sims, Keinhorst, Milnes, Richards, Garratt, Tate, Laulu-Togaga'e

Huddersfield: Senior, Ashall-Bott, Wardle, Senior, Golding, Cogger, Lolohea, Lawrence, O'Brien, Trout, Ashworth, Jones, Stevens
Interchanges: McGillvary, Ikahihifo, Rogers, Mason, Rush, Roberts, Roby, Cudjoe, Butler, Wainwright, Dayes

Craven Streat would be having its first run-out of the year, although in a streamlined fashion. 'Storm Malik', as it was known as, was no joke. The fierce storm ran roughshod over not just the UK, but Europe too, claiming human lives, causing damage and effecting people's everyday life. It also led to Craven Park being hit by high winds over the weekend of the game, leading to the club taking measures in preparation for the ground's first game in over four months. The Carling beer tent would be closed due to the inevitable potential issues.

As for the game itself, a step up in opposition meant that Tony Smith would ring in some changes. The vast majority of the youngsters that featured against Dewsbury would drop out altogether, making way for the big guns such as George King and Matt Parcell. On the other side of the field, Ian Watson picked a reasonably inexperienced side compared to Smith, but one that still had enough menace to trouble Rovers.

The opening period showed similarities to the Robins' previous outing as the game remained scoreless, but it was clear that the cobwebs had just about been blown off. Rovers broke the ice on the 14-minute mark, with Ryan Hall benefitting from multiple Huddersfield errors. Parcell, who had started lively, was soon brought back down to earth after missing a one-on-one tackle which led to Huddersfield levelling matters up at the other end.

Scrums had been missing for most of 2020 and throughout 2021 due to Coronavirus concerns, but they were back for 2022 and Rovers' next try was very much a set-piece from the scrum, with Sam Wood getting on the end of a fine piece of play. Rovers then picked an ideal time to score, with Jordan Abdull sending Kane Linnett through with just 40 seconds left until half-time.

As expected, the second half brought a lot of changes for both sides, which disrupted Rovers' flow despite them holding an 18-6 lead. But that didn't stop Shaun Kenny-Dowall and Linnett from linking up to extend the lead to 24-6; Linnett was in for his second try of the game. The Giants then marched their way back into the contest through back-to-back converted tries, but it was the Robins who held on for a 24-18 victory in the second and final pre-season fixture.

It was a mixed game for the playing side. With the result paling into insignificance regardless, Smith would've been happy at the attacking intent and execution that his boys showed, but he would have been less than thrilled at their deficiencies at the other end of the pitch, with the main issue being missed tackles. Still, Smith felt that it was something that his side could fix.

A lot of attention was understandably centered around Rovers' new signings, who themselves were in sparse numbers after a quiet winter. Sam Wood was once again the pick of the bunch, producing a strong display and bagging himself a try. There was some concern expressed around Tom Garratt. The prop clearly needed more time to acclimatize to life as a full-time pro; his lower-league origins were apparent in his run-in style which made life easier for Huddersfield's defence. Although Garratt would rightly be given time, it would still be a concern to some since the 26-year-old was part of the squad depth.

Injuries also surfaced on the consciousness of everybody involved during pre-season and it was no different for this contest, especially when Albert Vete and Will Dagger were seen limping after the warm-ups. It would be later revealed that Vete and Dagger had clashed with one another, with Vete standing on Dagger's foot and rolling his ankle. An omen such as that was enough to frighten any level-headed supporter ahead of a long and hard season ahead, but Vete shook it off and went on to produce a strong showing. Meanwhile, Dagger was also fine and like Vete, would go on to have a strong game. Unfortunately, the same couldn't be said for Luis Johnson. He had suffered a foot injury during the game, damaging his fifth metatarsal.

The Robins would be sweating on the news over his injury, especially with it being the biggest concern of the lot after a day which saw numerous players sustain knocks.

All in all, it was a good run-out for the players, and the fans that paid the admission were treat to a close-run match by the time the final hooter had blown. From then on, all attention and anticipation would turn to the season opener. After all, 2021's success had lifted expectations at Craven Park.

Full-Time Score: Hull Kingston Rovers 24-18 Huddersfield Giants

Attendance: 2,303

While parts of Western Europe and the Robins themselves had already felt the effects of Storm Malik, on the other side of the world, Tonga was suffering from its own issues. The Polynesian country was host to tsunami and volcano disasters after an eruption of an underwater volcano. The eruption caused chaos on the island, with the message to its residents being clear: run. As such, communication was few and far between for Tongan natives. Luckily, Albert Vete had managed to contact his family but many hadn't been so fortunate in doing so. Paying homage to his country in its hour of need, Vete teamed up with Rovers. With the season opener fast approaching, fans could get ten percent off tickets for the game if they used the promo code 'TONGA10'. Rovers would donate the difference on all tickets towards fundraising, helping Tongans rebuild their lives after such a harrowing period of time.

Overall, pre-season brought mixed fortunes. Friendlies are never a true yardstick, but even so, the Robins produced some entertaining rugby - with their most notable period being an annihilation of Dewsbury. Sam Wood's strong showings in both games also whet the appetite of everybody involved. The injuries that took place were rather limited in numbers and not as severe as they could have been.
There was an influx of negatives. The Tenerife cancellation was out of the club's hands, but either way, a hot and sizzling Tenerife would have made for better preparation than the cold and windy surroundings of Northern England. Brad Takairangi's error of judgement was a sideshow that the club could have done without and would no doubt rumble on in the early months of the season. It was also a poor example to set for his younger peers, especially as one of the most senior members of the squad. Although Rovers' injury front could have been worse, they weren't completely unscathed and the setbacks for Frankie Halton and Luis Johnson were unfortunate.

A YEAR OF CHANGE

FEBRUARY

With just a week remaining until the big kick-off against Wigan, Rovers received further disappointing news regarding Luis Johnson. His injury was worse than first feared. The initial timeframe was around six weeks, but after being advised by a medical consultant to go under the knife, Johnson was looking at 12 weeks on the sidelines instead. The injury itself was sustained during the Huddersfield friendly when he slipped after backing up Jordan Abdull. Given that the 22-year-old not only went about his 2021 season diligently, the consensus was that he would have claimed a starting place in the Robins' back row for the Wigan game; especially after starting in both pre-season games.
Since Johnson, Ethan Ryan and Will Maher had all been ruled out of round one, the news that Frankie Halton was making a much speedier recovery than previously anticipated was welcomed. Halton's trademark characteristic of determination was at the fore throughout his recovery process, resulting in Rovers' physio team giving him the green light ahead of the Wigan fixture.

While Lachlan Coote was named as part of the 21-man squad, one man that certainly wouldn't be appearing was Elliott Minchella. On 9 February, it was announced that the club's vice-captain would be temporarily joining Dewsbury, a move that firmly aligned with the purpose of the dual-registration agreement. Minchella had missed both pre-season games after suffering a devastating ACL injury in round two of 2021. With no reserve game taking place during the weekend of the Wigan game, the move presented a strong case of the advantages of the agreement.

Injuries aside, things were looking up for the Robins ahead of their season opener. With Coote being heavily tipped to feature, the side's pivots were all in place. In fact, the halves were arguably Rovers' greatest strength. The club held the proud distinction of being the only Super League side in 2022 to possess an all-English halves line-up, including Rowan Milnes, who was painfully unlucky to be in a set-up that featured two adept halves.

Rovers' supporters had been crying out for the club to sign bigger forwards for many years before 2021. In some ways, their wishes had been granted throughout the years in the form of some bigger forwards that had made their way to Craven Park – most notably Michael Weyman and Mose Masoe in the intervening years between the coaching periods of Justin Morgan and Tony Smith. Yet in spite of 100kg-plus forwards such as those named, it wouldn't be until 2021 when it felt like the wheels had finally turned and the forward pack was capable of mixing it up on a more consistent basis, evidenced by a stronger league finish. George King proved all of his doubters wrong, becoming one of the stand-out forwards heading into his peak years; meanwhile, Albert Vete came packing a lot of size and punch, endearing himself to the supporters with strong performances towards the back end of the season after a troublesome start with fitness and injuries. If Shaun Kenny-Dowall was anything to go by, then the likes of Vete and fellow 2021 recruit Korbin Sims were in for strong second seasons. The additions of the likes of Frankie Halton and Tom Garratt would only increase the size of the forward pack – even if the duo weren't tipped to be first-team ready in the early goings of the campaign.

Things weren't all prim and rosy. The likes of Kenny-Dowall and Kane Linnett had been some of the best imports seen in years, yet time is everybody's common enemy and both men were aged 34 and 33 respectively. Kenny-Dowall's captaincy and Linnett's 2021 Dream Team induction spoke volumes of their importance to Rovers heading into 2022, but at the same time the club had to be looking into longer-term replacements. Even Sims was reaching the end of his two-year contract with no extension in sight amid rumours of a potential return home to be closer to his son.

Perhaps the most important Australian that was also reaching the end of his contract was Tony Smith. When Smith originally signed his three-year contract halfway through 2019, Rovers' Super League status was firmly in the balance. At the time, it was a huge shot in the arm for the club and its fans considering that the prospect of dropping back into the Championship with no permanent head coach in place was daunting to say the least – and from the club's point of view, most replacements would have appeared as a downgrade when compared to Smith. He had since changed the ethos at Rovers, proverbially turning a frown upside down. The thought of losing him would rightfully be perceived as the biggest blow since Paul Lakin had returned to the club, making John Bastian's 2021 departure seem tame in comparison, and it would have certainly dwarfed any blow that people felt from George Lawler's untimely exit. Although Smith had openly admitted to the press that his stint at Craven Park had rejuvenated his passion for the sport after a lacklustre final year at Warrington, nerves would still be jangling until he actually signed on the dotted line. Nonetheless, Danny McGuire was continuing to spread his appeal as a viable succession plan in the event of Smith departing.

The name of the game at Rovers was to restore the club as a great power once more. But any talk of competing for silverware would be fruitless if the side failed to build on its sixth-placed finish from 2021. After all, prior to 2021, the mood around the club was a dour one; accompanied by a cocktail that tasted like never-ending disappointment. It felt like matters were reaching an impasse. The underachievement couldn't continue, and in 2021, it was curbed in favour of a confident and reasonably young side, and then later complemented by a new-look brand altogether. But they had only secured a play-off spot for the first time in eight years. A real foundation is built over a longer period of time and that's something that everybody involved would be hoping to create. The true test had finally arrived…

A YEAR OF CHANGE

10/2/2022
Hull Kingston Rovers vs. Wigan Warriors
Betfred Super League (Round 1)

Rovers: Coote, Wood, Takairangi, Kenny-Dowall, Hall, Abdull, Lewis, Vete, Litten, King, Storton, Linnett, Sims
Interchanges: Parcell, Keinhorst, Richards, Halton

Wigan: Field, Marshall, Pearce-Paul, Thornley, Bibby, Cust, Leuluai, Singleton, Powell, Ellis, Farrell, Bateman, Isa
Interchanges: Hardaker, Mago, Smithies, Byrne

A bumper gate of 9,044 turned up for the season opener and such a strong attendance translated into further profit, with the club setting a new record for matchday retail sales. It wasn't a surprise that fans were willing to dip into their pockets to support the club, especially since so many of them were beaming beforehand; filled with excitement and anticipation for what may lie ahead. An impressive display of fireworks just minutes before kick-off encapsulated the mood and feeling around Craven Park.
Although Rovers had earned the lions share of possession, Wigan went ahead through a try which was presented to them by Sam Wood, who failed to catch the ball after a Cade Cust bomb. It led to Jake Bibby going over, sending Wigan into an early 6-0 lead. The early try quickly quietened the home crowd down after they witnessed such a deflating error, but they shared no sympathy for ex-Robin Iain Thornley, who went off injured. Thornley had left the club in unamicable fashion following the club's 2016 relegation.
Just when a dark part of Rovers' past left the field, a new one lit it up as Mikey Lewis produced a piece of individual magic to deceive the Wigan defensive line with a dummy and then evade them, going over for a much-needed try to lift a crowd that was starting to diminish in atmosphere. Unfortunately, the good feeling didn't last long. Rovers were out at sea when an inspired Cust showed excellent vision with a kick through that exposed wide gaps among the Robins' backline, sending Jai Field in to increase Wigan's advantage.
Wigan's next try came from the other end of the field. The Warriors retrieved the ball after yet another failed Rovers attempt to breach their line, and then some quick hands got the ball over to Liam

Marshall, who had no issue in burning off the retreating defence; exposing a lack of pace in the process. The next try was all too easy. With 500-plus Wigan fans jeering Wood from behind, he once again failed to retrieve a bomb, spilling it, which allowed Bibby in for his second try of the night. With the half-time hooter blowing, the only thing that was keeping Rovers in the game was Wigan's lack of accuracy in front of goal. The Warriors led 18-4.

The second half was similar to the first, as the Robins huffed and puffed but couldn't break down a formidable Wigan defence that had already been forced to make unforeseen changes. After the Warriors withstood more pressure, they turned up at the other end of the field and produced some slick rugby to score again and take the score up to 24-4. With under 20 minutes left, the writing was on the wall. A late, scrappy Matt Parcell try was only a scant consolation, with Wigan emerging as 24-10 winners in the end.

A defeat to Wigan for the Rovers of old would have been fairly routine, yet this one evoked disappointment in spades. Tony Smith had previously spoken of wanting to 'entertain and win', but Rovers did neither on the night. Their attack felt very flat and it was only mirrored by the big attendance – the fans themselves quietened down after the first few minutes of the game. Aside from Lewis' moment of magic, they had very little to cheer. Naturally, a spotlight was placed on Brad Takairangi after his well-publicised off-field incident, and not only that, but the fact that *Sky Sports* pundit Phil Clarke had tipped him for the Man of Steel award, too. Although it was only early doors, Takairangi would have made Clarke wince when he spurned two opportunities which summed up Rovers' lack of execution on the night.

Although Rovers lacked in many areas of their game, it would have been unfair not to commend Wigan on a terrific defensive performance that was the bedrock behind their victory. They shut down Rovers' threats, and even when the Robins began to perk up and improve, the Warriors found a way to keep them at bay. Wigan also managed to disrupt one of Rovers' main strengths in 2021 – their speed at the ruck. Rovers had beaten Wigan away in the previous year with their defence playing a huge part. This time, the Robins had received a lethal dose of their own medicine.

Yet for all of Wigan's efforts, it was still Rovers who were the architects of their own downfall.

Unfortunately, Sam Wood would prove synonymous with Rovers' misfortune on the night due to his two fateful errors which led to two of Wigan's tries. It truly was a nightmare debut for the 24-year-old. Sportsmen and coaches often speak about the anxiety behind the prospect of losing heavily and/or badly underperforming live on television. Regrettably, Wood had underperformed and the game was televised on *Sky* with little competition from other sports. The vast majority of Rovers' fans felt sorry for him, but even so, there was an element that had been affected by the cold East Hull weather. During a moment in the second half, Wood had successfully caught the ball which prompted some ironic jeers from the home fans. The previous events had already made things difficult for Wood, but the ugly situation was only compounded by further abusive comments aimed towards him on social media. Tony Smith had already acknowledged the potential issue, encouraging Wood to stay away from reading the vitriol.

Smith himself wasn't entirely blameless for the defeat. It felt like he had played his hand too quickly, considering that Albert Vete and Korbin Sims were both starting together. The bench lacked firepower, especially compared to Wigan's, which featured two big forwards in Byrne and Mago.

Aside from the on-field woes, Rovers were potentially looking at yet another lay-off for Dean Hadley. The second rower had pulled up during training, presenting Frankie Halton with an opportunity to make his Super League debut; an opportunity he took, performing decently. Elsewhere, Albert Vete was potentially looking at a stint on the sidelines after being placed on report following a challenge on Iain Thornley. Rovers' fans would be more than happy to look the other way at such an incident, but the RFL's disciplinary panel would soon be placing it under a microscope.

Full-Time Score: Hull Kingston Rovers 10-24 Wigan Warriors
Attendance: 9,044
League Position: 10th; 10 points scored; 24 points conceded; -14 points difference; 0 points

14 February marked a day of sorrow on both sides of the River Hull, as it was announced that Johnny Whiteley MBE had passed away at the age of 91.

Being a Hessle Road lad and having enjoyed a decorated career with the Black and Whites as well as overseeing a five-year coaching stint, Whiteley grew to become an all-time legendary figure at Hull FC. Yet in 1970, he crossed the city divide and joined Rovers as their head coach.

During his time as coach, Rovers were in a transitional period; heading out of the swinging sixties and ushering in the 1970s, a decade in which Roger Millward, alongside a raft of home-grown stars, would prosper. Unfortunately, Whiteley would be robbed of some of those stars due to long-term injuries. In spite of that, there was a notable success under 'Gentleman' John. The Robins triumphed against Castleford in the 1972 Yorkshire Cup final, winning 11-7. Later that year, Whiteley tendered his resignation, having grown frustrated at his inability to select the team. Back then, the board of directors had the final say in such matters.

Whiteley would also coach Great Britain twice, leading them to a 1970 Ashes success in Australia which, up until the point of his death, had not been replicated since. Despite leaving the club under a dark cloud, Whiteley was always welcomed back at Craven Park. In fact, he would regularly attend the club's games, enjoying a natter with his former colleague and good friend, Colin Hutton. At the 21 August 2021 Hull derby clash at the MKM Stadium, Whiteley was honoured on the pitch. In what would turn out to be his final farewell to the Hull KR fans, he acknowledged the travelling contingent.

Whiteley gave back to his local community, setting up a working man's club in West Hull, as well as establishing the West Hull amateur club which would later supply the professional sport with top-flight players and others. He once said that 'It's hard to be a part of both East and West Hull unless you're something special' when referring to Clive Sullivan. Well, it was clear that Whiteley was something special, too. He would be sorely missed, but there was no doubt in the mind that some place, somewhere, Whiteley would be watching rugby league from afar alongside Hutton, laughing and debating over some thing or another.

Later that day, Rovers received the news that Albert Vete would be missing their next two games after receiving a grade 'C' ban. The RFL's explanation read: 'Defender uses any part of their body forcefully to twist, bend or otherwise apply pressure to the limb or limbs of an opposing player in a way that involves an unacceptable risk of injury to that player.' It wasn't a surprise that Vete copped a ban, but many still felt it was harsh despite the injury that Thornley sustained as a result of the challenge. Vete was also cautioned for dangerous contact.

Since the Robins had already started the season with a loss, the Vete news signalled that some problems were starting to mount up. Vete was one of Rovers' most important forwards. With Tom Garratt not yet looking first-team ready and Will Maher still not fully recovered after his pre-season injury, Rovers would appear light up front ahead of two big games against Huddersfield and Castleford. Given those two opponents were tipped to be battling Rovers for a play-off spot, one victory, or ideally two out of two seemed essential – even in the early goings of the season.

Just two days before Rovers' game against Huddersfield, Lachlan Coote was the latest player to be added to the sidelines. The 31-year-old had suffered a hamstring issue and would be missing the Huddersfield and Castleford games at a minimum. He had originally been named as part of the 21-man squad on the same day as the injury announcement. Although he didn't pull up any trees in his debut, Coote's absence was sure to be felt and the news also disrupted his rhythm from the point of view of adjusting to his new team, especially considering that he missed both pre-season games.

19/2/2022
Huddersfield Giants vs. Hull Kingston Rovers
Betfred Super League (Round 2)

Huddersfield: Lolohea, McGillvary, Cudjoe, Leutele, Senior, Fages, Russell, Hill, Levi, Trout, McQueen, Jones, Yates
Interchanges: English, Ikahihifo, Greenwood, O'Brien

Rovers: Dagger, Wood, Takairangi, Kenny-Dowall, Hall, Abdull, Lewis, King, Litten, Sims, Hadley, Linnett, Halton
Interchanges: Parcell, Keinhorst, Richards, Garratt

The list of absentees was already starting to mount up, yet nobody could have predicted the bizarre circumstances behind Matty Storton's absence. The second rower, travelling to the game from Keighley, failed to make it to the ground in time on what was a day filled with snow and sleet. He was originally supposed to be part of the starting line-up. Nevertheless, it presented Frankie Halton with an opportunity, likewise for Tom Garratt whom made the bench. Dean Hadley was also making his first appearance in over six months after an injury-ridden end to his 2021 campaign.

The Storton incident showed early potential as a bad omen for Rovers, with Huddersfield starting much brighter on their home turf. The Giants dominated the opening 15 minutes of the game, with sturdy defence from the Robins being the only thing standing between Huddersfield and the try line. Huddersfield finally opened their account through Leroy Cudjoe, who beat Ryan Hall in the air to open up the scoring. The Giants built on their deserved lead with more tries through Luke Yates and Josh Jones. Both tries were too easy and certainly preventable.

As the half-time hooter sounded, the Robins were 16-0 down and looked like a beaten side with 40 minutes still left to play. They resembled a lethargic group of players, and aside from Theo Fages cruelly ankle tapping Kane Linnett, thus denying him a try, there were little signs that suggested Tony Smith's men were going to launch a second half comeback.

Once again outgunned and outnumbered by their Huddersfield counterparts, Rovers conceded another try less than ten minutes into the second half. Tui Lolohea was the surprise courier, given that he could have touched down himself. Instead, he opted to kick through to Jermaine McGillvary who added another four points. After all, no Rovers player was in the vicinity as the game threatened to turn into a rout.

With just over 20 minutes to go, the game looked out of sight – but not out of mind – as Rovers started to display an unflinching attitude, reverting back to 2021 type with expansive play. Their upturn in performance rewarded them with a try through Brad Takairangi; the score was now 20-6 with 20 minutes remaining.

The Robins then continued their assault on Huddersfield's try line, forcing goal-line drop-outs and being held over the line. The natives would have been restless, wondering whether they were watching Huddersfield Giants or Huddersfield Town, as Mikey Lewis showed some silky football skills to control the ball and eventually score a try to make it 20-12 with just six minutes left to play. The enthusiasm from the away end only grew as Chris Hill was sinbinned not long after.

Unfortunately, Rovers once again failed to convert pressure into another try. Instead, Huddersfield had the final say on the game as Chris McQueen scored at the other end of the field to seal an impressive 26-12 win for the home side.

It was another frustrating game for Rovers, although it differed when compared to their first outing. They were lethargic and unimpressive, wilting to a Giants side that reeked of enthusiasm and energy. The manner of the defeat was particularly disappointing since it was likely that if Rovers were to once again challenge for a top-six position, then Huddersfield were among the sides that they should have been competing with. Instead, one would have been forgiven for thinking that it wasn't just Storton that didn't turn up – at least for the first 60 minutes.

Korbin Sims was one of Rovers' few decent performers against Wigan, something that he would take into this game with another solid showing following the speculation that surrounded him in the winter. He had precious little company aside from the likes of George King and Mikey Lewis. Jordan Abdull tried to make things happen, but nothing materialised in another frustrating afternoon for the 26-year-old. Even Matt Parcell – who many would have tipped to have stirred

Rovers following his introduction after 30 minutes – failed to get things going.

One of the few positives was the last 20 minutes. With the pressure somewhat alleviated, Rovers started to produce some good rugby and for one moment, it truly felt like they were about to make a fist of things. Ultimately, the damage had already been done beforehand, but the belief in the away end was indicative of the standard that had suddenly risen up many levels, as well as the quality that Rovers possessed. Plus, they still had plenty of credit in the bank given what they had achieved in 2021.

It wasn't unlimited credit, however, and the Robins had to shape up ahead of what was fast becoming a big home game against Castleford in the following week. The Tigers, now coached by ex-Hull FC boss Lee Radford, had also started with two losses out of two. Some of Rovers' fans were already growing apprehensive at what was rightfully perceived as a slow start by their team; a defeat would have only increased that feeling, making it more widespread. A first win of the season was looking important. If Rovers could perform over the full duration of the match rather than just 20 minutes then it was attainable, yet such a performance still remained to be seen at this early point of the season.

Full-Time Score: Huddersfield Giants 26-12 Hull Kingston Rovers
Attendance: 5,724
League Position: 10th; 22 points scored; 50 points conceded; -28 points difference; 0 points

A YEAR OF CHANGE

25/2/2022
Hull Kingston Rovers vs. Castleford Tigers
Betfred Super League (Round 3)

Rovers: Dagger, Wood, Takairangi, Kenny-Dowall, Hall, Abdull, Lewis, Storton, Parcell, King, Halton, Linnett, Minchella
Interchanges: Litten, Richards, Garratt, Laulu-Togaga'e

Castleford: Evalds, Olpherts, Turner, Fonua, Faraimo, Trueman, O'Brien, Massey, McShane, Griffin, Sutcliffe, Blair, Westerman
Interchanges: Watts, Smith, Matagi, Robb

On a night in which Rovers were looking to earn their first Super League win of the season, they were dealt an early blow when Dean Hadley and Korbin Sims both dropped out due to unspecified injuries. Elliott Minchella and Phoenix Laulu-Togaga'e took their place; the former making his first Rovers appearance for the first time in almost a year, and the latter potentially looking at a top-flight debut. PLT was a contender for the starting full-back position before Will Dagger overcame shoulder issues from the Huddersfield game.

The *Sky Sports* cameras were fixated on two sides that were both looking to avoid a third successive defeat, and the signs were on show early on as both sets of players made errors. It was particularly frustrating for Rovers, since they were seeing most of the ball and were starting to build pressure. Mikey Lewis would launch a looping pass into the electronic boards on the first tackle of a set, thus increasing the ever-growing angst that loomed amongst the home supporters.

Opportunity beckoned for the Robins as Castleford went down to 12 men after ex-Hull FC man Bureta Faraimo hit Dagger late, following a brave take from the full-back. It stirred up chants of 'Dirty black and white bastard!' from the home terraces. Faraimo would then endure more taunting as he was sinbinned by referee Liam Moore. With just over 20 minutes gone, Rovers made sure their advantage counted, as skipper Shaun Kenny-Dowall led from the front, bouncing off multiple Castleford bodies to put Rovers 4-0 ahead.

Things would get much better for the Robins soon afterwards, as Liam Watts joined Faraimo in the sinbin following a late shot on Lewis, reducing the Tigers to 11 men. Thankfully, Lewis later passed a head injury assessment. However, in his absence, Rovers dredged up unpleasant memories of years gone by, as they failed to take advantage of a golden opportunity. Despite playing five minutes of having a two-man advantage over Castleford, they failed to break them down and coughed up errors which led to precious possession for Radford's troops. To rub further salt into the wounds, Cas went ahead despite having one man less – Jordan Turner powered his way through a gap, leaving Dagger and Sam Wood in his wake. With the away side now back to a full complement of players, anxiety grew.

As half-time loomed, both sides went set-for-set and it would be Rovers who earned possession deep into Castleford's half. With two grey shirts swarming him, Brad Takairangi managed to pull off a sublime offload, handing it to Lewis who then did the honours for Wood, who scored in the corner. After the disappointing conclusion to their numerical advantage, Rovers managed to bounce back and led 8-6 as the hooter sounded.

A big turning point in the game took place ten minutes into the second half. Having just received a six again call, Matty Storton faced a wall of Castleford bodies and he laid siege to them, knocking over Joe Westerman, with two defenders finally holding him for the tackle. The moment not only reinforced belief in Storton's ability for both then and the future, but it also lifted the crowd. A bloodied and groggy Westerman could only look on, as Rovers extended their lead during the same set, with Wood producing a tremendous finish in the corner, beating off the attempts of Derrell Olpherts in the process. A fantastic Jordan Abdull sideline conversion was the cherry on top.

Rovers' next try started from in their own half. The running and evasion of Wood caused Castleford many issues, creating space for Lewis who sprinted through a gap; he timed his pass perfectly, handing it to Parcell who then went over, finishing off a well-executed move. In amongst the celebrations was a fresh-faced Laulu-Togaga'e, who had come off the bench.

Smelling tiger blood, Rovers effectively wrapped up the game after Takairangi crashed over near the sticks to extend the lead to 26-6. A gloomy-faced Lee Radford watched on as Faraimo scored a late consolation, finishing the game at 26-10.

Despite securing their first league victory of the season, Rovers were far from at their best which made the win more encouraging in one sense. They clicked in the second half, but it was their defence in both halves that was key in their win. Rovers' victory in the forward battle against a team coached by Radford was especially pleasing, considering that the Robins were missing both of their overseas props in Korbin Sims and Albert Vete. In fact, the trio of Frankie Halton, Greg Richards and Tom Garratt were all playing in the Championship in 2021 – but they certainly didn't look out of place in a night which raised auspicious vibes on the depth that Rovers possessed.

Halton in particular displayed an admirable amount of work rate, and it was already looking like he had the makings of being another valued member of Rovers' engine room. Meanwhile in the front row, George King enjoyed a standout game and continued to show his worth. It was no coincidence that King made the most metres once again (153), while Halton made the most tackles once more with 45 – missing none.

Sam Wood showed mental fortitude by consigning his nightmare debut to the history books after enjoying an excellent display which saw him pick up the home man of the match award. However, the *Sky* version went to Matt Parcell, who was rightfully delighted with his stellar performance which was instrumental in the win. During his post-match interview, Parcell acknowledged that the team had started slow in their first two games – but this win was 'more like it'.

Although it was very early in the season, the outcome signified progress. Rovers had only broken the mould once in 2021 when they finished in the play-offs for the first time since 2013. It was nearly a decade of underachievement, so outsiders should have been forgiven for wondering if Rovers were 'one-season wonders' or not. It was still hard to tell either way, but one thing that was more apparent was Tony Smith's belief in younger English talent. Wood, Lewis, King, Halton, Garratt, Minchella and Storton all flourished in their respective tasks on the night, and best of all, they were all aged either 27 or below. The future had the potential to be a bright one.

Full-Time Score: Hull Kingston Rovers 26-10 Castleford Tigers
Attendance: 7,119
League Position: 8th; 48 points scored; 60 points conceded; -12 points difference; 2 points

The most unfortunate moment of Rovers' 26-10 victory over Castleford was the violence that surfaced in the North Stand towards the end of the second half. Although reports were conflicted, it was generally believed that both Rovers and Castleford supporters clashed in ugly scenes. Many stewards rushed towards the vicinity as punches flew, and most disturbingly, a disabled supporter was almost dragged out of his wheelchair by a set of fans. He was also drenched in alcohol. For what was intended as a 'family game', rugby league was getting dragged into disrepute by mindless thugs. Hooliganism had plagued the sport in the past; especially in the 1970s and 1980s, most notably on 17 April 1981, when a Good Friday Hull derby clash turned into a brick-throwing contest on the terraces of the Boulevard. It was described by then *Hull Daily Mail* reporter John Sexton as 'Hull rugby's darkest hour'.

On the other side of the Pennines, two weeks before Rovers' game with Castleford, a seven-year-old boy was subjected to racist abuse after wearing a Catalans shirt to a game between St Helens and the Dragons. Although the scenes at Craven Park and St Helens didn't eclipse or match the horrid scenes of 1981 and that time period in general, it still had the potential to set an undesirable precedent. Castleford, Rovers and the RFL were all said to be looking into the incident.

A YEAR OF CHANGE

MARCH

The beginning of March brought some bad news from an injury standpoint, with Tony Smith announcing to the press that a stomach bug was lingering around the camp. Five or six of his players were suffering from it and Dean Hadley had missed the 26-10 victory over Castleford because of it. Nevertheless, Smith named a very strong 21-man squad for his side's upcoming game with St Helens. It was almost a full-strength squad, aside from the likes of Ben Crooks, Luis Johnson and Will Maher, who were all still recovering from their injuries.

On the same day, there was better news as Ryan Hall was reintroduced back into the England set-up by coach Shaun Wane. Hall's impressive 2021 form, which saw him bag 16 tries in 20 Super League appearances, had seemingly convinced Wane to include Hall in his training squad. With a World Cup on home soil waiting at the end of the year, Hall needed no further motivation. However, the 34-year-old wouldn't be joined by teammate Jordan Abdull, who missed out on the squad despite being handed his first international cap in the previous October.

2 March saw the possibility of Hull KR ground-sharing with rugby union outfit Doncaster Knights emerge upon the media spotlight. The Knights were topping the RFU Championship with just two games remaining at the time the development occurred, yet despite such promise on the field they were facing troubles away from it. In June 2021, it was agreed that the Gallagher Premiership – the top-flight of English rugby union – would effectively be a closed shop unless the promoted club(s) met the requirements, which primarily centered around their stadia. Doncaster's Castle Park ground held a capacity of around 5,183 with 1,926 seats, which was less than the number required to host top-flight games (10,001), per RFU rules. Doncaster were planning to extend the capacity, but the extension wouldn't be complete until 2022-23 and that's how Craven Park came into the equation.

Craven Park itself was the subject of intense focus after Paul Lakin had revealed that the club were zoning in on a stadium purchase just months prior, and this time it was back under the spotlight. The stadium's capacity was 10,525 (with Craven Streat installed) at the time, making it eligible if the Knights could strike a deal with the Robins. Doncaster Rovers' Eco-Power Stadium would seem like the natural temporary home for Doncaster, but the ground was deemed ineligible due to it being a host of the 2021 Rugby League World Cup. If Rovers and the Knights came to an agreement, then it would be the first time that Rovers had agreed to share Craven Park on a short-to-medium term basis since 2015-16, when local amateur football club Hull United enjoyed a short stint at the stadium.

From stadiums to the courtroom, 3 March brought the serious nature of Brad Takairangi's situation to the attention of everybody concerned with the club. After appearing at Hull Magistrates' Court, the 32-year-old admitted to dangerous driving. On 2 January, Takairangi had driven his car on Hull's A63, having consumed so much alcohol that the proportion of it in his blood had exceeded the prescribed limit (201 milligrams of alcohol in 100 millilitres of blood). While driving his car, he collided with a police vehicle and injured a police officer while doing so.

District Judge Mark Daley informed Takairangi that due to the manner in which he was driving, the incident 'could have been way worse'. As such, Takairangi would be sent to Hull Crown Court for committal for sentence on 31 March. He was also disqualified from driving, with the length of his disqualification to be decided at Crown Court.

Although the situation was always bubbling under the surface despite Tony Smith handing him three consecutive league starts, the news cast further doubt upon Takaraingi's future, given the details of the incident. It was unwelcoming news regardless, but especially since it broke on the eve of a big clash at home to St Helens. A prison sentence would more than likely spell the end of his time with the club, but since everybody was in the dark regarding the outcome, the attention on Takairangi and the club would only grow. The countdown to 31 March had begun...

4/3/2022
Hull Kingston Rovers vs. St Helens
Betfred Super League (Round 4)

Rovers: Coote, Wood, Takairangi, Kenny-Dowall, Hall, Lewis, Abdull, Vete, Parcell, King, Hadley, Halton, Storton
Interchanges: Litten, Sims, Minchella, Dagger

St Helens: Welsby, Hopoate, Hurrell, Percival, Makinson, Lomax, Dodd, Walmsley, Roby, Lees, Mata'utia, Batchelor, Knowles
Interchanges: Lussick, McCarthy-Scarsbrook, Amor, Paasi

Kane Linnett was the only casualty of Rovers' stomach bug dilemma, but arguably the biggest news was that Brad Takairangi was handed another league start following the details of his court case coming to light. Ahead of the visit of the champions, St Helens had won their last ten games against Rovers – a record which stretched back to 2015 – and had won three Super League titles and a Challenge Cup since their last visit to Craven Park which came in 2019.

The only relief that Rovers' fans gained from one of Saints' opening sets was comic. A tackle on Alex Walmsley resulted in the East Stand being treated to a full moon courtesy of Walmsley, whose shorts fell below desired height. In the same set, St Helens went over for their first score of the game through Sione Mata'utia; it was all too easy, with the forward powering through Rovers' defensive line.

Although Saints opened their account early, the Robins stuck to their task amid poor conditions on a rainy night. Both sides were making errors, and as the weather threatened to spoil the game, Konrad Hurrell delivered a late shot on Jordan Abdull, downing Rovers' star man as well as earning himself a ten-minute vacation in the sin bin. After huffing and puffing in the face of a resolute defence, Rovers finally made their breakthrough when Lachlan Coote found Ryan Hall in the corner after an excellent cut-out ball. Prior to this, Coote had been hobbling after receiving a rough reception from his old teammates. He would end up being replaced during the second half.

Despite taking advantage of their opportunity, the Robins looked second best to St Helens on the night. Saints' line speed was admirable, helping them on their way to stifling Rovers' pivots. While

Rovers looked ponderous, St Helens came across as imperious. There was a reason why supporters of other clubs wanted the Merseyside outfit to be shipped off to the NRL, and while some of Saints' aggression matched that of the hundreds of thousands of convicts that Britain had transported to Australia in the 17th and 18th centuries, it was all within the rules. Rovers were genuinely in the arm wrestle at one point, but ten minutes before the hooter, Tony Smith's men conceded three tries and were consequently on the wrong side of the 24-4 scoreline as half-time beckoned.

Things would get much worse. Firstly, Mata'utia would go in for his second after some poor defence. Following that, Jez Litten was sinbinned after being involved in a challenge with Hurrell. Saints followed up with tries from Tommy Makinson and Alex Walmsley. With the game petering out, Frankie Halton – Rovers' strongest performer on the night – bagged himself his first Super League try. It was Saints' night, however. Will Dagger made a mess of a Saints kick, allowing Makinson to grab a hat-trick and finish the game at 42-8.

It was clear to most observers that St Helens were the stand-out team in the division, yet Rovers failed to do themselves justice on an awful night. The Robins had managed to keep up with Saints for a period of 20 minutes or so, but after around the 30-minute mark, Kristian Woolf's men were always on top and the result was only going one way.

The frustrations from supporters were mainly aimed at the club's overseas contingent – namely Brad Takairangi, who did himself no favours on the night with a poor showing. He wasn't alone in that, and it was the likes of him, Albert Vete and Korbin Sims that were questioned. Defeats that come wrapped with a poor performance inevitably draw scepticism with regards to players, and questions were even asked of Tony Smith since he started Takairangi so soon after his off-field affairs. Elsewhere, it appeared that Coote wasn't fit enough to play through the entire game. His second half substitution concerned Smith, since Coote was feeling his hamstring. Takairangi had actually enjoyed a solid game in the week prior against Castleford, scoring and assisting. Smith had faced a dilemma in whether to persist with the centre or not, and he clearly chose to, but decisions over Takairangi were perhaps about to be taken out of Smith's hands depending on the court verdict.

Frankie Halton was one of Rovers' standout performers in a grim night. It was both pleasing and concerning in equal measure. Halton had made 44 tackles with zero misses in a game in which Rovers tackles were missed; his try was the icing on the cake. Still, it was quite a concern that a Super League 'rookie' - only in relative experience rather than performances and statistics - was the Robins' best performer. Most of the other players failed to perform, with the exception of the likes of George King, Matt Parcell and Elliott Minchella who all performed solidly given the circumstances. In the case of King, the times in which he was resting once again led to most of the opposition's tries. That pattern began to occur during 2021 and it was an early worry since nothing had changed.

Up to this point, the Robins had only played one half of good competitive rugby, which came in their second half against Castleford. They had failed to put a full performance together. Although St Helens were very good on the night, they weren't quite at their very best. They nailed the basic requirements in the way of effort and commitment, and Rovers faltered because of it. Rovers' fans were excited ahead of a new season, and rightfully so after the way the side played in the previous year. But so far, they had lost to Wigan and St Helens on home soil and both defeats came in very disappointing fashion. The results simmered expectations somewhat. The season was still very young and there was plenty of rugby to be played. Even so, this game begged many questions: were Rovers as good as the fans thought they were? Perhaps one win from four was just an early blip? The questions would be answered in due course, but on evidence, the stark chasm between the two outfits on the night suggested that Rovers had a long way to go in terms of becoming a top side. With an away trip to Salford approaching, a positive result seemed like the perfect antidote for the growing concern – one win from five would be a sickener.

Full-Time Score: Hull Kingston Rovers 8-42 St Helens
Attendance: 7,256
League Position: 10th; 56 points scored; 102 points conceded; -46 points difference; 2 points

On 8 March, Tony Smith revealed that Brad Takairangi would be stood down until the 32-year-old discovered his court sentence on 31 March. Smith cited factors such as the player welfare and attention generated by the press behind his reasoning. He also admitted that the previous week had been very mentally tough for Takairangi, stating: 'It's been tough, real tough. Real tough. This is his life and it's been turned on its head, through some of his own actions. We're yet to see how long and how much he pays for those bad actions. That's worrying. If he was a serial offender or somebody who does those things on a regular basis... sometimes having a brain explosion, how much damage they do depends. It can be minute differences sometimes that make somebody find out about it or not find out about it. Unfortunately, Brad's is fairly public and he's doing it tough.'

Takairangi would miss two games: Salford (away) and Catalans (home). Depending on his court sentence, it was plausible that the centre had played his final game for the club during the 42-8 defeat against St Helens.

On the same day as the Takairangi news, Smith also revealed that Ben Crooks had been given the green light to return to first-team action. Crooks had largely played on the wing under Smith. If that continued, it would allow Sam Wood to play in his more natural position in the centre since he started all four of Rovers' games on the wing. Kane Linnett, who would also be returning to action against Salford, had played centre for most of his career. But still, it was unlikely that he would be replacing Takairangi in the centre position due to his incredible 2021 success in the second-row which saw him claim a Dream Team spot. Regardless, Smith had decisions to make. For the time being, he was already one player down in squad depth.

11/3/2022
Salford Red Devils vs. Hull Kingston Rovers
Betfred Super League (Round 5)

Salford: Brierley, Sio, Cross, Lafai, Burgess, Croft, Sneyd, Akauola, Ackers, Vuniyayawa, Wright, Greenwood, Addy
Interchanges: Taylor, Lannon, Ormondroyd, Gerrard

Rovers: Dagger, Wood, Keinhorst, Kenny-Dowall, Hall, Lewis, Abdull, Garratt, Parcell, King, Halton, Linnett, Minchella
Interchanges: Vete, Hadley, Storton, Litten

One of the biggest talking points in the build-up to the away trip to Salford concerned team selection. After all, it was the first time that Tony Smith would have to pick a side after Brad Takairangi was stood down. Jimmy Keinhorst, who had earned a contract renewal at the end of 2021, filled his place. Smith also dropped Korbin Sims altogether, since he felt that the 30-year-old hadn't performed well enough in his outing against St Helens. Whether Smith was vindicated in his decision or not would remain to be seen. Either way, it had to be viewed as a brave decision since one of Rovers' high earners and overseas players was missing out due to performance, rather than fitness or injury concerns.

The travelling Rovers faithful were celebrating in the early goings of the match, albeit prematurely. Elliott Minchella thought he had crossed over, but was adjudged to have spilt the ball over the line. Rovers had started strong but failed to make it count in terms of points, and instead Salford came into the game with a mean spell of their own. It was Rovers who would get their noses in front, though. Albert Vete attracted four defenders, and in the next tackle, a Jordan Abdull kick was fumbled in the in-goal area; rather than a two-horse race between a Rovers and Salford player, it was a race between Minchella and George King to touch the ball down. Minchella was believed to be the winner and Rovers were 6-0 ahead. Vete's charge had created chaos for the Salford defence.

Although the Robins had taken the lead and performed better during the first 20-plus minutes of the game, their discipline was once again letting them down, as it had against St Helens. This time, though, they could afford to make more mistakes against weaker opposition. Rovers were clearly beating Salford down the middle, and although the penalties were a cause for concern, Smith's men were still in the ascendency. Salford themselves were suffering from disciplinary issues; with five minutes left of the first half, former Rovers player Ryan Lannon was sinbinned due to constant infringements.

Finally, more pressure paid off as Mikey Lewis sent Matty Storton in to put the side 12-0 up. Then, Lewis assisted himself with a chip and chase, beating another ex-Robin, Ryan Brierley, to the punch to score an excellent solo try in front of the travelling fans. This kind of try from Lewis was now starting to be dubbed as a 'Mikey Lewis special', and it was certainly a special way to end the half with Rovers holding a commanding 18-0 lead. Prior to Lewis' try, former Rovers favourite Ken Sio had spurned a golden opportunity to get Salford back into the game by intercepting a Will Dagger pass, only to stumble over himself at the halfway mark. Both moments appeared to have sealed the destiny of the game.

Salford made the perfect start to the second half proceedings. Dagger produced another error, which led to Sio getting on the scoresheet against his former side. The all-too-familiar, even haunting chants of 'SSSNNEEEYYYYDDD' were heard from the home fans after a successful conversion, but Rovers still had the game in their own hands at 18-6. With both sides battling for a crucial score, it was Salford's Marc Sneyd – an iconic figure behind Hull FC's back-to-back 2016 and 2017 Challenge Cup successes – who came up with a moment of inspiration to bring his side back into the game. A lovely kick found Salford new boy Shane Wright, who went over for the try. Somehow, Sneyd, a notoriously good goal kicker, missed a straightforward conversion which kept the score at 18-10. Although the miss was important, Salford were firmly back in the contest.

Knowing that they were now in a game, Rovers worked hard to try and once again turn the screw on the home side. Positioned near the try-line, Jordan Abdull thought he had sent the ever-impressive Frankie Halton through for a try, but Abdull's face would look on in horror, as Sneyd hooked the ball to make it a second interception for Salford. This time, the Red Devils were desperate to make it count. Sneyd launched a devastating counter-attack, with winger Joe Burgess getting on the end of it. The score was now 18-16 and Rovers were rocking with over 15 minutes left to play.

Again, Rovers worked their way back into Salford territory. It was imperative that they didn't throw this result away and they knew it. Abdull launched a bomb, and after beating Brierley in the air, Halton handed the ball to Lewis who went over under the sticks! It was a crucial score and Rovers played out the remaining nine minutes in a professional manner, even coming close to adding another try. In the end, Abdull kicked over a penalty which made it five out of five for him, and Rovers' second league victory of the season at 26-16 after a BPM-soaring second half.

The most important part of the night was the victory. The 2022 Super League season was still in its early infancy, yet two points felt like a must even at this stage due to the slow start made by the side. Rovers had come up against a decent team that also featured a number of former Robins players – winning wasn't a foregone conclusion, especially since Salford had won two out of their first four league games.

One of the main concerns of the performance was Rovers' lack of discipline. The same issue was prevalent throughout the thorough beating they had taken from St Helens. It needed to be addressed because the top teams would punish them. Salford's opportunity to get back into the game wouldn't have existed had Rovers kept things cleaner, so it served as a warning sign for future games.

Mikey Lewis went a long way in proving why he was one of the hottest young commodities in the competition by inspiring the Robins on their way to victory. In the previous game at St Helens, Lewis endured a torrid night in which he was given rough attention. Rovers were outmatched up and down the pitch during that contest, but in this one it was clear that Tony Smith's side were the alpha, and as a result, Lewis was allowed to shine. His performance brought two tries, two assists (if you included his 'special' in which he assisted himself) and an all-round strong performance.

Elsewhere, Jordan Abdull had a good game. His boot was back to its wicked best, tormenting Ryan Brierley throughout the game. Both of Rovers' halves generally inspired and led the side to victory. In the pack, Tom Garratt took a step further in proving that he was worth a starting place in Super League. He had missed out against St Helens after a solid showing the week before that against Castleford, but once again he took his opportunity well and was a key figure behind Rovers' success in the middle of the pack, alongside his fellow forwards. It was another indication that the Robins had better strength in depth for 2022 – especially since Korbin Sims was dropped altogether for the game.

For fans of a certain vintage, the Robins were either called 'Good old Rovers' or 'Bloody Rovers', dependent on the result on that given day. On this night they had picked up a win, but in the following week they were travelling to Perpignan – a city in which their 2021 Super League Grand Final dream was shattered. In order to exact a modicum of revenge, it would have to be 'good old' Rovers, rather than the 'bloody' sort.

Full-Time Score: Salford Red Devils 16-26 Hull Kingston Rovers
Attendance: 3,950
League Position: 7th; 82 points scored; 118 points conceded; -36 points difference; 4 points

The start of the Robins' Challenge Cup journey was written on 14 March, as they were drawn at home against either Bradford Bulls or Leigh Centurions. The two Championship outfits played against each other later that day, with Leigh edging out the Bulls at Odsal with a 20-16 victory. It meant that Rovers would be playing Leigh for the fourth time in six years and it was also the third Craven Park cup meeting between the two in the space of four years.

Rovers had defeated Leigh in all of the previous encounters, including a 23-10 win at the Leigh Sports Village in 2017 when the Robins were a second-tier outfit after Leigh had replaced them in the top-flight after the previous season. The omens were good, but nonetheless, the Centurions' squad had been revamped under ex-Wigan boss Adrian Lam. At the time of the draw, Leigh were sitting second in the division after a start which saw them win four of their first five games, with the loss coming at fellow promotion challengers Featherstone. It was set to be an interesting challenge, especially when other Super League sides like Hull FC and St Helens had drawn Sheffield and Whitehaven respectively. If Rovers had any aspirations of progressing further in the cup, then they could ill-afford to rest too many players – unlike other clubs.

Any extra revenue from the tie would be limited at best, since Challenge Cup broadcasters BBC, Premier Sports and The Sportsman chose to show other games. However, the club received good news on 15 March. The 21 May clash with Catalans Dragons was to be televised on Channel 4, thus turning it into a 12:30 pm kick-off at Craven Park. It was the first time that Rovers had been selected since Channel 4 gained rights to show Super League action.

The first two games (Leeds vs. Warrington and Hull FC vs. St Helens) had drawn an average viewing figure of 531,000 and 515,000 respectively, which was deemed impressive for a sport that was apparently on the wane. The quality of the coverage and presentation itself had also drawn widespread praise from across the game and now Rovers were about to be dissected by the same broadcasting team in addition to being exposed to the nation.

A YEAR OF CHANGE

18/3/2022
Catalans Dragons vs. Hull Kingston Rovers
Betfred Super League (Round 6)

Catalans: Tomkins, Davies, Whare, Langi, Yaha, Pearce, Drinkwater, McMeeken, McIlorum, Napa, Jullien, Whitley, Garcia
Interchanges: Goudemand, May, Chan, Kasiano

Rovers: Dagger, Wood, Keinhorst, Kenny-Dowall, Hall, Lewis, Abdull, Garratt, Litten, King, Halton, Storton, Minchella
Interchanges: Vete, Sims, Ryan, Richards

In search of back-to-back Super League victories for the first time in 2022, Tony Smith named a forward heavy bench against a Catalans side that was typically packed with sizeable forwards. The anomaly to this was Ethan Ryan, whose appearance on the bench had the potential to lead to his first first-team appearance since August 2021.
Meanwhile, Dean Hadley, Kane Linnett and Matt Parcell all missed out. Hadley had picked up a calf injury in the win over Salford; Linnett had seen a recurrence of a quad injury he originally sustained against St Helens; and Parcell was missing out due to a dead leg.
The opening stages of the game were pretty relentless for both sides, with either barely taking a breather. They finally got a break when Catalans opted to take a conversion after a dangerous tackle from Jordan Abdull led to a penalty. The Dragons then extended their lead after an overread from Mikey Lewis exposed Sam Wood to a two-on-one situation, with Fouad Yaha crashing over to give Catalans an 8-0 lead.
One might have been forgiven for thinking that it wouldn't be Rovers' night when the Perpignan wind played its part in halting an Abdull penalty from reaching touch. But things soon changed as the Dragons' star half-back Mitchell Pearce was sinbinned after a dangerous challenge on Will Dagger. The resulting numerical advantage paid dividends for the Robins, as Ryan Hall squeezed in to make it 8-4.
Catalans had stifled Rovers until the sinbinning, but now it was a different ball game as Rovers were in control. A cut-out ball from Abdull seemed to send Rovers' fearless skipper Shaun Kenny-Dowall

in for a try but it was deemed to be a forward pass. Lewis also came close, but alas, it was no dice. Instead, Catalans had the final say of the half by once again deciding to take a penalty, with Sam Tomkins slotting it over. 10-4 was the half-time scoreline and the game was far from done.

The Robins' upward turn in attacking promise continued into the second half. A break from Hall laid the platform for Kenny-Dowall to spin out of a challenge from Jullien and deservedly get himself on the score sheet. The game was now looking promising for Rovers. They had defended well enough but failed to show enough attacking prowess, but now Catalans were showing vulnerability, particularly on their left edge. Still, there was something in the Perpignan wind that dictated it would never be the Robins' night, as a Pearce grubber kick hit the post and conveniently landed for Jason Chan to touch down and put Catalans back in the lead at 16-10.

Although the weather on the night paled in comparison to hot summer nights in southern France, the same couldn't be said for the on-field action as things had steadily become heated over the course of the game. Sam Tomkins, a serial arguer, had been 'debating' with the likes of Lewis throughout the night. In general, the team had also grown frustrated and Catalans' game-sealing penalty was born out of the same frustration, with Rovers kicking the ball away after being adjudged to have knocked on in their own half. Tomkins hit his fifth and final two points of the night and the Dragons were once again victorious, having beaten Rovers by the score of 18-10.

Compared to the last time they lost to a 2021 grand finalist, this performance and result was a lot healthier. Rovers, who once again flew to France on the same day as the game, backed themselves and only came up short due to a lack of cutting edge in the attacking phases of their game. Just when it seemed like Rovers were about to take control of the game and were looking like the better side out of the two, the Chan try was a cruel twist of fate which ultimately turned the game in Catalans' favour.

Before the game, Tom Garratt displayed no fear ahead of facing a pack that contained seasoned NRL brutes such as Dylan Napa, Sam Kasiano and others. 'I don't get swept up in the talk about reputations. Once you do that, you fall into a trap of thinking you're playing against Superman. At the end of the day, Catalans' players are blokes with two arms and two legs, just like me' said Garratt, who himself proved to be a large part of Catalans' kryptonite in the form of a strong performance which gave the Robins a chance to compete. A man that had clearly backed up his words with actions, Garratt was joined by the likes of George King, Shaun Kenny-Dowall and fellow new recruit Frankie Halton in the key players behind Rovers' fight. But it was Garratt's rise that captured the imagination on this night.

Once an estate agent, the thought of the 26-year-old turning professional so soon and then taking the fight to the likes of Kasiano, McMeeken and Napa was staggering, at least in theory. But for Garratt it had become reality, and in the land of giants, he belonged – after all, Garratt possessed a 6'5" frame. Others that had graced similar circles to him also shared a similar frame, but Garratt was different; he had the heart of a lion and was performing on the pitch. He had only been playing semi-professional rugby for just two years when Tony Smith decided that Garratt fitted into his vision for a bright future, and with each passing game, Garratt's signature was growing in value.

Smith would be praised for searching the lower leagues and returning home with the likes of Garratt and Halton, but Rovers' head coach wasn't immune from criticism. Ethan Ryan received zero playing time on the night despite his place on the bench, and many were also wondering why Albert Vete didn't feature as much in the second half. After all, Vete had influenced the game well when on the field.

Rovers gave an aura of a professional, well-ran club only going in the right direction from the football point of view. As a result, there would rightfully be zero signs of pressure on Smith since he was a valued part of a sporting project which eventually aimed to restore the club as a domestic giant, yet the league table didn't lie. With six games played, Rovers had only won two games and were languishing in the bottom-half of the division. It was still early days, but they were fast approaching a run of fixtures which would dictate whether they were ready for another crack at reaching Old Trafford, or alternatively, if they were heading back to their previous habitat of being further down the Super League ladder. With games about to come thick and fast and the weather itself starting to pick up, Rovers needed to start to put a winning run together in order to keep pace with the top-six.

Full-Time Score: Catalans Dragons 18-10 Hull Kingston Rovers
Attendance: 6,782
League Position: 9th; 92 points scored; 136 points conceded; -44 points difference; 4 points

On 23 March, speculation that Tony Smith would be returning to Leeds Rhinos intensified when the head coach was absent from his pre-match press conference. The line from his replacement, Stanley Gene, was that Smith was 'finishing his lunch'. Even so, *Hull Daily Mail*'s journalist, James O'Brien, noted that he could count the times that Smith missed a presser on one hand.

At the start of the week, Richard Agar had stood down from his position as Leeds' head coach after presiding over a dismal start of one win in their first six games. The consensus was that Leeds' squad was far better than the league table had suggested, with some feeling that with better coaching, the team's potential could be unlocked with much of the season still to play. The situation drew parallels with the Rhinos' situation in 2004 when Smith took charge. With the likes of Danny McGuire at his disposal, he managed to inspire Leeds' 'golden generation' to two Grand Final successes during his three-year stint, as well as a World Club Challenge victory. Naturally, Leeds fans were clamouring for his and McGuire's return.

It wasn't all one-way traffic in the way of Smith leaving. On the previous day, the club had announced a trial partnership with the League Managers Association, a trade union for association football managers across the top four divisions as well as the national team. The arrangement saw members of the LMA visit Craven Park and observe the team's review sessions and get an overview on how the club's operations were being run. It would end up being beneficial, at least in the eyes of Smith, since it would allow the two parties to share ideas that they gained from their respective sports. The partnership likely wouldn't have had any legs if not for Smith, since he had worked at the LMA on a consultancy basis before returning to rugby league with Rovers. For the club to commit to such a partner with the knowledge that the man who orchestrated it would soon be leaving seemed unlikely.

At the start of the year, Smith was linked with the coaching job at Leeds while Agar was still the incumbent. He rubbished the report, and while addressing the rumour, Smith told Australian journalist John Davidson, 'There's no intention or thought of that. I loved my time and enjoyed my time with the Rhinos many years ago, and I'm very close to Rich Agar. As for me, I'll make a decision on my future whenever I'm happy to go beyond this year. That doesn't mean it's with this [Hull KR] club or any other club, it's certainly not the case...

I'll coach while I'm happy coaching - that's what my brief time out of rugby league helped me with, making those decisions.'

Smith's contract was due to expire at the end of the season and there were no signs of an extension. O'Brien himself felt it was the perfect chance for Smith to put the rumour to bed, something that was hard to argue against. After all, the lack of communication paled in comparison to mid-2019, when Smith announced that he was signing a new three-year contract despite the club's Super League status being in jeopardy at the time. The 55-year-old may well have been finishing his lunch, but the supporters' reaction to the prospect of him leaving was unanimous: many of them were apprehensive about a future without Smith. The fans were desperately hoping that he wasn't about to pull the plug on his Craven Park project with so much left to achieve. With a weekend game coming up against Leigh, questions would be asked – one way or another.

A day later, the rumour mill was turning once again as a press conference – later revealed to be a rumour itself – was set to be hosted at 5 pm, announcing Smith's departure. On Twitter, the club published photos from a training session, featuring Smith and McGuire with the caption 'business as usual.' Although they didn't outright confirm that Smith would be staying, it went some way in confirming it. Still, fans wouldn't be satisfied until official confirmation, and on the same day, Smith had jumped to evens favourite to take the Leeds job with major bookmaker William Hill.

A YEAR OF CHANGE

26/3/2022
Hull Kingston Rovers vs. Leigh Centurions
Betfred Challenge Cup (Round 6)

Rovers: Dagger, Keinhorst, Wood, Kenny-Dowall, Crooks, Lewis, Abdull, Garratt, Parcell, King, Halton, Linnett, Minchella
Interchanges: Storton, Sims, Milnes, Maher

Leigh: Aekins, Brand, Chamberlain, MacDonald, Inu, Reynolds, Mellor, Sidlow, Smith, Amone, Wardle, Stone, Asiata
Interchanges: Ipape, Nisbet, Hingano, Jones

While much of the talk was centered around Tony Smith's future at Rovers, the immediate priority was his team selection. Aside from the returns of Ben Crooks and Will Maher, the starting line-up was what you would expect from a Super League fixture. Smith's choices naturally aroused debate. On one hand, you could see the reasoning behind it: Leigh seemed like a Super League club in waiting and the Challenge Cup was increasingly looking like Rovers' best chance of silverware. But on the other hand, players such as Ethan Ryan and Rowan Milnes were omitted despite being available. It felt like a few changes wouldn't rock the boat, yet Smith stuck to his guns and the wait to make their first appearances in 2022 would go on.

Leigh showed up well during the opening exchanges of the contest and Ben Reynolds put them into an early 2-0 lead. The early points helped Leigh settle into the game and they started to pile the pressure on Rovers, who were distinctively second best to their Championship counterparts. The Centurions had earned two goal-line drop-outs in the space of 20 minutes; the Robins weren't helping themselves, having made mistakes and given away penalties. But things sparked into life following some neat footwork from Mikey Lewis who ended up in acres of space, eventually passing to the supporting Frankie Halton for Rovers' first try of the game.

It seemed like things were finally cooking. The next move was sublime; a piece of play that would have belonged in Rovers' 2021 highlight reel. A full flowing team move, it comprised of great decision-making from Kane Linnett and ended with Lewis finishing it off after Leigh were caught short in numbers. Attacking again, Matt Parcell looked to have been just short of the line before getting the ball over the whitewash, extending Rovers' lead to 18-2 as half-time beckoned. It seemed like an unlikely scoreline only 20 minutes or so beforehand, but Rovers' turnaround was admirable. Leigh had seen their strong start to the game amount to little in the way of points due to strong resistance from Rovers on their own line, and as a result, Adrian Lam's men were growing frustrated. Their penalty count grew as the half reached its end.

The second half began in the fashion that the first did; Leigh were enjoying more possession and looking more dangerous despite being way behind on the scoreboard. Still, the Robins managed to continue to defend their line well, and at the other end Matty Storton went over to put the game further beyond the visitors at 24-2. But Leigh didn't want to go to bed just yet; they finally breached Rovers' defence after posting their first try of the game through Keanan Brand.

For a sustained period, the game's tempo sunk to pitiful depths and it appeared that the contest was waxing away, nearing to an inevitable conclusion with Rovers as the victors. Suddenly, the script pages would turn and an unexpected twist took place. The Centurions kept the ball alive in trying circumstances, allowing Jacob Jones to cross over. This was then followed by another try just minutes later as the Robins were split down the middle, Joe Mellor being the man that touched down. Krisnan Inu coolly dispatched a tricky conversion to make the score 24-18 with under a minute to go. The fans held their breath. Surely Rovers couldn't screw up another Challenge Cup home tie two years on the bounce?! They could, but they didn't. Much to the relief of the home fans, Nene MacDonald, one of Leigh's star men, knocked on and brought the game to its end.

In the build-up to the tie, Shaun Kenny-Dowall had spoken about wanting the team to put a full 80 minutes together for the first time during the season, but unfortunately it didn't happen during this game. Instead, it was another fixture in which the Robins had an inspired period in, but failed to sustain it throughout the entire game, and as a result, the score was closer than what it should have been. They had allowed their concentration levels to drop once again, and it had to be addressed sooner rather than later.

Kenny-Dowall, true to his form from 2021 onwards, was one of Rovers' better players on the day. It was no coincidence that as soon as the skipper was taken off for a rest with 20 minutes to go, the direction of the team suffered. Meanwhile, there was a compelling case to rest Mikey Lewis ahead of this game but it was a good job that didn't happen because without the 20-year-old's participation, the cup run may have ended early. It would have been unfair not to mention the returning Will Maher, either. The Cumbria-born forward had a solid outing since sustaining a fractured eye socket in pre-season and had to get through many more minutes than he originally anticipated after Tom Garratt withdrew halfway through the game with sickness. When Tony Smith was talking to the media about the match, the topic of the vacancy at Headingley came up once again. Smith did not commit his future to the club, nor did he deny the Leeds rumours: 'I don't owe anybody or have to please my supporters by telling them what I'm doing next year at the moment.' The statement did draw some ire from a small number of supporters since they clearly felt that Smith did owe them some form of communication. However, he did reaffirm that his focus was on Hull KR, rather than elsewhere. The latest belief on rumour street was that the relationship between Smith and Paul Lakin had deteriorated. Compared to the phantom press conference, this one theoretically had some legs.

One quote from Smith that stood out was 'I'm quite at ease not knowing what my future is.' Although that was seemingly all good from Smith's perspective, from the club's it must have been anything but. They were fast approaching the time of year in which off-field movements happened, and with a head coach that was yet to commit, the Robins were in a spot of bother. It was made worse given that they had key decisions to make on several imports since their deals were up at the end of the year. Out of Albert Vete, Brad Takairangi, Kane Linnett, Korbin Sims and Matt Parcell, only Linnett was the one that hadn't been signed by Smith. Decisions had to be made and fast. For now, Rovers were in the hat for the next round of the Challenge Cup, but bigger challenges would surely await them – on and off the field.

Full-Time Score: Hull Kingston Rovers 24-18 Leigh Centurions
Attendance: 3,088

Supporters didn't have to wait long to find out who the Robins would be coming up against in the quarter-final stage of the Challenge Cup. The draw was made on BBC1 at the half-time interval between Leeds Rhinos and Castleford Tigers, which took place on the same day. Incidentally, it was the same two sides that Rovers were drawn against at home for the next stage. Castleford were already 28-0 up at half-time in what was easily the lowest ebb in Leeds' poor start to the season. The Tigers would win 40-16 in the end, thus setting up a quarter-final clash at Craven Park for the first week of April. In spite of the uncertainty surrounding Tony Smith, Rovers were 80 minutes away from reaching the semi-final of a glamorous competition that had eluded them for over four decades.

28 March marked a historical date in the modern-day history of Hull Kingston Rovers as it was announced that the club had purchased its Craven Park home. The purchase had been mooted for a few years by this point, and now the acquisition had finally been completed, much to the delight of every single person involved with Rovers. Paul Lakin told the club's website, 'The deal, coming in a significant year for us on our 140th anniversary, is fantastic news for Hull Kingston Rovers, East Hull in particular, and the wider city. We now have the opportunity to explore our vision of delivering a special project with both the stadium and surrounding land. The exclusive purchase option on the land can be drawn down in separate parcels of estate over the next seven years. We will start the thought process immediately of how we can create an exciting, generational project.' While acknowledging a bright new future filled with many possibilities, Lakin also made note of the club's dark days by referencing the Rovers Supporters Group, and he also commended the supporters who stuck by the club when it truly needed their support in the late 1990s and early 2000s. After all, Rovers were flirting with insolvency at the time which is what triggered a £450,000 sale of the ground to Hull City Council in December 1999. The council leased it back to Gaingroup, who later became Kingston Community Development Ltd. KCD would then rent Craven Park to Rovers, but played their part in the club's survival at the time by purchasing an interest for £200,000 which helped finance the Creditors Voluntary Agreement, in turn making a huge step forward in the way of Rovers' solvency. The agreement between the club and KCD continued for over 20 years

until the landmark purchase was made. Even though the ground had vastly improved since 1999, the Robins were still visitors in their own home up until this point. Throughout the club's entire history, Rovers never had a great amount of fortune from the point of view of stadia. The ground that they could truly call home, the 'Old' Craven Park, didn't take long to show its 1922 origins once a few decades had passed. The Rovers board had enough foresight to see potential problems in 1970, purchasing a site on Winchester Avenue for £22,000 with a new stadium in mind. Things never materialised as originally planned, however, and they sold it soon afterwards. Craven Park ended up being a catalyst in the club's sharp decline at the back end of the 1980s, and by 1989, they had the keys to their new home: 'New' Craven Park.

It was generally accepted that Rovers didn't obtain the sum of money from the sale of their old stadium that they had originally anticipated. Consequently, they were left with a ground that was essentially half-built and lacking the aura and spirit of its predecessor. From the bustling Holderness Road scene, to the comparatively lonely passes of Preston Road, it didn't quite feel the same for many supporters. Their spirits were only dampened by the team's declining fortunes as they eventually succumbed to the third tier by 1995. The ground was exposed to swirling North Sea wind during a game against Barrow, a match in which Rovers lost by the infamous scoreline of 1-0; a moment in time which was indicative of the Robins' plight and the ground's lack of completion. For what was originally supposed to usher in a new era for Rovers, the ground had quickly turned into a poisoned chalice.

Neil Hudgell's purchase of the club in 2004 was more representative of a new era, and so it proved with Rovers' promotion and consolidation of their top-flight status in the subsequent years. The new-found financial security led to improvements both on the pitch and around the terraces. The pitch was relayed, the East Stand was extended and a North Stand had been built. 'New' Craven Park was starting to look the part at long last. Even so, the East Stand still didn't cover the length of the field and neither did the West Stand. The latter screamed of being outdated in the fashion that the Holderness Road ground had done previously.

Upon the purchase, Rovers still had a lot of work to do to modernise Craven Park and increase its stock. Although it was a new build, Warrington's Halliwell Jones Stadium was a glimpse into what an ideal ground could look like for a club of Rovers' size. Possessing both terraced and seated stands, Warrington's stadium had the best of both worlds in terms of retaining its family image as well as appealing to old-school, diehard fans. On special occasions for the Wolves, the ground had the potential to become a cauldron of noise; but Rovers fans would tell you that those occasions were few and far between, and instead they were the loudest fans in the league. The supporters naturally felt that their potential was greater.

Interestingly, plans were allegedly afoot to completely tear down the outdated West Stand and replace it with a stand befitting of the times that Rovers were living in. In addition to that, the East Stand was also apparently going to be extended to match the full length of the playing field. Time would eventually tell if the plans were legitimate, but one thing that was certified was that as part of the deal, Rovers had the option to buy 15 acres of the land that surrounded Craven Park. Lakin suggested that it would be utilised for the benefit of the community, often describing it as an 'exciting, generational project'.

28 March 2022 had the potential to be reflected upon as a date which changed the course of history for Hull KR. Not only was the stadium about to undergo changes, but it was also part of the plan to make the club self-sustainable well into the future. The potential changes and implementations felt endless and only time would tell on what would exactly happen. Either way, it was a thrilling moment. For decades, 'New' Craven Park had been Rovers' castle; a dilapidated one in parts. Now, it had the potential to be modernised into a palace, one befitting of a club side with ambitions to conquer once more.

On the same day, further good news rolled in. Aside from the confirmation that Rovers would be playing Castleford on 8 April in front of the *Premier Sports* cameras for their Challenge Cup quarter-final, it was revealed that Leeds chairman Gary Hetherington would be looking elsewhere for his new head coach. When talking to Leeds' official club website, the 68-year-old said that his search was taking him to Australia. It was a relief for any Rovers fans who felt that Tony Smith was about to pack his bags and head back up the M62 and return to his former employers. Although his future beyond 2022 was still in doubt, the news was the icing on the cake on what was a wonderful day for the club.

A day later, Danny McGuire verbally committed his future to Hull KR. He had previously stated that he wasn't ready for a head coach role and he reiterated the fact to *Sky Sports*. He went on to say, 'I've only been an assistant coach for 18 months since I finished playing so it's way too early for me to be thinking about being in charge of one of the biggest clubs in world rugby.' McGuire usually acknowledged his connection with Rovers and there was no change in this interview, 'I'm really enjoying my time at Hull KR and loved my time playing there. I played there for two seasons and obviously I'm an assistant coach there. It's a fantastic club with great people and I love going to work every day so I'm really settled at the minute.' If Smith followed suit by committing his future, then the club would well and truly settle down. But there was no sign of any commitment at this point.

31 March was supposed to be the date in which Brad Takairangi would discover the outcome of his court hearing. However, the hearing was pushed back a week. March had proved to be a month of ups and downs. The club's infrastructure had taken a massive step in the right direction. Meanwhile, the playing side had more convincing to do ahead of an important run of fixtures. A big month awaited both the club and Takairangi…

DAN CROWTHER

A YEAR OF CHANGE

DAN CROWTHER

A WOMEN'S REVOLUTION

The 21st century has seen changes in equality. Not just in rugby league, but at Hull Kingston Rovers too. The pathway in which women can take up the sport is generally clearer than ever before, however, it wasn't always this way.

Female interest in the code dates all the way back to the 1880s – even before the great rugby split had taken place. For example, a large number of spectators that flocked to see a game between Cheshire and Yorkshire in 1883 were female, and they were said to be just as passionate about the proceedings as their male counterparts. A little closer to home, females made up a quarter of the 5,000 gate when Manningham played Hull FC in 1884. Despite the strong interest, there is no records of women taking the game up during the Edwardian and Victorian times. In spite of the setback on the playing front, women would take up positions as administrators and volunteer workers at clubs following the formation of rugby league in 1895.

Women tried to take the game up after the outbreak of the First World War, but the male players told them to take up football instead, regarding that code as more feminine. It wasn't until a decade later in the '20s that the ladies would start to climb further up the ladder as they toiled to prop up up local amateur sides and supporters' clubs.
On the other side of the world, 17 September 1921 marked an important day in Australia as it was the first time that two female sides - Sydney Reds and Metropolitan Blues - took to the field in a rugby league game on Australian shores. It drew a tremendous gate, believed to be around 20-30,000, and was an early indicator on the potential that the women's game possessed.

One of Hull's own, Kay Ibbetson, would write herself into the rugby league history books. She formed what would become East Hull A.R.L.F.C. in 1958 and then became the first female coach in the sport's history in 1960. The club was highly successful; Ibbetson even organised a pioneering tour of France in 1963. She was a lifelong fan of the Robins and although she lived a very private life, her legacy is not forgotten.

Lesley McNicol would end up becoming known to Rovers fans as a diligent front-office worker during some of the club's most turbulent times in the early part of the millennium, as well as the wife of former chairman Colin. Unbeknownst to many, she was also part of Hull Kingston Rovers' ladies team during the spring of 1968. It was one of the first instances, if not the first, in which a Hull KR women's team could be traced.

John Hickson, a member of Rovers' 'A' team at the time, volunteered to coach a group of young women – aged between 16 and their early twenties. McNicol remembered Hickson as a very helpful, kind and unassuming member of the playing staff, who like her, was from an East Hull family and lived locally. The girls would train twice a week for one hour, as McNicol recalls: 'We trained in East Park opposite the 'Old' Craven Park, behind the almshouses on the grass area and further round behind Tower Grange.'

The team became involved in their first fixture: a curtain-raiser at Thrum Hall, taking on Halifax's ladies. For McNicol, it became a memorable day for all of the wrong reasons: 'One of Halifax's forwards played with running spikes on. I didn't realise until I had an "ow!" moment. I'd been tackled, or gone down, either way I didn't know what had happened. But gee whiz, there was blood all over the place. The spikes had gone into the back of my calf.'

Johnny Williams, Rovers' physio at the time, tried his best to clean the wound up. But in the end, McNicol was consigned to a trip to Hull Royal Infirmary to allay any fears of a potential infection.

The Halifax game would prove to be her first and last. It wasn't due to her ghastly injury, nor was it a game-wide repercussion of her wounds. It was because of a lack of interest and players. After coming close to fulfilling another fixture, this time against Castleford, the women's team faded into obscurity during the same spring that it arose.

The 1970s generally ushered in demand for more equality for females, and that included a demand for female's to be able to play rugby league on a more regular basis. Women clubs began forming up and down the M62 corridor, and by 1991, 18 sides were split into two divisions.

An iconic moment came in 1993 when 11-year-old Rochdale schoolgirl Sophie Cox became the first female to play rugby league on the hollowed Wembley soil. It was 1 May 1993. The Challenge Cup final: 'The Cup Kings' of the 1970s and '80s, Widnes, against the unstoppable juggernaut that was Wigan. It didn't get much bigger than that, especially on the grandest stage. The traditional schoolboys' curtain-raiser that year was between Rochdale U11s and Sheffield schools side. Cox had a blistering season in 1991-92, captaining her school's mixed sex football and rugby league teams and scoring 67 tries. She was duly chosen to represent Rochdale for the big occasion. However, the authorities had other ideas. In December 1992, a week before her eleventh birthday, Cox was told that she wasn't permitted to play due to a rule in the English Schools Rugby League constitution that stated that curtain-raisers were meant to be played by boys. The rule was 25 years old by that point. Nevertheless, it still stood.

Sophie was inevitably distraught, but she was still determined to have her day by playing at Wembley. The story of her snub ended up reaching the national news. After many television appearances and numerous debates, the 'Sophie Cox Affair', as it was known as, was arguably receiving more public attention than the sport of rugby league ever did. Cox had become a symbol for gender equality and was well on her way to receiving what she wanted: the opportunity to play the game she loved on the biggest stage that England had to offer. In the end, the authorities backed down and Cox was allowed to grace Wembley's hallowed turf.

To add the cherry on top, the game was a success. Rochdale won 12-6 and Cox set up the winning try in front of a crowd of over 60,000; legendary commentator Ray French would exclaim: 'And that's a beautiful long pass from Sophie Cox!'

After the game, Cox was quoted as saying: 'It might have been nice to be a boy so I could have gone professional but the ladies game is spreading and maybe when I grow up there will be a women's professional league.' A stronger league would materialise, but long after Cox had matured. Instead of providing a catalyst for growth, the whole chain of events is now a footnote in history; a piece of trivia;

and Cox is just a *Guinness Book of Records* awardee when so much more could have happened.

The ladies game did take a step forward in 1996 when the first-ever women's tour of Australia was organised by the Women's Amateur Rugby League Association. The Lionesses made the most of the opportunity too, winning the test series 2-1. But still, the growth of the entire game was stunted by a lack of exposure and investment. At that time, the eyes of the English fans were fixated on the formation of the Super League and all of the changes that came with it.
The all too familiar changes would keep happening well into the 2000s and 2010s. From the debate and changes surrounding promotion and relegation and then to the licensing system; the women's game was not on the agenda, especially since the male sport was still finding its own direction amid decades that had seen it frustratingly lose ground to rugby union.

In 2014, everything started to change. Although the male side of things would change course again, this time choosing the path of the 'Super 8s' system, a new women's league would be formed. Set up by the Rugby Football League, the RFL Women's Rugby League was an amateur division made up almost entirely of community clubs, aside from Featherstone, Hunslet and Rochdale. The league only lasted a total of three seasons and had a relatively low profile throughout its run, but it led to something even bigger and better.
The league was replaced in 2017 by the RFL Women's Super League, mirroring the male counterpart's name. Just like its predecessor, it was made up of mainly community clubs, but Bradford Bulls most notably lent a hand by taking the place of the previous club, Bradford Thunderbirds.
The first season only saw four teams participate. That went up by three for 2018; one for 2019; and then two for 2020. More professional clubs filtered in as well. Bradford, Castleford and Featherstone were three founding members out of four (the other being Thatto Heath Crusaders), but in the intervening years Huddersfield, Leeds, St Helens (replacing Thatto Heath), Wakefield, Wigan and York would all join the division and enhance the professional feel to it. It was a slow burn, but the league was starting to catch on after a couple of

years, in part thanks to the skill and combativeness of its athletes, as well as the credibility of the Super League brand that it now enjoyed.

Hull Kingston Rovers' women's team was launched in 2019 with the help of the Hull KR Community Trust, who supported the venture separately from the club. They would be coached by Ben Parker, a local man that had been working at the club as a community coach since 2015, having had previous experience in similar roles at Castleford and Leeds. The side would start in the third tier (League 1), a division made up of fellow community clubs.
While Parker and his team would be temporarily looking up at the bright lights of Super League, and even the Championship at that point, 2019 reminded everybody of the potential that the female game had. A tremendous cover tackle from England international Kelsey Gentles went viral, drawing a staggering 34 million viewers. It became the most viewed clip from the Facebook page of a sport's national governing body from the UK in 2020, contributing to the ever-growing buzz that was emanating from the women's game.
It's said that there is untapped value from men's international rugby league, but the same can be said for the women's game, evidenced by how the internet blew up at the sight of Gentles' tackle. In 2021, things took a step further when history was made as the England Lionesses' game with France was part of a BBC2 double-header with Shaun Wane's England men's team taking on France on the same day. It was the first ever time that a women's international had been shown on terrestrial television and the monumental achievement wasn't lost on former international Danika Priim, who told the BBC: 'In 2015/16/17 we were playing in front of maybe 20, 30, 40 people on a field that had been walked on in the morning by the dog walkers. To 2021, we're at Headingley, which is a great stadium, in front of nearly 4,500 people (for the Challenge Cup final). The girls are having to adapt to being on TV, the cues, the timings of all that, coming out to fire cannons, to an opera singer, to a crowd where you are playing and you can't hear the calls because we are just not used to having that.'

England were too much for France in the end, running out 40-4 winners on French soil. Priim's description of just how far the women's game had come in a short space of time also rang true with one of the leading names of the English game, Jodie Cunningham. The

30-year-old captained St Helens to a historic treble, winning the League Leaders' Shield, Grand Final and the Challenge Cup in 2021. To cap off a perfect season, she was crowned the Woman of Steel. Cunningham reflected upon her and the game's ascension to notability: 'It's quite strange to think of myself as a role model because when I got into rugby league there was no profile or visibility of the women's game, and therefore I had no female player role models. The exposure of the women's game over recent years has allowed young girls to look up to the women in the game and see a clear pathway to what they can achieve in this great game. Every time someone asks for a photograph or autograph it blows me away at how far the women's game has come. Not too many years ago if I told someone I played rugby league their usual response was "I didn't know women played, is it tag?" so to have people recognise us as players and want photographs is just incredible.'

Cunningham was not the only success story, but the St Helens club, too. After all, they had only been admitted to Super League in 2018 and after two seasons of near-misses with the Grand Final (2020 was curtailed due to the Coronavirus), they fired on all cylinders throughout 2021; only losing one league game all season. On the flip side, they scored a whopping 138 unanswered points en route to their Grand Final triumph, with Cunningham proving integral to their success.

One noticeable element about St Helens was their connection between their men's and women's team. The women's team have their own section on the club's main website, which includes detailed player profiles and statistics. That isn't always the case with other sides, including Hull KR. Another thing that made Saints' strong bond with their women's team even more distinguishable was the fact that they paraded their women alongside their men after both sides had won their respective Challenge Cup titles in 2021. Cunningham reflected upon how St Helens have unified the men's and women's team as one strong club: 'The club have been brilliant for us as a team and myself as an individual since they established their women's team for the 2018 season. Particularly towards the back end of this year (2021) I have seen first-hand how much the women's team has now been adopted and celebrated by the community of St Helens town thanks to the profile and support the club have given us. Our head coach Derek Hardman has been instrumental in driving the standards of our women's team on the pitch, and the club has given Dek and us players all the tools we need to do that which has resulted in the success we have had this year. It wasn't about having everything on a plate instantly, we have shown the effort and commitment as a team throughout the last four years and the club support has built on that year on year.'

Being a part of the open top bus celebrations along with the men's team clearly meant a lot to her and her teammates: 'One of the most unbelievable experiences of my life was being part of the open top bus parade alongside the men's team when we both were crowned Challenge Cup champions earlier this year, the town of St Helens were out in their masses to cheer us on and for us as players it was a real "pinch me" moment. Proving these types of money can't buy opportunities for players is evidence of the respect the club has and the value it sees in the women's team and players.'

One of the greater challenges that Rovers face with regards to their women's team is ingraining it into the consciousness of their fans and making them more aware and supportive of their ladies team – especially since they currently play outside of the top-flight and don't enjoy the notoriety that other sides do. The truth is that some fans won't be reasoned with; they fell in love with Hull KR due to the male aspect of the sport – it's all they want to know, and it's all they will ever want to know. The same applies for some female fans, too. Every club wishing to further integrate their female team faces this same issue.

I proposed to Jodie Cunningham a hypothetical situation in which the Hull Kingston Rovers brain trust were directly listening to her – how would she advise them on how to further incorporate the women's team into Hull KR? Drawing from her success with St Helens, she replied: 'Rugby league clubs don't have huge budgets to spend on immersing the women's teams into their club so it has to be a gradual and sustainable process but there are lots of little things you can do to raise the profile and awareness of your women's team, and also make your female players feel valued. That doesn't cost a lot, if anything. When advertising a new kit, hosting club events or doing social media promotion, integrating the women onto these club wide activities is really powerful, fans value and admire the male superstars at the club they support and therefore seeing content with both the men's and women's team together can help to change mindsets towards the women's team and just raise awareness throughout the fanbase that there is an official women's team at the club.'

Halfway through 2021, Rovers' supporters were exposed to short videos of players expressing their mental anguish and/or telling stories of different scenarios they had faced in their lives. The videos were part of the club's partnership with Mind Charity. It gave supporters a different outlook on matters, including how abuse can affect players, as well as the situation that Korbin Sims endured in travelling to the Northern Hemisphere without his young son. Cunningham had a similar idea for further female integration in terms of connecting and introducing the fans to female players through videos: 'There are some incredible women that play rugby league and have really interesting stories, providing opportunities to tell these stories for fans and allowing them to buy into the women who represent their club is a great way of growing the fan base of the women's team.'

One other idea was double headers. After all, there was some instances of women's games being a curtain raiser at Craven Park and only Covid cut its momentum. Cunningham said: 'It isn't always feasible but a hugely successful element of the women's Super League which we will also see at the World Cup in 2022 is the introduction of doubleheaders with the men's and women's teams. Fans will be much more likely to get down to a game early to support their women's team than they would to seek out the women's game separately but often when fans witness a game for the first time, they are impressed by what they see and are much more likely to follow their women's team going forward. It also allows young girls in the stadium to see the amazing opportunities that are available now in the women's game to represent their club of Hull KR, wear the badge and play in their stadium, just like the men.'

Hull KR Women's first season in League 1 was one of consolidation. When they were first formed, a five-year plan was formulated. The thought of such a plan will probably give many supporters an eerie throwback to the days of Jamie Peacock being the club's 'Head of

Rugby'. However, this plan was much more transparent: reach Super League by 2024. Unfortunately, they couldn't foresee a global pandemic when formulating the plan, so 2020 was essentially a write-off since the league season was cancelled.

In 2021, the team improved and reached a League 1 play-off position. Due to logistical issues, Warrington couldn't fulfil their fixture, and it granted Parker's team a passage into the final where they travelled to Dewsbury Moor Ladies. It was expected to be a close-fought affair and it lived up to expectations as both sides went into half-time drawing 6-6. It was proving to be a up and down affair since Dewsbury went ahead twice, only for the Robins to peg them back for the second time in the half and third overall time. Thankfully, it would be the last time that Dewsbury scored, as two tries from Madison Kendall sealed her hat-trick, a 28-16 victory and promotion to the Championship for 2022. The news would also mean that a first competitive league derby with Hull FC was on the cards for the following season.

Parker was rightfully delighted about the result and promotion, telling the club's website: 'Our last game prior to playing yesterday was a month ago due to postponements with Covid-19. The team went a month between games and really dug in. Full credit to the side for digging in and believing in themselves all the way through. Me and Harry Cooke (assistant coach) have believed in them from the get-go.' He would go on to point out the success of his homegrown players and the club's overall system. After all, hat-trick hero Madison Kendall, Abbie Kudla and Georgia Skibowski had all come through the U16s and more than played their part in the Grand Final success.

Further great news followed the promotion success. Not only would the side be gaining an U18s team, but the division would be fully integrated into the club for 2022, following its origins with the Community Trust. Parker spoke with excitement about the announcement and what it meant for the side: 'With that, it means we'll be getting even more support than what we've been getting, from nutrition, player welfare and media support – going forward it can only benefit everybody playing for the club. The newly-formed U18s team will be perfect for the development of our graduating U16s' girls. We have girls in our women's team that are still young enough to play U18s rugby so that gives them the opportunity for more regular game time and that's only going to help strengthen those pathways to women's rugby.'

When discussing the announcement, Paul Lakin told Rovers' official website: 'As women's rugby league continues to grow it's important our women's side and their youth pathways are an integral part of 'One Club, One Team' at Hull KR. Following their promotion on the back of an excellent season, Hull KR Women will receive the full backing of the club to face the next set of challenges that come with the RFL Women's Championship. We're excited to see what the future holds for this group as we continue to strive for Hull KR Women to one day be promoted to the Betfred Women's Super League.'

Looking ahead to the future of the club's ladies team, it's hard to ignore the upward trajectory that they are currently enjoying. I asked Jodie Cunningham her views on the standard of the division that would await Ben Parker's team – the Championship – as well as if she thought that the club's five-year plan was attainable: 'Naturally, there is some disparity in competitions due to the resource and investment some of the Super League clubs are able to provide for the women. The formation of Super League has driven standards so much on and off the pitch with players becoming much more athletic and robust thanks to uplift in the strength and conditioning and physio support provided by the professional clubs. Coaching standards have also been driven up by Super League clubs with better quality coaches being attracted to coach in women's rugby league thanks to the added exposure we have had in recent years, seeing huge increases in the core skill level of our players. Even between teams in the Super League we have seen quite big score lines between the top and bottom sides but the more clubs that see the value in the women's game, the more the gap between teams in the Super League and teams across the other tiers will close.' Cunningham was conscious of Hull KR's potential, adding: 'Clubs such as Hull KR have the capability to close the gap pretty quickly with the resources they can provide to support their women's team, just as we have seen with really successful seasons from Huddersfield and Warrington in 2021 despite it being their first year in the top tier of the competition.'
'I think a goal to push for a Super League spot in 2024 is definitely achievable.'

DAN CROWTHER

A YEAR OF CHANGE

APRIL

The month of April had arrived and it had all the makings of being a big month for Rovers' season. Their run of fixtures included Warrington (home), Castleford (home), Hull FC (home), Toulouse (away), Wakefield (home) and Leeds (away). All things considered, the side had gotten off to a slow start to the season but this run pitted them against teams that were in and around them, including the Challenge Cup tie against Castleford. The Robins had the potential to reach the end of April safe in the knowledge that they were once again competing for the top-six and booked in for a Challenge Cup semi-final. Alternatively, a less than desirable run would see them dumped out of the cup, stuck in the bottom-half of the division or even worse after Toulouse gave all of the sides near the bottom jitters after pulling off the shock of the season by beating St Helens at home during March. In short, Rovers needed to produce the goods.

A YEAR OF CHANGE

1/4/2022
Hull Kingston Rovers vs. Warrington Wolves
Betfred Super League (Round 7)

Rovers: Coote, Keinhorst, Wood, Kenny-Dowall, Hall, Lewis, Milnes, Garratt, Parcell, King, Halton, Linnett, Minchella
Interchanges: Storton, Litten, Sims, Maher

Warrington: Thewlis, Charnley, Mata'utia, King, Wrench, Widdop, Williams, Mulhern, Clark, Cooper, Currie, Holmes, Hughes
Interchanges: Philbin, Bullock, Walker, Magoulias

Over 10,000 fans packed into Craven Park for a non-televised Friday night clash with Warrington. The club had launched an initiative in March where fans could buy tickets for £1, appealing to the future generation of potential fans, as well as supporters without season tickets. The scheme sold out within days. In many ways it was the most apt way to start the new era of Rovers owning their home ground since they not only had a bumper gate, but they also had the potential to maintain the attention of some the new eyeballs that they had attracted if they could take the two points on offer.

The pre-match discussion was centered around two matters: the absence of Jordan Abdull and two kick-off delays. Many scratched their heads during the Leigh cup tie when Abdull was taken off goal-kicking duties mid-game, only to later discover that he was suffering through a hip issue. It wasn't his hip that would keep him out of this game, but an ear infection. Rowan Milnes was taking his place, making it Milnes' first start of the campaign. Meanwhile, on the M62, Warrington's team coach was the victim of lane closures. At first, the game was delayed until 8.10 pm, and then 8.15 pm, much to the bemusement of the Robins' supporters. Many East Standers greeted the latecomers with derogatory chants during the warm-ups.

Some supporters did fancy their team's chances against the Wire, especially since Daryl Powell's men had lost their four previous matches and possessed what seemed to be a soft underbelly, yet few could have predicted the opening salvo of tries. Frankie Halton scored the first, smashing his way through Warrington's line. The ball was spread wide for Rovers' next try, with Ryan Hall retrieving a tricky-looking pass and then bundling himself over in the corner. The next started centrally. Elliott Minchella broke from midfield and passed to the supporting Mikey Lewis who then provided the honours for Lachlan Coote, who scored upon his first-team return to cap off a very fine move. Coote was involved in the next try; near the opposition's line he displayed excellent vision by sending a kick through to Jimmy Keinhorst, who only had to touch down to increase the score to 20-0 with just 18 minutes gone.

Warrington had defended poorly for Rovers' onslaught, but it was time for the Robins themselves to showcase some poor defence as Peter Mata'utia crashed through a tame defensive effort to earn his side some points on the board at last. Before and after the try, Rovers had plenty of opportunities to put the game to bed but couldn't find another score before the half-time whistle blew. Although the game wasn't finished just yet, it was close because the away side were starting to teeter; demonstrated by constant infringements and a Joe Bullock sinbinning towards the end of the half.

For the second half, the first try was always going to be crucial and it didn't take long for it to happen. A Coote pass went stray and instead it was retrieved by Lewis who zoomed past some gaping holes to score under the sticks and strengthen Rovers' lead. Some quick hands at the back saw Hall in some space, and he passed to Jez Litten at the right time to allow the speedster to finish off another exciting move. April Fools had already passed but that didn't stop George Williams from fooling Kane Linnett with a dummy, going over for what was another disappointing try for the Robins to concede. It was Rovers' night, though, and they responded again with another Hall try in the corner after more quick hands. Warrington had the final say with a Josh Thewlis try which looked forward, but was nonetheless given to end the game at 34-18.

Barring some sloppy moments in defence, the result was by far the best outcome that everybody could have hoped for. Given both the month ahead and Warrington's form in the league, a win seemed imperative but it was achieved in style. During 2021, Rovers had established a reputation of being 'entertainers', and this was the game which proved that the tag could be earned once more. On the night, they had scored some terrific tries, including some in the opening four which blew Warrington away.

Most people would find it difficult to pick out one outstanding performer due to the nature of the all-round attacking performance, yet Lachlan Coote couldn't be ignored. The returning Coote, who would turn 32 just five days later, produced by far his best performance in a Rovers shirt thanks to his attacking presence. His previous absences were starting to create fickleness within small parts of the fanbase, but he went a long way in shutting them up by becoming one of the biggest stars of the show. Simply put, a performance like this worth the wait.

Rovers' success may not have been as fast and intense without the influence of Matt Parcell, who continued his great early season form by tearing Warrington apart at the ruck. Elliott Minchella's performances had gone under the radar, but his levels were up there with the likes of ever-dependable figures such as Frankie Halton and George King.

One of the few negatives that could be taken from the night was the scoreline; it flattered Warrington. Aside from their final try which was almost certainly born out of a forward pass, Rovers showed up weak in defence. Since virtually no rugby league side could replicate a red-hot start week in, week out, it was imperative that they fixed that aspect of their game for closer encounters that would lie ahead.

After the game, Daryl Powell told the media that he would happily meet with any Warrington fans that travelled to Craven Park on the night, with the offer of an insight on his plans for the club on the table. Given the state of the uncertainty surrounding the head coach position at Hull KR, many of Rovers' supporters would have probably appreciated a similar meeting with Tony Smith but with a different agenda in mind. It was one of those nights which reinforced the belief that Smith could take the club to the next level. Following a great start to a hugely important month, everybody could now look forward to a home Challenge Cup quarter-final…

Full-Time Score: Hull Kingston Rovers 34-18 Warrington Wolves
Attendance: 10,069
League Position: 8th; 126 points scored; 154 points conceded; -28 points difference; 6 points

5 April saw Rovers launch their 2022 third strip, described by the club as an 'alternative', rather than a charity incentive. The charity-based designs had largely dominated Rovers' third strip scene after they came to the fore in 2014. However, for 2022, the design would be dedicated as a homage to the club's foundations in 1882 – even before it was named 'Rovers' or wore red and white jerseys. Marketed as 'The Spirit of the Boilermakers', the design was a tribute to the local boilermakers that met on Vauxhall Grove, Hessle Road during the winter of 1882 to form Kingston Amateurs – the team that would later become the institution known as Hull Kingston Rovers.

Although a teaser video was posted on 4 April, the true seeds were planted during the pre-match build-up to the Warrington game. The line from the pitch announcer Neil Rudd was, 'We'd also like to welcome a very special group of apprentice boilermakers who have joined us from Vauxhall Grove tonight. We are looking forward to working closely with you soon.' It was accompanied by a graphic that appeared on the big screen which featured a stylish-looking text stating 'The Boilermakers'. It went over most people's heads. Not many of them stopped and wondered why a 'very special group of young boilermakers' – who didn't even appear on the pitch – were being announced as part of the build-up. It would soon become clear. On 5 April, the kit was officially revealed at 7 pm. It was green and gold, the colours of the United Society of Boilermakers, Shipbuilders and Structural Workers' logo. The trade union itself had been long since dissolved, but it was a prevalent union in 1882 and its membership was reaching record heights at the time. However, that was just the tip of the iceberg in relation to the shirt's design and features. At the back, it featured the club's founding year – 1882 – with the match-worn version featuring the player's unique heritage number instead. Sublimated in the design was blueprints for old boilers, the same blueprints that were used at the point in time that Rovers were established. The sleeves were the home of intertwining lines; a nod to how the club and its local community 'intertwined together from day one'.

The shirt itself drew huge praise from many supporters. For many, it was love at first sight and instantly their favourite strip of the season. The club had ordered just 1,000 shirts, and less than 24 hours after the full unveiling, the only available male sizes were 4-6XL. The 'Boilermakers' shirts hadn't just flown off the shelves, but they had also quickly become the fastest-selling Hull KR replica shirts in history.

6 April was the date in which Brad Takairangi was back at Hull Crown Court to finally hear what his fate would be following his ill-fated episode at the start of the year. He was given a 12-month prison sentence suspended for two years and was hit with 300 hours of community service. He would be paying £2,000 to the police officer that he injured and was also banned from driving for two years.
Unsurprisingly, Takairangi was relieved. The 32-year-old was said to have been laughing and smiling outside of the building, the same vicinity in which he shook the hands of the Rovers supporters that had gathered to support him on his big day. It wasn't just Takairangi that had smiled, but also fate, since the incident could have easily seen the demise of the police officer that got caught up in the mess. It was fortuitous, yet Takairangi could now start to put his unwanted past behind him and look ahead, since Hull KR would confirm that he was once again available for team selection.
The club's official statement read: 'Court has today sentenced Brad Takairangi to a 12-month prison sentence suspended for 2 years and 300 hours community service for serious driving offences. The club have also undertaken and concluded an internal disciplinary procedure and Brad is now available for selection if, and when required. The club are satisfied that Brad understands the gravity of this one-off incident and its potential consequences on an otherwise exemplary record, that he is genuinely remorseful and is keen to make reparation through his work in the community. The club do not condone anti-social behaviour of any kind, and the steps taken by the court and club today reflect that. Neither the club or player will comment further on the matter.'
The subject was divisive. Some supporters wanted Takairangi to be dismissed, while others were willing Rovers on to give him a second chance. Given his import status and wealth of NRL experience, he hadn't started the season in the way he would have wanted to. That wasn't a surprise, given all of the uncertainty about his life going forward, never mind his career. But now the shackles had finally come off, figuratively rather than literally. He now had a second chance to repay the faith that the club had shown in him, and with a large portion of April still to play, he was very much needed. Takairangi's episode,

up until this point, was one of the few dark spots on a bright couple of weeks in the history of Hull KR. It wouldn't be easy, especially considering that the left edge partnership of Jimmy Keinhorst and Sam Wood had meshed well for the four games in his absence, but Takairangi now possessed the opportunity to return to the field and make history shine a little more fondly on him.

In the press, more details began to emerge surrounding Hull KR's plans for Craven Park. In an interview with Rugby League Live, Paul Lakin revealed a seven-year plan had been formed to transform the ground. The full-length plans had been discussed privately, yet no drawings were forthcoming at this point because of the uncertainty over how long the work itself would take. Still, he was confident that the deal would save the club a six-figure sum, a fee described by Lakin as 'significant'.

Another aspect of the purchase involved training facilities and other areas. When discussing the ground acquisition, Lakin said: 'For a club like ourselves a six-figure sum is a huge amount of money, and another step closer to breaking even. That money could be used on improving the stadium, which we now own of course, it could be invested into on-field recruitment, it could go into the academy. Suddenly, it changes how we do business as a club.'

The importance of training at Craven Park was evidently important to Lakin: 'A lot of professional clubs have training facilities which aren't at the ground and that means you can't build that 'we as one' approach. The staff and the players interact every day and once we can do that, it'll be huge.'

Interestingly, the West Stand was revealed as 'phase one' of the seven-year plan. Lakin said: 'Phase one is about looking at the West Stand. We see that as our immediate target. It's a big area and a big chance to do something great there and have events happening every day of the week. Breaking even at the very least as a club is always our goal and with a redeveloped West Stand, it's a step in that direction and not having to rely on that external investment.'

The West Stand itself housed many different areas of the club, from the players' changing rooms to corporate areas and bars – it made sense that it became the first port of call with relation to the grand plans that the club were yet to fully reveal. A potential transformation of the West Stand was arguably the most exciting prospect of the whole purchase for many fans and observers, since it aroused fascination on how the club would replace the ageing stand.

The fans themselves were also part of the seven-year plan, as Lakin revealed: 'The community is in our DNA. That might sound cliche but it genuinely is. We live and breathe the local area and we want to support it as well as we can. It's a chance to do brilliant things for Hull KR but also for Hull in general. There aren't many opportunities in a built-up area like this to purchase land around a sports club and we'll seize the moment.'

8/4/2022
Hull Kingston Rovers vs. Castleford Tigers
Betfred Challenge Cup (Quarter-Final)
Rovers: Coote, Keinhorst, Wood, Kenny-Dowall, Hall, Lewis, Milnes, Maher, Parcell, King, Halton, Linnett, Minchella
Interchanges: Abdull, Storton, Litten, Richards

Castleford: Evalds, Eden, Turner, Mamo, Faraimo, Trueman, O'Brien, Massey, McShane, Smith, Edwards, Griffin, Westerman
Interchanges: Watts, Milner, Fonua, Matagi

Tony Smith's biggest dilemma was rooted in the halves – would he stick or twist with Rowan Milnes? In the end, he stuck with the 22-year-old but Jordan Abdull made the bench. Conspicuous by his absence was Korbin Sims, whose 20-minute cameo in the previous week against Warrington only drew further doubt as to his Craven Park future. Instead, Sims would be passing Castleford on the way to Leeds for a reserve game alongside the likes of Brad Takairangi, Ben Crooks and Will Dagger. There was some good news for Sims away from the field as his son was landing in England for the easter period. The match-up had a different feel to the previous meeting between the two sides. Even though just seven Super League rounds had passed, the Challenge Cup was looking like the best opportunity of silverware for both sides. Lee Radford was not only a past master with the competition, but his side had picked up a little steam after a disappointing start to his tenure; they had comprehensively defeated Leeds away and Toulouse at home. Rovers themselves had improved too, and on the night neither side could afford to hide with a semi-final on the line.

Starting strong was the foundation behind the Robins' victory against Warrington and it continued here. Just three minutes into the game, Milnes displayed game intelligence by sending a neat kick through on the last tackle, with Elliott Minchella touching down. Minchella looked to be in again, but the *Premier Sports* cameras were present on the night, and as a result the decision would fall into the hands of the video referee, James Child. Although the on-field referee, Robert Hicks, had sent it up as a try, Child overruled him and judged

Minchella to have lost control of the ball as well as been short of the line. A longer than normal delay for the decision, which eventually would be 'no try', only served to annoyed the home fans further.

Throughout the contest, Castleford undermined most of their time in possession by producing handling errors and lacking discipline at important times. Yet they burst into life out of nothing when Bureta Faraimo raised many eyebrows after launching a kick on the second tackle, which led to a high-speed footrace between Matt Parcell and Jake Mamo who were both racing towards empty field. In the end, both men crashed into the advertising boards – with Mamo almost going straight through them – but the Cas man managed to touch the ball back into the in-goal area, only for Ryan Hall to clear the danger. Rovers had survived a scene which wouldn't have looked out of place in an action-packed blockbuster. Faraimo was at the centre of Castleford's next big moment, as he spurred a golden opportunity by mishandling the ball, just as space opened up on the right flank. The Robins faithful promptly reminded him about his past employment with the ground's next visitors, Hull FC. Still, the supporters would admit that it was a firm warning sign.

Castleford and Faraimo's misfortune soon turned into joy for Rovers, and ultimately, redemption for Minchella. In the set that followed Faraimo's error, Milnes launched a high kick which was batted back by Lachlan Coote, eventually finding Milnes again. Milnes, met by a wall of grey Castleford shirts, spotted space in behind and made another simple kick through which was duly finished off by Minchella. The Bradford connection had struck again in what was a case of déjà vu – Rovers were now 12-0 up and looking in control of the tie despite a few dicey moments.

Tony Smith's men had looked more competent and generally more dangerous in possession, but Castleford hit back with a try of their own through ex-Rovers man Greg Eden, who benefitted from lacklustre defending. From looking comfortable at 12-0, mistakes were now starting to creep into Rovers' game and the Tigers went close to scoring again until a knock-on denied them. Rovers regained their poise but Castleford enjoyed a breakaway try. Greg Eden, three tries away from his Castleford century before the game began, had scored his second. The difficult conversion was dispatched and Rovers were now under the cosh at 12-10. Rovers' problems continued as Sam Wood departed the field after taking a knock around the solar plexus; he was replaced in the centre by Jordan Abdull.

Half-time had arrived and it couldn't come soon enough, since the pendulum had swung in the Tigers' favour. A few minutes before the interval, a supporter in the East Stand showed their frustration by hurling a bottle onto the pitch. But their arm wasn't as strong as they had perhaps hoped, and instead they came desperately close to striking a Rovers physio instead. It was a stark reminder on how innocent people could easily get caught up in somebody else's reckless actions. Rovers could ill-afford to lose their heads in a similar manner as another important 40 minutes beckoned.

Just under five minutes into the second half, a nightmare scenario had been realised at Craven Park. Mikey Lewis was badly hurt; everybody knew straight away as he clutched his leg in agony. While in the background, Jordan Abdull was being helped off the field after sustaining a head knock. It felt like doomsday to many supporters, especially given that their side was in the midst of a real battle with the score still remaining at 12-10. 'Mikey Lewis, he's one of our own!' rang out from the East Stand, as Lewis desperately tried to continue. For a very short period of time, Lewis remained on the field but he embodied the walking wounded, rather than a 20-year-old future superstar, as he fed a scrum and limped to and from the Rovers line before finally being withdrawn. The same fans that were chanting Lewis' name needed to get behind their team more than ever since the Robins now had an even bigger fight on their hands. Despite the affair being lowly-attended, as many Challenge Cup matches were across the game, the atmosphere was noticeably better than most of, if not all of the home games that had come before it.

Rovers met fire with fire by competing as they had done in the first 20 or so minutes of the first half. Castleford were now facing an onslaught. A slick combination between Coote and Kane Linnett allowed the full-back to fire a cut-out pass to Hall, who scored in the corner in what was a much-needed try. The stadium lifted thanks to the sensational piece of play that led to the score, and the cavalry had arrived in the form of Sam Wood. He overcame his knock to re-enter the field and he would soon be followed by Jordan Abdull who had passed his head injury assessment.

Both men would soon play their part. In Rovers' half of the field, Wood was well-placed to prevent what would have been a sure-fire

Castleford try, and then five minutes later at the other end, Abdull kicked towards the posts. It was collected by Milnes who scored, placing Rovers back into the driving seat with 15 minutes remaining. With defeat staring them in the face, Castleford starting to lose their temperament and also their tackling ability at a crucial time, as Wood stormed through some slack defending to leave the result in no doubt. Abdull then placed the cherry on top of the juicy cake by breaking the Tigers' line and racing 60 yards to end the game at 34-10. The Robins were in the hat for their first Challenge Cup semi-final since 2015.

This game was different to any other that they had won so far. They displayed character and grit that they hadn't showed all season up until this point. Rovers were impressive when they stemmed the Salford tie in March to hold out for their victory, but this time they were down on troops for periods against a sizeable Tigers outfit that smelt blood. The Castleford side were well-versed in the art of knock-out football, especially considering a bulk of their side had been 2021 Challenge Cup finalists. For Rovers to outperform them and then outwork them despite the adversary that they had gone through was a testament to their character, and was also in line with the upward trajectory in performances, which had started with their win against Warrington.

Tony Smith had been vindicated with his decision to once again start Rowan Milnes. Through 2021, Milnes appeared to have developed into a Super League standard half. He complimented the team with his consistency and steadiness; his two assists for Elliott Minchella demonstrated that. Everybody was still sweating on the fitness of Mikey Lewis, who was seen around the ground on crutches, but the night also reminded everyone involved that Milnes was equally adept. On another fantastic Friday night at Craven Park, one of the few downsides was that Rovers once again took their foot off the gas. They had started well but had dipped again, leading to some hairy moments in both halves. It was acknowledged that they had yet to put together a full 80 minutes or close to that, but with the ability and potential that the side possessed, it wouldn't have been a surprise to see a side be truly put to the sword at some point if Rovers could reach their top performance levels. For now, the great start to April continued and a semi-final draw was just days away.

Full-Time Score: Hull Kingston Rovers 34-10 Castleford Tigers
Attendance: 4,887

A YEAR OF CHANGE

Rovers were drawn against Huddersfield Giants. The semi-final, which would be taking place on 7 May at Elland Road, was probably the best tie that the Robins could have hoped for. St Helens and Wigan – two sides that had already comprehensively beaten Rovers – were pitted against each other in the other tie. Huddersfield had already defeated Rovers, however, it was in the early stages of the season. Still, the Giants' fine form had continued, with Ian Watson's men nestled into a top-five spot at the time of the draw. They had recently knocked Hull FC out of the competition, 24-16 in front of their own fans, ending any chance of a second all-Hull Challenge Cup final on 28 May. Rovers had improved since their 26-12 loss at the John Smith's Stadium – arguably not well enough to be too confident about a victory, but confident nonetheless after a terrific all-round start to the month.

12 April brought in a mixed bag of news. Starting with the bad, it was revealed that Mikey Lewis had ruptured ligaments in his ankle and would be missing for up to six to eight weeks. It was a cruel blow for a young man that had continued to light up Super League, especially since it meant that if Rovers could successfully negotiate the Elland Road tie against Huddersfield, then Lewis would be a doubt for the final itself since the recovery was never likely to be straightforward.

The good news was a development that concerned Tony Smith. It was reported by various newspaper outlets that the Robins' head coach was close to signing a one-year extension to remain with the club. Although one year wasn't long, it was far better than what would have felt like a premature departure at the end of the season. When questioned about his future by the media, Smith often spoke about one-year extensions, as opposed to a longer stay like the time he signed a three-year contract in 2019. The Australian was aged 55 by this point and admitted that he was in the 'twilight' of his coaching career, so few could have blamed him for not committing to a longer stint.

On 13 April, the youthful duo of Connor Moore and Daniel Okoro were announced to be joining League 1 side Hunslet for an initial two-week loan spell. The two props, both aged 19, actually had ties rooted in West Yorkshire. Both of them had played for Leeds amateur side Milford Marlins before signing for Rovers, and incidentally Moore's family were staunch Parksiders. Moore and Okoro were promoted to Rovers' first-team at the back end of the 2021 season, yet they had both failed to break into the first-team due to stiff competition. Time would tell on whether they would eventually make the grade; at this point a loan spell in the third tier seemed like the right step for their development.

On the eve of the first Hull derby of the season, Will Tate became the latest young Rovers player to head out on loan. The 20-year-old was heading to Championship outfit Workington Town in what was initially a two-week deal. Unlike the other departing youngsters, Tate had featured under Smith during 2020 and 2021 – and was even called upon during the side's play-off semi-final defeat. In 2022, he had failed to make a competitive first-team appearance up to this point, with the likes of Jimmy Keinhorst, Ryan Hall and Sam Wood keeping him firmly down the pecking order. If the past was anything to go by, Rovers still had a plan for Tate in the coming years, but for now first-team experience elsewhere was the priority.

2019 wasn't just a bunch of numbers or a year – it held meaning for the Robins. Up until this moment, it was the last year in which they had hosted Hull FC at Craven Park. The date was 27 June 2019. It was Tony Smith's first derby as Rovers' head coach, and it was his side that won 18-10, with debutant Matt Parcell scoring and driving the team forward on a warm night. 2019 was the last full season of supporters being able to attend games until 2022, when they were finally allowed back in from the start. In 2019, the average attendance for the entire league was 8,828. At this point, Hull KR were one of the clubs that were lifting that figure since this game was announced as a sell-out just under a week before kick-off, although there was a limited number of tickets reserved for anybody buying a 2022 membership. Given that they had sold all of their allocated tickets against Warrington, and ignoring the limited tickets for anyone enticed into buying a late membership, they had sold out back-to-back Super League games, with the club itself announcing that they were the first Super League outfit in over ten years to sell out two consecutive league fixtures. It was an impressive achievement.

In recent years, the Easter period would cause *Sky Sports* to ask the question: what is bigger? What is better? The Hull derby or St Helens versus Wigan? The answer would vary depending on who was asked, but a more pertinent discussion would revolve around the state of both Hull clubs ahead of the first derby of the season.

Hull FC's off-field issues were well-publicised before a ball was kicked. The Black and Whites posted a small £23,000 profit off the back of a government loan following the Coronavirus outbreak in 2020; in the next financial year, they announced a staggering £1.2m loss. Their financial woes stemmed from a number of issues; the pandemic; a 30% drop in memberships; a 33% drop in Super League revenue; and increased costs. FC chairman Adam Pearson would name it a 'perfect storm'. The details of FC's misfortune came at a time when Rovers were on a high, having just announced their stadium purchase.

Hull had started the campaign with 4 wins and 3 losses and were riding high in fifth place at the time of their visit to Craven Park, while Rovers sat in eighth. Throughout history, Hull had always been viewed by outsiders as the more glamorous club out of the two, in part thanks to their longer history and generally higher attendances. Between the years of 1998 and 2006, FC were the only top-flight club in the city. It not only strengthened FC's image, something that was felt even years after Rovers' Super League arrival, but it also placed Hull in an advantageous position when it came down to their playing staff. After all, they had an eight year start on Rovers. Hull FC's Super League identity, aside from a few years of struggle following promotion, consisted of being big-spenders with lofty ambitions, but ultimately underachievers. Their greatest achievements in the league came in 2005 and 2006; homegrown talent such as Paul Cooke and Richard Horne came to the fore, helping them win a Challenge Cup in 2005 and then fired them to a Grand Final appearance the year afterwards. Rovers made their Super League bow after that season.

In hindsight, 2015 was a pivotal year for both clubs. Before then, in the eight seasons that they had played one another, they were tied four each in terms of finishing above the other which was very impressive from Rovers' perspective given the standing of both clubs at the start of 2007. Things were bound to change one way or the other in 2015, however, as the 'Middle 8s' system was introduced; and as fate would have it, the final spot for the 'Super 8s' side of the split was fiercely contested between Hull and Rovers. FC won a decider between the two at Craven Park, condemning the Robins to a Middle 8s spot and confirming themselves in the Super 8s in the process. Just over a month later, Rovers would make the Challenge Cup final against Leeds but lost 50-0 in dismal, record-breaking fashion. In the following year, Rovers' malaise deepened as they went on to suffer a heart-breaking relegation. Meanwhile, FC got to Wembley themselves and actually won, ending a drought that had started in 1959 but was popularised by KR fans after the 1980s, a decade which saw Hull fail to win at the famous venue three times – including against Rovers themselves. In 2017, FC went back-to-back at Wembley while the Robins successfully regained their place back in Super League. Rovers' return to the top table wasn't initially as successful as first hoped, and although Hull's fortunes also dipped, the Airlie Birds won six out of nine competitive first-team meetings between the two from 2018 to 2021. Some of the losses were extra hard to take, considering two of them included a home defeat in which Hull played out most of the game with 12 men, and the other being a 56-12 defeat which became the heaviest derby loss in history.

Until the end of 2021, Hull doubtlessly enjoyed the stranglehold when it came to bragging rights and overall dominance. 2021 itself ended up becoming a transformative season for Rovers. Finishing above Hull for the first time since 2014 was merely a footnote as they landed a play-off place at the expense of FC and came 80 minutes away from a Grand Final – which in itself was the closest Hull had come winning the competition since 2006 (they reached the semi-final stage in 2017). In the same year, Rovers remodeled their look by introducing a new crest, whereas FC stayed true to their three coronets badge. 2021 also underlined the wealth of young talent that Rovers possessed. The likes of Jordan Abdull and Mikey Lewis had strong potential to be the Cooke and Horne of yesteryear. And the two halves were just the pick of the bunch since Rovers had acquired more players with plenty of upside since Tony Smith's arrival. For Hull KR, it was a new look and a potential new dynasty in the years to come if they could retain their talent and build around them.

On the flip side, Hull FC had one of the biggest wage bills in the entire division, and as a result, their squad was impressive on paper. As usual, FC had lofty ambitions with an expensively-assembled side at their disposal but the majority of their key players didn't have age on their side, unlike Rovers'. Incidentally, Craven Park was the butt of Hull FC's fans' jokes when it came to mocking KR. It was somewhat ironic that the MKM Stadium, which was part of many FC fans' pride, was actually turning out to be their club's Achilles heel. Stadium Management Company, the company that were in charge of the ground's affairs, was helping bleed FC dry due to rental demands. Many of Hull's fans sneered and looked down upon Craven Park, yet Rovers now owned their home and enjoyed the profits that came with it; including the ever-popular Craven Streat, a venture that FC could only dream of in their situation.

Ahead of the game, the two clubs painted two different pictures off the field. By Adam Pearson's own admission, Hull were facing homelessness in five years' time unless their situation improved, not to mention the possibility of repaying the government loans that they had taken out in 2020. Meanwhile, Rovers appeared healthier. They now owned their home and had announced a seven-year plan to renovate it. One of their few worries was breaking even, something the club was working tirelessly towards achieving.

Even though the future seemed bright, nothing was won away from the field, but on it.

The time for talk was over. The first derby of the year had arrived…

15/4/2022
Hull Kingston Rovers vs. Hull FC
Betfred Super League (Round 8)

Rovers: Coote, Ryan, Wood, Kenny-Dowall, Hall, Milnes, Abdull, Maher, Parcell, King, Halton, Linnett, Minchella
Interchanges: Storton, Litten, Keinhorst, Richards

Hull: Connor, Swift, Tuimavave, Griffin, McIntosh, Reynolds, Gale, Sao, Houghton, Fash, Savelio, Ma'u, Lovodua
Interchanges: Brown, Evans, Lane, Satae

There were a few interesting selection decisions from Tony Smith. Ethan Ryan was starting on the wing, displacing Keinhorst who made the bench. It was Ryan's first competitive appearance since August 2021, when he had featured against Wigan. Korbin Sims failed to make the bench, even though he was named as part of the 21-man squad. Since Rovers were facing a heavier pack than theirs, it was expected that Sims would return to action, but it wasn't to be and fans continued to wonder about his future at the club with time continuing to tick away on his contract.

The excitable atmosphere around Craven Park was telling even 40 minutes from kick-off as the home fans welcomed the visiting Hull supporters with several pleasantries that came from the East Stand. Luke Gale, out on his own, was practising his goal-kicking. Each time he missed, he would be met with jeers and he promptly laughed it all off. Gale was new to this derby, so he would quickly learn that his cheerfulness was to be short-lived in the land of blood and thunder. The pre-match build-up was also a special occasion for indie rock band The Reytons, who performed live in front of the *Sky Sports* cameras. The group, who hailed from Doncaster, played two of their songs, 'Mind the Gap' and 'Red Smoke'. For each song, smoke bombs fired away in the background, the same background which featured a vibrant East Stand. The band had provided their songs for the club to use since 2021; 'Red Smoke' was used in 2021, while 'Mind the Gap' became synonymous with matchdays throughout 2022. The band were performing at the University of Hull on the night – it was perfectly timed for both parties.

For all of the expectation and atmosphere surrounding the occasion, the game itself dissolved into a tense affair with mistakes occurring from both sides. With the 30-minute mark approaching, FC's plan to stop KR's trademark fast start, which had seen them on their way to victory in the past two games, worked. But it didn't stop Rovers from being the more dangerous of the two, and their pressure finally paid off. On the last tackle of a Rovers set, a delayed kick through from Lachlan Coote found Ryan Hall, who touched down in the corner. The try went up to the video referee, Ben Thaler, who would be looking for a knock-on. The replays showed that Shaun Kenny-Dowall had a masterful sense of awareness since he had only just spotted the onrushing Hall in time to leave the ball for the winger to finish the play off. It was awarded as a try.

It wouldn't take long for Hull to hit back. Showing attacking intent, FC showed some quick hands on their last tackle, catching Rovers cold and allowing Josh Reynolds to get on the end of the move. Gale's happy nature soon withered away. He stabbed a kick towards the goal, only for the ball to crack against the posts, keeping the game level at 4-4. A late Jordan Abdull drop-goal attempt at the end of the first half suggested that the players were in for a tight contest. The scoreline remained 4-4 as the half-time hooter sounded. Rovers had seen more of the ball, but their wastefulness created some angst with the score still remaining level. Hull had already proved to be dangerous due to their quality, even if their chances had been few and far between.

Rovers came out like they had done in the first half: ready to fight for everything and anything, but this time they brought some additional X factor to the table. Following a scrum near Hull's line, the ball was quickly moved to the right. Coote passed to Wood, who drew the attention of four defenders, before passing it back to Coote who darted into the space that was in front of him and touched down. The next try was something else. Ethan Ryan demonstrated brilliant footwork to evade four defenders and then passed the ball to… who else but Lachlan Coote? The roof lifted off Craven Park! Coote broke through open field and finished the move off. In a tight game, Ryan had caught a high kick from Gale and turned what looked to be a tough set into four points after flipping the field.

Fortunately, or unfortunately, that was as entertaining as the game would get. The remainder was played out in professional fashion. Hull did have some chances to get themselves back in the contest. Although

Rovers had done themselves proud over the past few weeks, few fans could trust them with a 20-point lead, so a 12-point advantage was not to be trusted. When Hull did come close to troubling the Robins' line, there was some worry, but Rovers' scrambling defence matched FC each time and ensured that it was Hull KR who would be celebrating this time. It was Rovers' fourth straight victory and their first derby win since 27 June 2019.

Lachlan Coote was the star of the show and thoroughly deserved his man of the match award. He was involved in every Rovers try and had been proving his worth with each passing game following his return from injury. St Helens' fans had created a chant called 'He's the reason'; and on the day, Coote was one of the main reasons behind Rovers emerging victorious. One of the only times that he could be criticised was his failure to send Elliott Minchella away for a try. Instead, Coote tried to seal a hat-trick but it backfired. In the process, he accentuated the reality of the scoreline since the game was still far from over despite the 16-4 lead. Plenty of beating hearts didn't thank him for that. Regardless, if he could stay fit, Coote was showing signs of becoming the club's best full-back of the Super League era and integral to any future success.

In an all-round good team performance, Ethan Ryan was another standout. The moment in which he set up Rovers' decisive try was worth the admission fee alone. In a tense game, it was a moment of magic that inspired the team on their way to victory. Ryan was also very capable in defence. He made a number of impressive reads throughout the game which protected Rovers from harm's way when FC targeted his edge. On the whole, Ryan's performance was a huge statement that he was back and ready to stay in the first-team after his injury woes. Given that he hadn't played since the previous August, he had become a forgotten man since new figures such as Halton, Wood and others had emerged. But the 25-year-old still had a very big part to play and he showed it during one of the biggest occasions that the calendar had to offer.

Hull FC had one of the biggest forward packs in the entire league, yet they were well-matched by Rovers', which was down on numbers. The pack leader George King was the stand-out, but he was joined by his comrades Greg Richards and Will Maher, who both helped sway the forward battle in the Robins' favour. It was yet another sign that the squad's depth had improved in 2022.

That same depth would be tested further, as it was revealed after the game by Tony Smith that Tom Garatt would be missing more games after showing some worrying concussion symptoms. Also, Frankie Halton was ruled out of the following fixture against Toulouse after suffering a knee issue which forced an early withdrawal from the game.

One of the more interesting incidents of the derby was a moment between Brad Fash and Elliott Minchella. Perhaps Fash was absolved from FC's nutrition plan, as halfway through the game he was accused of biting Minchella's finger. The incident was filed on report and would be sent to the RFL for further examination, with a four to eight game ban potentially looming for Fash. If he was found guilty, then offerings of human flesh clearly came at a heavy price. The topic of teeth was also unkind to Maher, who lost one of his during the game. The bragging rights had been attained. Several supporters proclaimed that the city now belonged to Rovers. From a rational point of view, that was hardly the case at this point. Although the two sides were now level on points, there was much of the season still to play and Hull still had a strong outfit – although it was worth noting that they were at full-strength for this game, unlike Rovers. Still, nobody could blame the fans for their excitement. The whole vibe of the club matched with a first derby win in three years was bound to create such emotion, but the players could ill-afford to get caught up in it as they were soon about to fly over to Toulouse three days later after a bruising derby. Technically the city was still Hull FC's, at least while Rovers were in France anyway.

Full-Time Score: Hull Kingston Rovers 16-4 Hull FC
Attendance: 10,300
League Position: 7th; 142 points scored; 158 points conceded; -16 points difference; 8 points

18/4/2022
Toulouse Olympique vs. Hull Kingston Rovers
Betfred Super League (Round 9)

Rovers: Dagger, Ryan, Crooks, Kenny-Dowall, Hall, Milnes, Abdull, Storton, Litten, King, Hadley, Wood, Minchella
Interchanges: Parcell, Sims, Keinhorst, Richards

Toulouse: Ashall-Bott, Macron, Hankinson, Vaivai, Bergal, Gigot, Albert, Navarrete, Marion, Sangare, Stefani, Dixon, Puech
Interchanges: Pelissier, Springer, Garbutt, Hansen

A trip to France was never easy, especially when the side had just negotiated a punishing derby three days beforehand. Toulouse had recently competed in the first-ever Super League French derby with Catalans, although they had a day's rest over the Robins and also had no worries over logistical issues since they would still be stationed in France.

The newly-promoted side had joined the elite with very little in the way of major signings. In fact, their pre-season erupted into turmoil when two of their best players, Mark Kheirallah and Johnathan Ford, departed over COVID-related disagreements with the club. They had just one win to their name – albeit a highly creditable one against St Helens – but they needed points immediately to avoid being cut off at the foot of the division. In the eyes of ex-Robins forward Mitch Garbutt, Rovers presented a good opportunity to get two points on the board.

Of course, the Robins would have different ideas. They were chasing their first back-to-back wins over the Easter period since 2015. After a stunning performance against Hull, Lachlan Coote was rested and Will Dagger stepped into his place. Ben Crooks was brought back into the fold for his first Super League appearance of the season, while Sam Wood was moved into the second-row. Brad Takairangi missed out again despite the need for fresh bodies, but another man in the spotlight, Korbin Sims, made the bench.

Rovers had started well but they also wasted a few opportunities to score points. Typically, Toulouse would go up the other end and score. They exploited a gap on the right edge, with Lucas Albert getting on the end of a good move. Despite the inevitability of feeling tired, Rovers tried their hardest, with an instance of three defenders pushing full-back Olly Ashall-Bott from his ten-metre line, all the way back to his own tryline for a goal-line drop-out. But the follow-up never went anywhere and it was clear that Rovers were jaded. Toulouse were in once again, this time through Garbutt who enjoyed plenty of space to run through, increasing the home side's lead to 12-0.

After a half-time rollocking from Tony Smith, things appeared to have picked up. There was an element of luck when Garbutt dropped the ball seconds into the new half, yet there was only improvement in Rovers' move that followed. The tempo increased during a movement in which Ryan Hall got on the end of to reduce the deficit to eight. After that, the pattern from the first half emerged again as Toulouse found another gap, with Andrew Dixon eventually finding his way over in the corner after escaping the clutches of Sims. Rovers were now 18-4 down and it was looking like defeat was on the cards.

In a game of poor quality due to two tired sides, space could be obtained with regularity and it was once again when a cut-out ball from Rowan Milnes found Hall in the corner for his second try. Was it another false dawn? Not according to George King, who was the scorer of Rovers' next try. The Robins' star prop ran the ball up the gut of the Toulouse defence, finding something soft as he took Maxime Puech and Garbutt over the line with him.

With the score now 18-16, the momentum was with Rovers. Abdull lofted a kick into Toulouse's corner, where it was met by a group of players from both teams. It ended up getting knocked back to Abdull, who was well placed. He proceeded to evade two defenders before having the presence of mind to touch down more centrally. The Robins had taken the lead for the first time in the game and they were hungry for more. Matty Storton was the next scorer, pushing off defenders and scoring in a great position to allow Abdull to convert; Rovers were 28-18 up and looking good for the win.

Still, Rovers fans of all ages should have known that their side wasn't going to just see the game out and ride off into the French sunset. Tony Gigot, Toulouse's greatest inspiration on the day, kicked a fantastic 40/20 with just a few minutes remaining. During the set that followed, Macron bagged his second try of the game by wrong-footing three Rovers defenders simultaneously in what was a desperate scene.

The scoreboard now read 28-24 and there was under two minutes remaining. Toulouse, buoyed by their score, came right back at the Robins, and were now closing in on their tryline. Olympique's one final push was halted by Hall, who knocked the ball over for a goal-line drop-out. But there was no time to take it - Rovers could breathe at last. They had won, and for the team, it was time to get the hell out of France with the two points.

Up until this moment in time, this had to go down as one of Rovers' greatest league victories of the season. Not only had they risen up to the Easter challenge by winning both games, but they also came back from being 18-4 down. It would have been easy to melt in the sun, succumbing to a heavy defeat after their schedule, but no. The side meant business and showed it with a hugely impressive comeback. It certainly put a smile on Tony Smith's face. Rovers' boss, who was victorious in his 500th Super League game as a head coach, cut a very different figure at half-time but, like the team, was transformed by the hooter.

In his post-match press conference, Smith criticised the sport for its part in allowing the Easter period to continue. Ryan Hall also shared the same sentiment after posting his views on his Twitter account. He accused the RFL of thinking that he and the rest of the Super League players' bodies were tools that had been disrespected by the governing body. It was hard to argue against him. It wasn't just the players that suffered, but the game as a whole due to a plethora of poor-quality games. This was just one of many from the same day.

As a consequence of the poor standard, it was difficult to pick out too many stand-out performers. George King was once again at the heart of Rovers' battle and his sheer determination to successfully bamboozle the gut of Toulouse's defence was a key moment in the fightback. In general, most of the players performed adequately in trying times and made sure their teammates got over the line.

They hadn't won back-to-back during the Easter period since 2015. In the midst of a five-match winning run, anything felt possible and that just about summed up the morale of the team. They had won ugly in both games – but winning is everything – and it had been in short supply until the past few years when this grand new team was formed by Tony Smith.

Full-Time Score: Toulouse Olympique 24-28 Hull Kingston Rovers
Attendance: 6,180
League Position: 6th; 170 points scored; 182 points conceded; -12 points difference; 10 points

Just two days after the Toulouse aftermath, a bombshell hit the club. At the start of his afternoon press conference, Tony Smith announced that he would no longer be coaching Hull KR after the season's end. It wasn't just a surprise because of what his message meant, but also because Smith revealed that he had informed Neil Hudgell (who was away in America) and the playing staff shortly beforehand. Nobody else had been told about his decision. The revelation was such a shock to everybody at the club, as well as the journalists that were in virtual attendance.

Smith was tight-lipped about the specific reasons on why he was departing Rovers. He described his decision as the 'best thing' for the club, since in his eyes it wouldn't be healthy for him to remain for 2023 and beyond. He delved into the matter a little further, adding: 'I haven't been able to have the influence I'd like in the entire organisation and sometimes that happens within organisations' and would go on to say: 'Not everyone are best friends and some people operate better without other people around and I'm hoping that's the case' Smith was almost certainly referring to Paul Lakin. It had been murmured at the start of the season that all was not right between the two, yet it seemed the pair's issues hadn't been settled several months later. Lakin was not referenced or thanked at all throughout the near 40-minute press conference, but others were. Rovers' chief executive would later state that the two had no stand-out arguments during the course of their working relationship.

Smith would be remaining at Craven Park until the end of the season, at least all being well. After all, his announcement had taken the club's boardroom by surprise. Lakin was under the impression that Smith would be signing a one-year extension at the time of his great mischief, creating bigger disbelief inside the offices that were based just inches away from his presser.

Following the press conference, Rovers announced the departure themselves and revealed that a club statement would follow. The statement took four hours to arrive and naturally aroused a lot of anticipation. It read: 'Hull KR can confirm Tony Smith will leave the club at the end of the season. Much to our surprise during his weekly press conference, Tony announced his intention to bring the curtain down on his two-and-a-half-year reign at the Robins. We will now fully focus on ensuring we appoint a head coach for 2023 and beyond who builds on all the positive momentum and progress the club has made over the last two seasons. This season offers plenty of promise, we know the character and quality of our playing and coaching squad will ensure we give everything to make 2022 a great season.'

Smith quelled any speculation that he would be joining another club, at least not until he had left Rovers. He also told the press that he had nothing lined up. But he did admit that he would stay in rugby league if an appealing offer came along. Smith was in a different place to what he was after he had left Warrington at the end of 2017. He was leaving Rovers as a 'rejuvenated' man that was ready to go, and nobody could deny it since he was currently steering Rovers through a five-match winning run. He was hot property.

The nature in which Smith announced his departure left supporters wondering if the club would immediately dispense with his services, but that wasn't forthcoming. The thought was plausible since Lakin and Smith's relationship was said to be frosty at best, and this episode only diminished any chances of repairing it. There was no going back now.

Another factor was the appointment of Rohan Smith at Leeds Rhinos, which occurred on the same day. Rohan was Tony's nephew and it made not only Rovers fans draw a connection, but the rugby league media itself. The feeling was that Smith could head back to the Rhinos, fill a director of rugby position, mentor his nephew and help rebuild Leeds. This was one of many rumours and scenarios that could have triggered Smith's abrupt action.

Interestingly, another rumour had appeared on the previous night which linked Anthony Seibold with the Hull KR head coach position. It came from Mark "The Mole" Adams, an experienced Australian journalist. Adams suggested that Rovers wanted to move in a new direction after the season had ended and that Seibold would be the man to drive them there. Seibold had played for the Robins between 2003 and 2004, even captaining the side during his short stay. Since hanging his boots up, he had gone on to take highly prestigious coaching positions at Brisbane Broncos and South Sydney Rabbitohs. At this point in time, he was working in rugby union under Eddie Jones as a defence coach for England. The timing of the link and the timing of Smith's announcements could be seen as a coincidence, and they could also have been as linked.

There was the thought that Smith could have seen the Seibold link and decided his future on a whim, making sure that he was the alpha in the situation; he would be the one that would announce his departure, not the club. Other rumours persisted, like the handling of Brad Takairangi being a major bone of contention between Lakin and Smith.

Fans demanded answers. Some felt let down by Smith, whilst others felt let down by Lakin and the club since they hadn't managed to keep hold of the club's best head coach in over a decade. Those expecting answers shouldn't have been expecting any. Rovers, just like every other rugby league club, was a business and businesses didn't disclose every single decision they made – especially deep internal matters. The bottom line from Smith that he loved the club and its supporters. And with love, sometimes you have to let that person or thing go in order for it to prosper, and that's how Smith apparently felt about Hull KR and his situation.

You wouldn't have been able to find one supporter that wasn't disappointed and/or worried about the news. For all of the good vibes that surrounded the club, they were only there because of the on-field success and that was mainly down to the coach. Back-to-back league sell-outs were aided by what was described as the team's 'DNA'; an enterprising, winning brand of rugby league. It all stemmed from Tony Smith and his retinue, which itself was perfectly balanced for the first time since his 2019 arrival. Almost everything was in place. The only worry about the sustainability of Smith's success was how certain ageing professionals, as well as squad players, would be replaced over time. That would become somebody else's problem when so many desperately wanted it to be Smith's.

The date of 1 May was fast approaching. That was when clubs would be allowed to sign off-contract players from other sides, or conversely, lose them. Rovers had many out-of-contract players. Elliott Minchella and Sam Wood were the biggest domestic talents, while all of their overseas players barring Lachlan Coote still hadn't agreed terms on a new deal. In effect, it meant that Rovers had less than two weeks to secure a head coach before the deadline passed. After that, it was open warfare, and Rovers would already be behind the eight ball, even if they were sitting comfortably in the table. Smith's 'grenade' wasn't ideal in a few ways; however, it at least gave the club some time to bring their next man in before May came around.

When Paul Lakin returned to Rovers at the end of 2020, he had inherited Smith as the club's head coach. At that stage, Rovers had an awesome trio of figureheads in their respective roles: Lakin, Smith and John Bastian. It was a fantastic line-up – few other Super League sides had one like it. For personal reasons related to travel, Bastian headed home for Leeds in 2021, and now Smith was departing. Jason Netherton had big shoes to fill when he succeeded Bastian, and it was a blow to the club in general. But Smith's departure dwarfed that.

For a relatively calm club that was making all of the right noises on and off the field, this presented a huge challenge for Lakin. It marked the first time that he would be making a head coach appointment since his return and it was one of the most important ones in Rovers' history. If it backfired, then all of the hard work and foundations that had been built could have easily floated down the drain. On the other hand, if it did work, then the only direction was upwards for a club and playing staff that were generating startling momentum. A huge decision would have to be made. Modern-day Hull KR had never been so interesting.

On the same day, it was revealed that Hull FC's Brad Fash had escaped a ban following the biting incident with Elliott Minchella during the Good Friday derby. The tribunal released a statement, saying that both players had given 'fair and credible' evidence, but they weren't satisfied with the film footage. According to the tribunal, the clip didn't show evidence of a bite injury. In their eyes, it suggested a coming together of Fash's mouth and Minchella hand.

The Tony Smith fallout continued a day later when Neil Hudgell commented on the matter. The club's owner told the *Hull Daily Mail*: 'I think I deserved more than two minutes notice, but it's done as far as I'm concerned and I'm not losing any sleep over it. All I am bothered about now is maintaining progress.' Hudgell was as shocked as anybody else. It was his relationship with Smith, which itself pre-dated Smith's time at the club, that convinced the Australian to take the reins on a short-term basis in 2019.

Hudgell's words suggested that he was upset by the manner of Smith's departure and rightfully so. Although Lakin hadn't publicly commented on it himself, it wasn't hard to imagine that he wasn't best pleased with Smith's approach either. Hudgell was returning from his trip to America. Lakin had already been mindful that a coaching change could take place at the end of the year and had already drawn up a shortlist in search for a successor.

Everything had been going so well in every department. After a slow start to the season, the team clicked into gear and the five-match winning run was no fluke; it contained a mixture of strong performances, strong character and grinding results out. With a Challenge Cup semi-final on the horizon and a top-six spot starting to look like it was made for Rovers, nothing could go wrong. That was until Smith did what he did. It had the potential to change everything. The fans were already starting to become divided, and now, a few bad results had strong potential to turn Craven Park from one of the most vibrant grounds in the league, to one drowning in toxicity. Plus, with two unhappy sheriffs in Hudgell and Lakin, there would be no surprise if Smith was to take an early bullet. What good would that do? One dared to wonder. However, that was now the situation that the club found itself in due to the way Smith had handled the situation. For better or worse, life was never dull at Craven Park.

Some much-needed news did arrive on the same day as Hudgell's comments. In the evening, the club announced that vice-captain Elliott Minchella had signed a new four-year contract with them. The 26-year-old had been key behind the side's rich vein in form, showing his worth in spades after missing most of 2021 through injury. It was also a shot in the arm after the Tony Smith fiasco. One of Rovers' strong assets was staying for another four years. Smith, however, was mentioned during the announcement. Minchella paid tribute to him for giving him a second chance to shine in Super League, since Minchella had started his career at Leeds.

He didn't just praise Smith. He also lauded his teammates and even gave a potential glimpse into the players' attitude towards the future under a new coach: 'I'm looking forward to the future and we're going to have a new coach. We all rip in and buy in now and we'll all do the same for the next man in charge' Minchella backed up his words. Unbeknownst to some, he had actually penned a new deal after what was now the infamous Tony Smith press conference.

Minchella would be buying a house in Hull after signing the contract. The stability of a four-year deal also drew Rowan Milnes into house hunting around the city. After a few days filled with worry, the news of Minchella's commitment spread happiness and joy. It wasn't the first time that Rovers had managed to compel their better, younger talent into signing new, long-term deals. With Sam Wood still off-contract at the end of the season, it was hoped that this wasn't the last time.

On the day before the Robins would take to the field against Wakefield, Kane Linnett and Shaun Kenny-Dowall were announced as part of Ellery Hanley's Combined Nations All Stars squad. The All Stars would be playing England on 18 June. Both men were in contention for Tim Sheens' 2021 squad, but the previous year's game came during a COVID-19 outbreak at the club and both men subsequently became unavailable for selection.

23/4/2022
Hull Kingston Rovers vs. Wakefield Trinity
Betfred Super League (Round 10)

Rovers: Coote, Ryan, Crooks, Kenny-Dowall, Hall, Milnes, Abdull, Storton, Litten, King, Hadley, Linnett, Minchella
Interchanges: Vete, Sims, Keinhorst, Richards

Wakefield: Jowitt, Murphy, Lyne, Hall, Johnstone, Miller, Lino, Tanginoa, Walker, Arona, Ashurst, Pitts, Batchelor
Interchanges: Kay, Aydin, Battye, Crowther

Wakefield Trinity arrived in East Hull, posing the first threat to Rovers' quagmire. Trinity had won at Craven Park three out of four times since the Robins' return to the top-flight in 2018. Wakey were quite the plucky underdog, but more importantly to Rovers, they were the definition of a 'bogey team'. Huddersfield, Rovers' Challenge Cup opponents, were the same. But that was a different focus for a different day. If Rovers' players were serious about competing at the top of the game, they had to banish any of the Tony Smith drama to the back of their minds and stretch their winning run to six.

Albert Vete was returning to first-team action after missing the hectic Easter period, while the strength of Wakefield's forward pack was diminished due to the absence of David Fifita, who was initially expected to make the bench. Matt Parcell was missing out altogether due a concussion that he sustained against Toulouse, while Will Dagger was replaced by a refreshed Lachlan Coote. Dagger was about to undergo on a scan on his knee after picking up an injury in France. There was still no sign of Frankie Halton and Tom Garratt. Halton would be missing for the next few weeks due to an ankle sprain, and Garratt was still showing concussion symptoms in what was becoming a worrying situation. Still, Rovers had to march on ahead of what was another test of their squad depth.

The Robins had threatened, but it would be on the 11-minute mark when they made their early pressure tell through Kane Linnett. Coote was the architect; his break and inside pass made the try. Coote was involved in the next try. Rovers attacked the Wakefield line again but appeared to meet a dead end. That was until the ball was given to

Coote, who promptly cruised through a gap to increase Rovers' lead. The Robins' star full-back had been rested against Toulouse and it appeared like he had picked up from where he left off against Hull FC. With Rovers threatening to completely blow the travelling side away, Trinity fought back. For the spectators, they only had to cast their mind back to the previous season when Rovers were 12-0 up in the same fixture, only to go on and lose the game. However, this time, the Robins were made of sterner stuff. Wakefield had attacking sets near the Rovers line, only to be repelled each time by some excellent defensive efforts. At the other end, Shaun Kenny-Dowall powered through the attempted tackles of two Wakefield defenders to touch down and increase the lead to 16-0. Most sides would have been content to play out the remaining few minutes of the half and maintain their healthy lead, but Rovers' mentality was totally different. They came agonisingly close to making what would have been an amazing break, but came up just short after going through great lengths to keep the ball alive. The hooter then sounded.

Rovers' attacking prowess was shown early on in the second half. Jordan Abdull and Ben Crooks combined, with Crooks providing a slick offload for Ethan Ryan. It would be Ryan who would score the next and it was far from conventional. Coote sent Ryan in for a one-on-one showdown, but Rovers' winger was static upon receiving possession and instead kicked the ball through the gap between Max Jowitt's legs and then retrieved it, scoring in the corner. The try later earned acclaim from long-running football talk show Soccer AM, which appreciated the nature of the try, given its similarity to a 'nutmeg'.

The unforgiving East Hull wind had been tormenting Coote's conversion attempts all afternoon and the elements would also end up punishing Ryan, who was unable to take a ball which fell into the path of Jacob Miller who scored Wakefield's first try of the afternoon. Trinity then followed it up with another try; a long, searching pass from Mason Lino found Lewis Murphy, whose acrobatic effort in the corner made the score 24-10. The game was still firmly in the Robins' grasp but there was little doubting that they had switched off for a period and needed to reassert their dominance.

Rovers would get back on the front foot. After attracting the attention of two defenders, Kenny-Dowall managed to smuggle the ball to Coote, who timed his pass excellently, sending Ryan Hall into the corner, tightening Rovers' stranglehold. The final try of the afternoon came from Kane Linnett, who was enjoying a fine game. Linnett carried three defenders over the tryline with him to finish the game at 32-10. Rovers had run out comfortable winners in the end – a fine contrast to the last time they had faced Wakefield.

Lachlan Coote and Rowan Milnes were Rovers' main producers. Coote was already looking like the man of the match when the side went 12-0 up and his contributions list continued to grow as the game went on. With a run of games under his belt and his early injury issues behind him, Coote was now starting to live up to the 'big name signing' tag that followed him to Craven Park. Meanwhile, Milnes was at a different stage in his career. The 22-year-old was confirming what most fans had suspected about him: he was a special talent. His performances, which continued to show a maturing pattern, would only make Mikey Lewis' task of breaking back into the team more difficult.

Jimmy Keinhorst had been one of the unlikelier components of the success that was 2022 up to this point. He was always a utility player in the eyes of Tony Smith. This time, his utility value spread further as he enjoyed a stint as hooker in the absence of Parcell.

In general, one area of Rovers' game that was a traditional weakness prior to Smith's arrival as coach was their defence. This game showed just how far they had come along in such a short space of time. Although Wakefield did eventually breach the line twice, some of Rovers' defending was very admirable. For the longest time, the Robins' lack of ability to defend had cost them, even haunting them in their 2016 relegation. But now Smith had created major improvement in that department, making his own looming departure a bigger sore point. Above all, the team's willingness to defend and eke out a great amount of commitment and energy told the supporters and the entire division that the players were still playing for Smith despite a tumultuous week.

Smith's departure was for another day. At this moment, he had just guided his side to a sixth straight victory; Rovers' third win in just seven days. Although many had taken issue with the way in which Smith decided to announce his exit, there was no denying that he had turned a sinking ship around and then some. The last time that Rovers won six in a row in the top-flight was 2009. In that season, they ended up finishing fourth. This result did temporarily place them in fourth place, until a Hull FC win on the following day bumped them down to fifth. Either way, the top-six – and perhaps more – was firmly in Rovers' sights.

Full-Time Score: Hull Kingston Rovers 32-10 Wakefield Trinity
Attendance: 7,058
League Position: 5th; 202 points scored; 192 points conceded; 10 points difference; 12 points

Rovers received terrible injury news on 26 April when it was revealed that Kane Linnett would be missing up to three months of action after suffering a torn bicep. It would also mean that the 33-year-old was certain to miss the looming Challenge Cup semi-final and even the final – if Rovers were to get there. Linnett's injury was made crueller given the fact that it occurred during the closing moments of the Wakefield game. There was solace in the form of Luis Johnson's return. The back-rower had played for Dewsbury over the previous weekend, his first game since his pre-season injury. Even so, there was no doubting that Linnett's absence would be felt. Although his early season form didn't replicate his 2021 performances, the recent games before his injury suggested that he was well on his way to being back to his best. The Wakefield performance was arguably his greatest of the season to date. Since Linnett was one of the main engineers in Rovers' engine room, it remained to be seen how the likes of Johnson would cope when replacing him.

A YEAR OF CHANGE

29/4/2022
Leeds Rhinos vs. Hull Kingston Rovers
Betfred Super League (Round 11)

Leeds: Broadbent, Handley, Simpson, Martin, Tindall, Austin, Leeming, Prior, Dwyer, Oledzki, Donaldson, Gannon, Smith
Interchanges: Thompson, Mustapha, Sinfield, O'Connor

Rovers: Coote, Ryan, Crooks, Wood, Hall, Milnes, Abdull, Vete, Parcell, King, Hadley, Storton, Minchella
Interchanges: Sims, Keinhorst, Maher, Richards

Rovers marched to Headingley as favourites for the first time in the Super League era. It indicated how the fortunes of both clubs had changed in a short space of time. But for Tony Smith's men to live up to their favourites tag, then they would have to overcome the Rhinos without their skipper, Shaun Kenny-Dowall, who was being rested. Kenny-Dowall's absence ended his fantastic record of making 54 consecutive first-team appearances since his arrival in late 2019.
In the Leeds camp, Zak Hardaker's homecoming was delayed by a sudden seizure for the 29-year-old. On the Tuesday before the game, Hardaker collapsed while walking with his son. During his recovery, his teammates were hoping to claim just their third win of the season. For Rovers, it was about claiming their seventh consecutive win and laying down a marker ahead of a Challenge Cup semi-final in the following week.
The match started badly for Rovers when Ben Crooks made a mess of a Blake Austin kick, allowing Matt Prior to touch down under the sticks. It never got any better. Leeds enjoyed most of the possession. The Robins, on the other hand, continually made errors and lacked any discipline. After going into the dressing room at 6-0 down, the perfect example of Rovers' wastefulness came in the opening moments of the second half. Ryan Hall was free for a try, but Sam Wood threw a forward pass instead. It wasn't their only forward pass of the night.
Not only were Rovers poor with the ball in hand, but they were also out-enthused by their opposite numbers. Morgan Gannon went over for the home side after three defenders failed to deal with Leeming's kick. The writing was on the wall before Rhys Martin added an extra

two points after a penalty, as Rovers succumbed to a disappointing 12-0 loss in a game in which they never got started.

The result wasn't the most pressing matter, however. During the game, four concerning incidents took place. Lachlan Coote appeared to be knocked out cold after a heavy collision with Leeming. Although Coote recovered, his fitness ahead of the Huddersfield semi-final would be questionable due to the strong possibility of concussion. Sam Wood went off with a suspected knee injury, and Albert Vete would be facing an anxious wait over his availability for the semi-final after being sinbinned for the last ten minutes of the game after a high shot. That wasn't all. Matt Parcell, arguably Rovers' best performer of the season up until this moment, went off with minutes to go after suffering a neck injury. If the imagery of Jordan Abdull and Mikey Lewis going off during the Castleford cup game wasn't bad enough, this was truly haunting.

It was safe to say that the result was not what the club needed ahead of the trip to Elland Road. It was an abject performance, featuring all of the hallmarks that made Tony Smith's first full season in charge at the club such a miserable experience. The injuries made it even worse; Rovers were facing a real possibility of being without two key pivots, as well as two first-team regulars, while the consensus was that Huddersfield were about to welcome back a few of their key players after overcoming Wakefield during the night before.

A whirlwind month had ended in the worst possible way. Yet it was the month of April that had potentially set the platform for the Robins' 2022 season as a whole. It catapulted them into a position of strength in Super League and also presented them with a great opportunity to book themselves in their first Challenge Cup final since 2015. Things were still rosy, although it was safe to say that the Leeds debacle had tempered matters somewhat ahead of another big month.

Full-Time Score: Leeds Rhinos 12-0 Hull Kingston Rovers
Attendance: 13,333
League Position: 6th; 202 points scored; 204 points conceded; -2 points difference; 12 points

A YEAR OF CHANGE

MAY

The build-up to Rovers' biggest game of their season to date got off to a bad start when it was revealed that Albert Vete had been suspended for two games after delivering a high shot on Leeds' Cameron Smith. Vete, who was increasingly coming under criticism from fans as a result of his lack of first-team games, would miss the semi-final as well as the 15 May fixture at Castleford.

Better news would soon follow. Two days later on 4 May, England Knights boss Paul Anderson called Jez Litten and Mikey Lewis up to his 27-man squad. Litten's appearances from the bench had often proved to be an important intervention for the Robins throughout the early stages of the season, just like they did in 2021. With rumours linking Matt Parcell to the newly-formed NRL outfit The Dolphins, there was every chance that more responsibility was about to fall on Litten's shoulders in the years to come.

Even better news landed a day later, as Kane Linnett penned a one-year extension to extend his stay at Rovers to a fifth season. The club had activated a clause in his contract, triggering the extension. Linnett's ascension to becoming one of the Robins' best overseas players of the Super League era was boosted with performances like his committed display against Wakefield. It was, however, in that same game in which he suffered a torn bicep. Still, that didn't exclude him from Tony Smith's in 21-man squad for the semi-final in what was a shocking turn of events.

On the topic of injuries, another man that would be in line for a return to first-team action sooner than anticipated was Sam Wood. There were fears that Wood had torn his ACL, but instead he had actually dislocated his patella which meant that he would be facing weeks out, as opposed to a crushing season-ending injury.

A YEAR OF CHANGE

Leeds United's historic Elland Road home had never been a happy hunting ground for Hull KR. In February 1983, Robins legend Phil Lowe played his final Rovers game at the ground. The side would go on to lose 12-11 to Hunslet in what was an infamous Challenge Cup first round exit. Two years later, the chance for a second all-Hull Challenge Cup final was scuppered when Wigan defeated Rovers 18-11 in a gripping semi-final contest. More heartache followed when Mal Maninga ran rampant as St Helens cruised to a 36-16 success in the 1985 Premiership Final; and then in the following year, Wigan got one over the Robins again as they won 11-8 in the John Player final in what was another high-quality match between the two sides.

Rovers' finest hour at Elland Road came on 3 April 1986. In the previous week, 23,866 fans witnessed a Robins comeback as they drew 24-24 with hometown side Leeds. It set up a replay, and the thrilling first clash left fans wanting more; this one drew 32,485. Rovers won by the scoreline of 17-0 after delivering a complete performance which was still revered by those that witnessed it as one of the greatest Hull KR performances of all time.

The only reason why the Robins were back at Elland Road was because the club itself had gotten its act together. A trip to the venue was a backdrop to success in the competition. After overcoming Leigh and Castleford, only Huddersfield stood between Rovers and only their second final appearance in the 21st century.

8/5/2022
Hull Kingston Rovers vs. Huddersfield Giants
Betfred Challenge Cup Semi-Final

Rovers: Dagger, Ryan, Crooks, Kenny-Dowall, Hall, Milnes, Abdull, Storton, Parcell, King, Hadley, Linnett, Minichella
Interchanges: Litten, Sims, Keinhorst, Richards

Huddersfield: Lolohea, McGilvary, Cudjoe, Leutele, Senior, Russell, Fages, Hill, Levi, Wilson, Jones, McQueen, Yates
Interchanges: Ikahihifo, Greenwood, Trout, Golding

Huddersfield were heading into the game with an edge in more ways than one. Not only was their team fresher and injury free, but they had also beaten Rovers seven times in the previous eight competitive meetings between the two sides – including earlier on in the season. Regardless, the Rovers team enjoyed strong backing from their fans; over 6,000 supporters made the trip, the highest number out of all four semi-finalist clubs.
The biggest shock in the team news was that Kane Linnett was set to feature. It shouldn't have been too much of a surprise, given that Tony Smith had taken the same gamble in the previous season with Ryan Hall who had the exact same injury, but it was still a huge risk nonetheless. Despite being named in the squad, Brad Takairangi was once again missing, which was another questionable move given his experience, as well as his import and salary status.
Despite enjoying loud backing from their fans, Rovers started off jittery. Huddersfield were looking a lot more inventive with their play, while the Robins chanced their arm in possession all too often. After failing to capitalise on two early opportunities, the Giants took the lead through Josh Jones. Huddersfield's field position came from a Rovers error. Just before the 15-minute mark, Smith's gamble had already failed: Kane Linnett was in severe pain and could no longer continue.
The Robins weren't just an interchange down, but also another score down. A Jordan Abdull kick was caught by Innes Senior, who utilised his pace by breezing through open field since Rovers were painfully exposed at the back. At 12-0 down, it was imperative that Rovers

scored next. They were presented a great opportunity to do so, but instead of sending Ethan Ryan in, Ben Crooks found the advertising board instead. Moments later, the reeling Robins gave a penalty away and the frustrating pattern to the game continued. One of the few positives by the time the half-time hooter sounded was that they were only 12-0 down after surviving a late Giants attack.

That scoreline didn't last long. Some well-timed Huddersfield passing caught Rovers short, allowing Jermaine McGillvary to power through what was usually a strong right edge. He held Ryan off to touch down and increase the score to 16-0. Rovers were lacking in every department all afternoon, especially discipline, as back-to-back penalties concluded in Olly Russell knocking the ball over for two extra points.

With the outcome looking ominous, more problems arose. Elliot Minchella came off for a head injury assessment, only to return and immediately roll his ankle. The interchange bench was down to two. A simple try for Owen Trout only rubbed salt into the wounds, and then Huddersfield added a one-pointer through Theo Fages. There was more injury concern as Jordan Abdull went off with a dead leg. Even the Robins' only try of the game, which came through Kenny-Dowall, had a tinge of 'get this over with' due to the many minutes that it took video referee Robert Hicks to make the decision.

In the end, the full-time scenes showed a dejected set of Rovers players and a jubilant squadron of Giants. Huddersfield's players proudly marched over to their fans - who as a unit were at least twice as small as Rovers' - and celebrated the fact that they were heading to Tottenham for the final. Meanwhile, the Rovers supporters who had stayed behind, watched on soulfully. The club had been in existence for 140 years and had only won just one Challenge Cup. The mighty trophy was eluding Craven Park once again.

The side had been beaten in every department. It was clear from the opening part of the game that Huddersfield's line speed was superior to Rovers', and it laid the platform for them to physically dominate throughout the contest. Even George King, the club's leading forward, failed to shine in what was a dismal defeat up front. The halves had failed to inspire Rovers for the second week running. Mikey Lewis' speed and dynamism was missed, but as a senior half-back, this game brought home the fact that Jordan Abdull had failed to live up to expectations for most of the season and badly needed to step up for his team.

Tony Smith's decision to play Kane Linnett proved to be an ill-thought-out idea. He struck lucky with Ryan Hall's play-off semi-final appearance in 2021 with the same injury. However, playing as a winger and playing as a second-row was different. Linnett was usually involved in most phases of the game due to his position, and in such a physically-demanding game, he was pulverized by his opposite numbers. It was no surprise that he went off injured. With the likes of Luis Johnson and Brad Takairangi waiting in the wings, there was opportunity for fitter players to participate.

Smith's name had been on the lips of everybody concerned with the club since his April announcement and the post-match reaction was no different. On social media, Smith was severely criticised by some supporters who simply wanted him to go. They felt betrayed by his actions in April and also believed that he was now holding the team back. Following the 32-10 success over Wakefield, Smith had overseen two abject defeats and performances. A toxic atmosphere was always likely if the results turned, and since the Challenge Cup was realistically Rovers' best hope of winning silverware in 2022, tempers flared. It remained unclear as to whether the feeling would escalate into the terraces, or indeed into the boardroom.

The result refocused the team's ambitions for the rest of the season. Smith had spoken about wanting to go out on a high, and that high would now have to consist of lifting the Super League crown at Old Trafford in September. The Robins were sat in sixth at this point, but only two points separated them from eighth-placed Castleford, who were their next opponents. The side still had everything to play for, although there was little doubting that the semi-final result came as a huge disappointment. Viewing figures peaked at 700,000 (with an average of 600,000) for the BBC2 broadcast, and with another terrestrial broadcast appearance on the horizon, Rovers had to shape up to prove to the nation – and more importantly themselves – that they were still a rising force within the game.

Full-Time Score: Hull Kingston Rovers 4-25 Huddersfield Giants
Attendance: 22,141

A YEAR OF CHANGE

The wait to find out who Hull Kingston Rovers' next head coach would be ended on 9 May, when Willie Peters was announced as the club's new boss from 2023 onwards. Peters, 43, was signing a three-year contract and was an assistant coach to Adam O'Brien at Newcastle Knights at the time of the announcement. Peters was already familiar with Super League, having played at Gateshead, Widnes and Wigan during the late 1990s and early 2000s. But it was back home in Australia where Peters really cut his teeth. A half-back during his playing days, South Sydney Rabbitohs legend and Peters' former coach, Craig Coleman, once claimed that Peters could have been the 'next Peter Sterling'. Although such heights never materialised, Peters went on to make 76 first grade appearances in the NRL and Coleman backed his former player to thrive in his new job.

Coleman wasn't the only man to back Peters, either. Paul Lakin told the club's website: 'Willie knows Super League well, he's a fan of the competition, and he has six years' NRL assistant coaching experience across three clubs with high-quality cultures, who have consistently reached the play-offs' Lakin also gave a glimpse into how Peters fit the club's vision, adding: 'He initially worked as a development coach and is clearly passionate about promoting youth at every opportunity, again a key discipline that we believe in as a club.'

Rovers had a clear brief on what they wanted from their next head coach: a certain style of play, a level of experience, a knowledge of Super League and a background in promoting youth. When speaking to several contacts in Australia, Peters' name came up time and time again. After a handful of long conversations with him, the club's hierarchy was sold.

Peters was walking into a job that had been set up nicely for him. In most cases, head coaches would go into underachieving clubs in a bid to turn them around – be it an immediate battle for survival, or years of underachievement. Only the likes of St Helens and Wigan represented the land of milk and honey; the 'only' pressure that was included was one which demanded the coach to sustain the success, rather than build it (sometimes from scratch). Although it was nigh-on impossible to make a direct comparison, the most recent situation that could be best attributed to the state of affairs that Peters was heading into was 1977 when Roger Millward took over as head coach. At the time, Rovers had a contingent of young players with a tremendous amount of upside, as well as a rising league position following re-establishing themselves in the top-flight after relegation in 1974. It was tough to draw too many parallels given that many of Rovers' then young players would become fully-fledged internationals, yet it was still similar in its own right. It was also a reminder of just how long Rovers had been starved of such a position. For the first time in a long time, the Hull KR coaching role was one of the most promising job opportunities in England.

There was a risk attached to any appointment, no matter how experienced or inexperienced the successful candidate was. In Peters' case, he was the latter but it shouldn't have been held against him too much. After all, the likes of Nathan Brown, Michael Maguire and Justin Holbrook had all joined Super League having previously been assistant coaches in the NRL, and all of them came through with flying colours and re-joined the NRL as head coaches. But for every Brown there was a Rick Stone, for every Maguire there was a Peter Gentle, and so on. It didn't always work out, but after coming away from their conversations with Peters, Rovers were confident that they had landed a coach that could take them to the next level.

Whether Peters was 'the man' or not was a discussion for 2023 and beyond. At this point, most of the attention remained on Tony Smith and the conclusion of his final season in charge. Some goodwill was already demolished due to the way the side's Challenge Cup campaign ended on a whimper, but the Grand Final dream remained a possibility. With Peters' appointment confirmed, there was still a natural anticipation as to who the new boss would keep on, since a raft of players' contracts were due to expire at the end of the season.

Will Tate headed back to Workington on another two-week loan deal and this time he would be joined by second rower Tom Wilkinson. The 19-year-old's exit would be perfect timing, given that the reserve fixtures were about to enter a break period. The deal, which was announced on 11 May, served as another invaluable experience - particularly for Wilkinson. The move also suggested a blossoming working relationship between Rovers and Workington.

On the same day, Rovers received a post-cup blow when it was announced that Elliot Minchella would be looking at between four and six weeks on the sidelines after picking up an ankle ligament injury during the Huddersfield game. The injury list had a new entry, and it was another blow for Minchella, especially after the manner in which he overcame his 2021 ACL injury. By this point, he had produced strong showings throughout his return.

It never rained for Rovers – it poured. Following the news about Minchella's lay-off, two days later the club suffered an even bigger blow as it was revealed that Jordan Abdull's season was over after he suffered a quad injury. Abdull had played out a lacklustre season given the high standards that he had set himself throughout 2021. Nonetheless, his absence was sure to be felt, particularly with an injury list that was beginning to hit the floor due to its length. The news also spelled the end of Abdull's World Cup hopes, even though the chances of him being included were already slim due to his lack of form. From a Rovers perspective, they needed to see a marked improvement from 2023. They were relying on Abdull to be one of their key players. Judging from his 2022 showings, he wasn't matching up to players in the same positions at the very top clubs, and if Rovers had any aspirations to reach that stage, the likes of Abdull had to be counted on.

Although it floated under the radar due to the magnitude of the Abdull news, on the same afternoon two Rovers youngsters were heading to League 1 on loan. Phoenix Laulu-Togaga'e was joining Rochdale, while Adam Rusling would be getting a taste of first-team rugby with newly-formed Cornwall. Both deals were two weeks long.

After a tonne of speculation as to where his future would lie, Matt Parcell signed a new deal with the Robins on 14 May. The news came as a surprise to many, especially the *Hull Daily Mail*. Hull's local newspaper had drawn up a list of five replacements for Parcell, who, according to the paper, was set to return to the NRL. He was linked with the Dolphins ahead of their inaugural season, and although it was said that there was never any truth in that particular rumour, Paul Lakin did state that there was genuine NRL interest in Parcell.

The 29-year-old's signature was a huge boost. Not only due to his influence on the field, but the fact that it stretched over another two years. A conversation with Willie Peters played a big part in his decision to stay, and it was made more impressive by the fact that Parcell had previously worked by one-year extensions for the past few years, only to commit the bulk of his prime to Hull KR this time around. He revealed that Peters would continue where Tony Smith had left off in terms of utilising Parcell's running game - his greatest asset. A key piece of the attacking jigsaw was remaining in place for at least two more years.

A YEAR OF CHANGE

15/5/2022
Castleford Tigers vs. Hull Kingston Rovers
Betfred Super League (Round 12)

Castleford: Hampshire, Olpherts, Mamo, Fonua, Qareqare, Trueman, O'Brien, Watts, McShane, Griffin, Lawler, Edwards, Westerman
Interchanges: Milner, Massey, Smith, Matagi

Rovers: Coote, Ryan, Crooks, Kenny-Dowall, Hall, Takairangi, Milnes, Maher, Parcell, King, Johnson, Keinhorst, Hadley
Interchanges: Storton, Litten, Sims, Richards

This fixture's importance had already been heightened by the fact that Lee Radford's side were just two points behind Rovers at the start of the game, very much threatening the Robins' play-off position. A win for Castleford would have meant that they would overtake Rovers, while an away win would've been the best possible start to the race for the play-offs.

Brad Takairangi was making his first start since 4 March, joining Rowan Milnes in the halves. It had felt like a lifetime since Takairangi had last played, given both the circumstances behind his absence and also how Rovers' season had changed since early March. But in part due to injuries, he was back, and also playing in a pivotal role despite his relative lack of match sharpness. In normal circumstances, he would have been under pressure to perform, but the team's loss in form as a unit helped shield him from the supporters' full attention.

The game started off in the worst possible way when George Griffin eased through weak defensive efforts from Dean Hadley and Will Maher to open up the scoring at the five-minute mark. Then things seemed to turn in Rovers' favour when Liam Watts received his second sinbinning against the Robins in 2022, but in fact, it didn't change anything. Dean Hadley went off with a concussion-related issue, and then Castleford extended their lead to 12-0 through Kenny Edwards. The Tigers were fortunate not to have another player sinbinned when Jake Mamo remonstrated with the referee, even kicking the ball out of the stadium, but he somehow avoided punishment. Instead, it would be Rovers that would be punished. Just three minutes after Mamo's try, Cas were in again, and as luck would have it, Mamo was the scorer. 18-year-old Jason Qareqare was the next to score, rounding Lachlan Coote and leaving Rovers in a deeper hole. Going into half-time, Castleford were leading 24-0.

Things got much worse. Mamo rubbed further salt into the wounds by intercepting a Rowan Milnes pass, racing 90 metres downfield to leave the result in no doubt. While Mamo was hurtling towards his moment of glory, Takairangi collapsed in a world of pain while attempting to chase him, and had to be helped off the field despite a stretcher looking like the wiser option. It was another afternoon of woeful rugby and wretched injuries. Rovers did see more of the ball towards the end of the game, but they couldn't find a way through and instead Castleford added another to their tally; Qareqare was in again and Rovers had been beaten 32-0 in another dismal display.

For a side that prided itself on its expansive play, the Robins had scored just four points in over 200 minutes of rugby. It was a dreadful statistic, and it was now apparent that something was wrong in the camp. Whether injuries were biting, Tony Smith's announcement had affected the players, or maybe both, nobody but people inside the club knew. The significant drop-off was threatening to ruin Rovers' season altogether. Something had to change and quickly.

Full-Time Score: Castleford Tigers 32-0 Hull Kingston Rovers
Attendance: 8,175
League Position: 7th; 202 points scored; 236 points conceded; -34 points difference; 12 points

A YEAR OF CHANGE

A day on from the Castleford debacle, Tony Smith revealed that Brad Takairangi had been ruled out for the rest of the season after tearing his hamstring. Smith also admitted that it was unlikely that the fans would see Takairangi play for the club again. The depth chart would have to be stretched yet again, now that another player had suffered a season-ending injury. The 32-year-old's deal was up at the end of the season. In truth, the die was likely cast when the severity of his off-field incident came to light.

In better news, Rovers activated a clause in Sam Wood's contract to keep him at Craven Park for another year. The news, which broke on 19 May, was welcomed. Wood, 24, was primed as a figure that would play a part in any future success that Rovers could attain. He struggled for form in his first handful of games, but ended up proving his worth as the season wore on. Although the deal wasn't long-term, Wood admitted that he was 'grateful' for another year at Craven Park, while the Robins' supporters were relieved that one of the club's better prospects had extended his stay.

During the build-up to a Thursday night game between Warrington and St Helens, *Sky Sports*' pitchside reporter Jenna Brooks claimed that Rovers had signed Wakefield's James Batchelor for the 2023 season. Both James and his older brother Joe, who was playing for St Helens, had been highly-rated for years. With a number of star players mooted to be leaving Belle Vue for greener pastures, James was set to be the latest name. Although the 24-year-old second rower hadn't officially been confirmed by the club, it was starting to become an open secret after other news outlets more or less backed Brooks' claim. Sam Wood himself was an impressive capture in 2021 and was of a similar age to Batchelor. Both men were of the same prototype: young, hungry British players with a lot of potential to go on to greater things. Even though Tony Smith's time at Rovers was looking like it was crumbling, the club itself was still in great hands as it related to the future.

The feeling that Rovers were still on the upward trajectory was boosted a day later when they received the outstanding news that they'd been granted an Elite Academy License until 2027. Just under a year earlier, the club's future was unexpectedly thrown into uncertainty when they weren't awarded one. They soon launched legal action, before receiving a probational period. In 2022, the feeling was much different. The RFL noted that Rovers had 'driven up standards' following the 2021 snub, and the quick turnaround was made more impressive given the fact that neither Bradford or Castleford – who were both stripped alongside Hull KR in 2021 – had won back their elite status at the time of the announcement.

Credit also had to be given to the Rovers Supporters Group, who raised funds so that the club could employ an academy welfare officer, which itself was highlighted as a significant strength in the RFL's assessment on the club's bid. The RSG rushed to Rovers' aid when the 2021 misfortune struck, and unmistakably continued to be a unique pillar which few clubs in the sport possessed.

A YEAR OF CHANGE

21/5/2022
Hull Kingston Rovers vs. Catalans Dragons
Betfred Super League (Round 13)

Rovers: Coote, Ryan, Crooks, Kenny-Dowall, Hall, Dagger, Milnes, Maher, Litten, King, Hadley, Johnson, Minchella
Interchanges: Vete, Storton, Keinhorst, Halton

Catalans: Tomkins, Davies, May, Laguerre, Yaha, Pearce, Mourgue, Napa, McIlorum, Bousquet, Whitley, Jullien, Garcia
Interchanges: Dudson, Goudemand, Dezaria, Kasiano

Craven Park was looking more sparse than usual for a 12.30 pm kick-off against Catalans, with the earlier kick-off time being made due to Channel 4 covering the game. For the reported 7,000-plus that did make it, the weather ranged from sunny to cloudy – the gods from above were clearly aware of how Rovers' season had been patterned thus far.

Will Dagger was stationed in the halves, in part due to the injury casualties that had now defined themselves as one of the Robins' major misfortunes in 2022. Elsewhere, the bench was strengthened by the return of both Albert Vete and Frankie Halton, the latter recovering from his ankle injury. Elliot Minchella was also back after overcoming the worst of his ankle injury; he would be starting.

Unlike the previous game, this time the side got off to the best possible start when Ben Crooks leapt high into the air, taking a lofting Rowan Milnes kick and touching down to score Rovers' first Super League try since 23 April. The lead was extended to 8-0 after Catalans were caught offside. Rovers were on top, while the Dragons' turgid completion rate was hampering them from having any meaningful influence within the contest. However, it only took one spark of life and some poor Rovers defence to see Tom Davies squeeze through some tackles to get himself over in the corner. An error-strewn first half - which Rovers had dominated - ended with a scoreline of 8-4.

Things were looking promising early on in the second half when the Robins were attacking the Dragons' line, only for Dagger to throw an interception, allowing Mathieu Laguerre to burn the chasing defenders off to give Catalans the lead for the first time in the game.

It was a momentum changer and Rovers' third interception in as many games. Just over ten minutes later, a cut-out ball from Sam Tomkins exposed the Robins out wide, allowing Fouad Yaha to provide an acrobatic finish in the corner.

At this point, Rovers were suffering from more injuries. At times, they were reduced to just one interchange after Dagger, Dean Hadley and Matty Storton were all hurt. In part due to the injuries, Rovers looked directionless and started making poor decisions. Kicking off short at 16-8 down with over 20 minutes left to play was an ill-advised move and helped Catalans' cause once the move backfired. By the end, Catalans closed the game out, winning 20-8 after knocking over two penalties in the last 20-plus minutes.

The performance was much-improved compared to the previous four games. Rovers' inability to convert their dominance into points did cost them, but factors such as injuries and Catalans benefitting from most of the decisions made by referee Tom Grant conspired against a strong overall effort. It was clear that the side was down on troops, luck and confidence.

Regardless of effort, Rovers had still lost their fourth consecutive games in all competitions. Tony Smith's decision to play Dagger in the halves – something that he did in his very first game as coach in 2019 – could have been avoided. The club had invested money in the likes of young Adam Rusling, a natural half, only to loan him out as the injuries continued to mount. Rusling starred in a two-try performance on the same afternoon. Square pegs in round holes were hardly ever a good solution.

Catalans had once again given Rovers a bloody nose. The French outfit had won nine out of 11 Super League games against the Robins since Rovers' 2018 top-flight return, and the record became more relevant around this time since the Robins were starting to bridge the gap between themselves and the Dragons. Rovers had suffered a lot of bloody noses at the hands of Catalans over the years, and at this point in the season their nose was as shattered. But the Robins' beak wasn't completely broken. They still had time to get back into the play-off fight.

Full-Time Score: Hull Kingston Rovers 8-20 Catalans Dragons
Attendance: 7,199
League Position: 7th; 210 points scored; 256 points conceded; -46 points conceded; 12 points

25 May brought another contract extension, with Jimmy Keinhorst committing his future to the club for another year. Keinhorst, who would be turning 32 within two months of the extension, had one of the more interesting Rovers careers of the time period. When he joined Rovers from Leeds in 2019, he had a reputation of being underutilised in West Yorkshire, and as such, his move east allegedly saw a pay rise which made him one of Rovers' better earners upon arrival. Despite starting in the best possible fashion that season by scoring a game-winning try against Hull FC in the opening round, his form had suffered, and by 2021 he was no longer being consistently selected for first-team affairs. He looked to be on the outs. Yet when he was called upon from the bench or slotting in due to injuries, Keinhorst was a solid performer with immense utility value whose graft didn't go unnoticed. As a result, he was rewarded with a one-year extension and the exact same situation had occurred in this season. Keinhorst was called upon time and time again and rarely disappointed. Even if he wasn't the answer to how Rovers one day sustaining a top position in the years to come, his value on and off the field was still enough to convince Willie Peters to hand him another year.

Paul Lakin took the time to reflect on the progress that Rovers had made on the pitch over the last 12 months: 'The club has made really strong progress over the last year, with the fruits of our labour starting to show. Firstly, the purchase of the stadium and the agreement for a seven-year option of 15 acres surrounding the stadium gives us the exciting opportunity to develop the ground and surrounding area. Creating an improved stadium, an impressive surrounding infrastructure and club financial sustainability for years to come. We want to do this around health, education, environmental sustainability and community inclusion. We are delighted to have over 5,500 members; we have record levels of retail sales and significantly stronger sponsorship income. The Academy has been officially recognised with elite status until 2027 and we are determined to create as clear a pathway as possible through to the first-team.'
He continued: 'Whilst all focus is rightly on the 2022 season, in the background Willie, Danny and myself are talking on a daily basis regarding the 2023 squad. We are determined to only bring in signings that will, in our opinion, significantly improve our playing squad and give every possible chance of further on field growth. It's a big week

coming up, we are very optimistic that we'll be able to sign two of our key quota targets in the next few days.'

The components of the worst month of the season to date were also mentioned: 'I feel we are coming out of what has been a tough month. Firstly, the manner of Tony's announcement regarding his departure at the end of the season did, as reported, come as a surprise to everyone. We have since had some really bad luck with injuries and a poor run of results including a semi-final loss but I do sense we are starting to stabilise again, and after a break for the Challenge Cup final next week, I'm hopeful we will come back strong again.'

Lakin also confirmed that formal discussions with rugby union side Doncaster Knights took place over a potential groundshare, with Rovers having 'seriously' considered the proposal. However, since the Knights eventually missed out on top spot in the RFU Championship, the deal fell through. In the event of Doncaster securing promotion a year later, they would have already solved their capacity requirement dilemma.

May was over with and quite frankly, many were happy to see it end. The team had been dumped out of the Challenge Cup after a poor showing, and the subpar performances continued in the league. The injury situation was showing no signs of getting better, either. On the bright side, summer was around the corner and it was at that time of year in which Tony Smith's Hull KR had traditionally shined the most.

DAN CROWTHER

A YEAR OF CHANGE

THE REBRAND

In many cases, a sports club's crest represents a part of their geographical and/or local identity.

Tigers had no known affiliation with the city of Hull back in 1904 when Hull City were founded. Their 'Tigers' nickname is purported to have been coined by a *Hull Daily Mail* reporter in 1905, originating from their striped black and amber jerseys, and it stuck ever since. When City unveiled their first ever badge in 1935, it was more or less something that you would expect from Hull City Council: a blue shield with three coronets. It was nice enough for its time, but it gave the club no real identity – and it was thus replaced by the Tigers theme and look that people associate the club with to this day. Yet their first effort was a cautionary tale which told us that not every 'local' themed crest is necessarily the right call.

Manchester United is one of the most famous sporting brands to ever come out of the British Isles and yet some people will still wonder why they are nicknamed 'The Red Devils'. The club's path to their current nickname was interlinked with that of rugby league side Salford. During an October-November 1934 tour of France, the French press nicknamed Salford 'Les Diables Rouges' (which translates to 'The Red Devils') after a hugely successful tournament. Needing a new nickname to replace the 'Busby Babes' moniker after the tragic conclusion to the Munich air disaster of 1958, then manager Matt Busby eventually settled on the 'Red Devils' nickname.
Busby was inspired by the backstory behind how Salford earned their nickname and wanted his newly-built side to gain the same fearsome image. The new nickname was a great success, but it would take until 1973 for when the club would finally include the devil inside their badge. Devils have no place in Manchester – although such a claim would draw scepticism from some parts of the world. Either way, the

devil is now an iconic symbol, as is the crest itself. It's known throughout the entire world.

On the flip side, some club's badges are a genuine tribute to their local area – be it their city/town, or perhaps the region that they hail from. Eastbourne Borough, a football club that have spent their entire existence below the four-tier English Football League pyramid, don a crest that represents their area as well as a piece of British history.
Eastbourne's badge features a red and black (matching the team's playing colours) Martello Tower. The town itself is a southeast beach resort just 54 miles shy of the nation's capital and is a perfect holiday destination for Londoners. As well as providing a lovely outlet for sunny summer days, the town also provides one of the original 74 South Coast based Martello's that were built between 1804 and 1812. A Martello Tower is essentially a small, defensive fort that would predominantly be based on coasts. They were introduced at the start of the 19th century when Napoleon Bonaparte had already begun his reign of terror upon continental Europe, and eventually Great Britain and her empire during the height of the Napoleonic Wars. Many Martellos now cease to exist, but the Eastbourne-based one still stands and remains synonymous with the town, making it the key piece of the puzzle when the club began forming its first ever crest during the late 1970s.

By the late 1890s, Hull Kingston Rovers had already settled on what would become their iconic club name. All what needed to come next was their emblem. The world was totally different back then; even newspapers had barely figured out how to include their illustrations; and official merchandise was a dozen decades away from being sold. All of the playing venues were practically ramshackle at that point, so clubs would have been lucky to have had a half-decent terrace - let alone one that featured a club badge or anything exotic on the exterior. In spite of that, Rovers did introduce their first known crest. It was a shield design that featured a lion in the top section; 'HKR' in stylized gold text (surrounded by a green colour); two Yorkshire roses at either side of the text; and red and blue colours taking form in a wavey shape below the 'HKR'. It was a classy badge, perhaps more befitting of the aristocratic classes that lived in England during that time period, rather than a club that had started from the bottom and had just joined a breakaway working-class sport. Later generations would christen the emblem as the 'posh badge'.

This incarnation was believed to be specifically used for use on club caps. It was designed during an era in which such caps were common. However, that trend hit a decline sometime after 1900, and the crest gradually ended up falling into disuse in the early 20th century.

The design would resurface almost 100 years later when Rovers celebrated their centenary season during 1983-84. Although it wasn't used on the players' playing shirts, it featured prominently on the club's programmes and the previously mentioned stylized HKR text could be seen on merchandise. Over the decades that followed, the badge would be fully used for merchandise ranges.

In 2017, the club celebrated its 135th year in existence. To showcase the landmark, they introduced a merchandise range which featured a modified version of the same badge, removing the 'HKR' text and replacing it with '135' in a similar font, as well as adding the years of 1882 and 2017 below each Yorkshire rose.

The best was yet to come. Ahead of Rovers' vital Middle 8s campaign that season, they introduced a third strip which was based entirely on the anniversary. Featuring the modified badge, the shirt's design replicated the look of the crest, with all of the colours and wavey features intact. It didn't take long to be emptied off the shelves and would be remembered on the pitch too, since Rovers memorably clinched promotion while donning the same shirt in a close-run affair against Widnes at home.

Just when you thought it was obsolete, the badge's legacy was felt once again. At the back end of the year, the club introduced a new range called 'The Lion Collection'. It was based on the lion that had featured on the badge. The range was entirely made up of casual clothing but featured either the lion, or the same shaped badge but with a lion, or both, on it but in discrete fashion. It lasted for a few years before being discontinued.

In the modern day, the club refer to the badge as the 'heritage crest'. It's aptly used for the Hull Kingston Rovers Heritage Committee, who followed in the club's footsteps by sacrificing the HKR text, this time replacing it with their group name.

While Eastbourne Borough's badge epitomised the local feel and could be immediately identified by the town's inhabitants due to the

Martello Tower landmark, the heritage crest couldn't exactly say the same. Aside from the text, colours and Yorkshire rose, the badge resembled nothing to do with Hull or the club. The inclusion of the lion is likely down to the fact that it is England's national animal. International rugby league was virtually non-existent at the time, ruling out any possibility that it was made with Great Britain's 'Lions' nickname (first introduced in 1922) in mind. Still, the lion was befitting of the badge and greatly enhanced its overall presentation.

The crest could easily have been forgotten and left in dust, especially since it was anachronistic by the late 20th century. But over time the club found use for it in various ways and there's every chance that it will appear in some form for generations to come.

By 1948, the world had changed. Digital media was starting to become a little more prominent, but print media had definitely advanced since the club introduced its first emblem. Newspapers now featured photography in conjunction with columns and illustrations. Another important addition to print media was the introduction of club programmes, and by this time they were well in circulation. Still, despite the evolution in media, club badges were generally very rarely seen.

Samuel Littlefield of the Rovers Supporters Club saw the situation of the club having no real badge in an evolving world and addressed it by designing one. His design would become synonymous with the club – not just in Hull – but across two hemispheres.

Like its predecessor, it featured a shield design. This time, however, it contained 'HULL KINGSTON ROVERS R.F.C' on the top, left and right sections. In the centre were three coronets (or 'crowns' since the language of heraldry had evolved); they had appeared on Hull's coat of arms from the 1400s and were instantly recognisable to residents of Hull. They were also designed differently to the coronets that featured on the cities coat of arms. The badge was predominantly red and white – which were by then firmly established as the main colours of the club.

The playing shirts still had no crests attached to them by that point, but club suits were becoming all the rage by the 1960s, and they featured the new design. Keith Pollard, who played 22 games for the club between 1964 and 1966, later recalled that players needed to play at least 20 games to have the club's crest stitched onto their club suits. When Rovers reached Wembley for the first time in their history in 1964, Littlefield's design would make way for a newly-made crest designed specifically for the game. It was a very simple design: a shield, stylized HKR text (with emphasis on the 'H' while 'KR' was placed behind it) and a thin white outline around the whole red-coloured shape with 'WEMBLEY 1964' below it.

Despite the changes and growth in media, badges still weren't widely seen or viewed as important. Rovers only started placing the 1948 badge on their programmes in the 1960s and the internet was still yet to be accessed. Television was one of the rare instances where the badge would be shown, particularly during and after the '70s. Whenever the team line-ups were shown, the crests were invariably shown with them.

It wouldn't be until the 1979/80 season when Rovers players would pull on a shirt that featured a stitched badge on it again. It was mostly reserved for big occasions such as the BBC2 Floodlit Trophy final, as well as the Challenge Cup final during the same campaign. After that season, the stitched badges would be used regularly, ingraining it further into the consciousness of the fans and thus increasing its overall importance and sentimental value in later years.

Although the Littlefield design was predominantly red, the shirt version would feature inverted colours for over a decade, complimenting the shirt nicely since it was mostly white. One of the few anomalies to this was the 1983-85 shirt. Considering that it was mostly red, the badge was changed accordingly.

Several whacky designs were released throughout the early-to-mid part of the 1990s. In order to keep up with the changing times, Rovers' crest was altered. The shape of the shield was slightly changed and the font modernised. Also, the colourway of the entire crest would sometimes change. For example, the club's 1996-97 away shirt was blue and green, and in order to accommodate it, the badge had a green outline and a blue font. Similarly, the badge was altered in shape and sizes during the early 2000s.

The final change to the Littlefield design came ahead of the start of the memorable 2006 campaign. The shape of the shield was modernised and the font was made bolder and more defined. Even the dots between RFC were removed and the crowns had been modified. Yet it had a flaw that many people hadn't realised until the badge itself was about to be laid to rest. The 'N' at the end of 'KINGSTON' wasn't properly aligned with the 'R' at the start of 'ROVERS'. For many, it was very much filed under 'once you see it, you can't unsee it.'. If the truth be known, the previous iterations featured the same flaw. In any case, little did fans know that they wouldn't be seeing the badge for much longer.

Around the same point in time, Rovers' crest would be accompanied by the strapline of 'Pride of East Hull'. It started off as a means to expand the club's commercial opportunities and integrate the club and its supporters in the wider community with the new developments of the club, as former chief executive Nick Halafihi explains: 'I would go out to businesses and speak to them about investing/sponsoring the club, with developing the club's restaurant and other commercial revenues in mind – the bar is where a lot of our income came from. If supporters came in to eat, they'd come in earlier than usual and often stay, drinking later. While that may not seem like a lot of income, it was for us at the time.' During that period, all of the club's commercial pamphlets would feature the 'Pride of East Hull' slogan and Halafihi felt like it delivered a better presentation to new and old customers with the aim to harness wider support in new areas of the club's business ambitions.

While the Robins were very much a community club at the time, the slogan's addition below the badge helped drive the ethos. 'You need something for the club to hang their hat on. It's just like the Rhinos in Leeds – you can't go anywhere in Leeds without seeing a rhino. The Leeds Rhinos Foundation logo is a rhino with the strapline "changing lives through sport"' Halafihi, who now leads a marketing department and lectures in sport branding at Leeds Beckett University, added: 'It's the brand as well as the logo. At the time, branding wasn't a big thing and was more widely connected to blue chip companies. So, this helped to engage our market in a new and vibrant way while clearly demonstrating our ambitions.'

'I think it also differentiated Rovers from Hull FC. At the time, Hull were the cash kings, moving into the new stadium. But we were about the stability of grassroots, community, and local people, there was a kind of working-class pride in what we did. We needed an impetus.'

The slogan was also a feature on the club's playing kits until it was phased out by the start of 2009. For those that knew it and lived through the time period, the 'Pride of East Hull' line was associated with some of the greatest kinship that a club built from its community, had ever known.

By the late 2010s, digital and social media had completely risen to a whole new level of prominence. Television, merchandising, social media and many other aspects were now at the forefront. If you dragged Rovers' late 19th century pioneers into this new world from a cryogenic freeze, then they would be truly bewildered at how the world had changed in just over a century following on from when they were organising fixtures and so on.

In regards to the ever-growing digital world, European rugby league appeared to have been left behind. A big moving part in what led to many rebrands across the sports top division was when sports brand agency Nomad produced an audit of several clubs. The London-based company, who's most notable client was the Premier League, told Wigan Warriors that they had a workable nickname but that their crest had very little potential in terms of broadcast, digital or commercial opportunities. From barely mattering at all, badges were now of huge importance; they needed to tick numerous different boxes.

The message from *Sky Sports*, Super League's main broadcaster, was pretty clear: 'Rugby league has to evolve, or it will die.' When looking at the line-up of badges for 2020, *Sky* felt that the stark difference in badges – a prominent tiger in Castleford's and a dreadnought symbol in Wakefield's for example - meant that it didn't appear as though the clubs were playing the same sport. Likewise, some of the detailing in some badges was too much for the broadcasting and digital world. The penny dropped for Rovers' head of marketing, Craig Franklin, who was a lifelong supporter and lover of the Littlefield design. Something had to change.

Wigan would end up introducing a badge in November 2020, but at the outset of the 2020 season, many clubs were figuring out their options in light of the news that their badges had little pull in the way of digital potential. Hull Kingston Rovers were no different. In October 2019, internal dialogue at the club had already started on if their iconic, long-serving badge should be renewed or not. In the end, they decided to explore options of finding a potential replacement but in a considered manner.

A few months later, the club compiled a tonne of research on every single crest the club had throughout its history, including every variation, and also their 'Robins' nickname as well. After doing so, they submitted a brief to Nomad who then presented Rovers with 14 potential different routes to take. Unfortunately, the Coronavirus pandemic ensured that the project would be halted for several months, since staff members were placed on furlough.

Work resumed in September 2020 and the different designs presented by Nomad were narrowed down. There was to be a change in the boardroom as Paul Lakin returned to the club after 12 years away, but his arrival didn't halt the process since he gave the project the green light.

In November, the club showed initial concepts to a limited number of unidentified fans as well as club partners, in order to gauge the reactions. The feedback was said to be positive, but the supporters wanted to see a bigger change than what had originally been proposed. A month later, a more diverse feedback panel was set up. Fans aged from 4-75, club partners, former players, staff and ambassadors all made up the panel in order to better equip the club with what would turn out to be a historic decision.

After the formation of the panel, one specific crest was clearly winning the contest. A month later, the badge was tested in the form of digital and retail product trials. In March 2021, the final artwork was agreed and then in April, the 2022 season retail ranges were signed off with the new crest in place. The decision had finally been made after almost two years of planning.

Following that, more meticulous planning was in the works, centred around how and when the club would unveil their new look to their supporters, the same fanbase that had already caught wind that change was afoot. As well as that, a full audit took place at Craven Park since every location of the crest needed to be updated. In August, the first retail product featuring the new badge arrived. The clock was ticking away; the launch looming ever closer.

And then the clock stopped. 10 September 2021 was the date.

It seemed like a normal day. The weather was 25 degrees, quite typical of Hull weather at that time of year. The public were attending their daily business but something was quite different. A dozen red and white stickers had been stuck all around Hull, featuring eyes of some sort…? Perhaps an emblem? Later that day, a small, select number of sponsors and other individuals were arriving at Craven Park for 5 pm ahead of a presentation of sorts.
Speculation on a change of crest was fuelled throughout the day since the club had already removed their badge profile photo on all of their social media pages at 1 pm, replacing them all with a red wall. Could it be? Are those red and white stickers somehow tied in with the club's badge removal on social media? The speculation would continue to grow as the clock ticked ever closer to 5 pm.

The clock finally struck 5 o'clock. At Craven Park, Craig Franklin and Paul Lakin would convey the process and reasoning behind a change that was about to be unveiled to the world through the means of social media.

A video landed on social media at 6 pm. Entitled 'It's time to #RiseAgain', the short video was narrated by owner Neil Hudgell:
'The famous Hull Kingston Rovers. The Robins. Representing the three crowns of Hull for 140 years. Proud of our history, our tradition. But to truly grow, you have to look forwards and evolve,' As Hudgell read out his last line, the crowns on the screen turned to the all-too-familiar eyes that had appeared on the stickers around Hull.
'Let's create new memories together and look forward to new horizons with determination and fierce eyes. To build for our tomorrow. This is a symbol. A colour. An identity that shouts, "We are Hull KR!" The Robins. This is our city. This is our time. We are ready to rise again'

And with that, the new badge was fully revealed after an inspiring montage that would have tugged on the heartstrings of many ardent Rovers fans, considering the message that was delivered and given who delivered it, since it was Hudgell's first important dialogue since reaffirming his financial commitment to the club.

The new crest was striking. It retained the shield shape of its predecessors, yet it was different to all of them. The three crowns were replaced by the robin eyes and there was no sign of the Hull Kingston Rovers name. Instead, it was replaced by 'HULL KR', which featured boldly above the eyes. The colour scheme was predominantly red, with white featuring for the robin eyes and outline which also surrounded the text. Although the crowns had been removed there was a form of compromise, since they looked similar to the crowns in terms of shape.

One immediate noticeable aspect of the new crest was the removal of the Hull Kingston Rovers name. It provoked fears from supporters that the club's historical name was about to be wiped in favour of a shortened moniker. It was no surprise that such fears were brought to the fore considering that all of the club's emails were also shortened and that in their statements, the club referred to themselves as just 'Hull KR' as well. However, it wasn't the case, as Paul Lakin told the *Yorkshire Post*: 'As a company and a club we're Hull Kingston Rovers overall but this [Hull KR] is our brand. The vast majority of people call us Hull KR so it's not like we're changing what most people say anyway. It keeps it lean and clean.'

Reactions to the new badge went from one extreme to another. Some lavished praise on it, proclaiming that they 'loved' it, with one gentleman getting it tattooed on his skin just weeks after the reveal. On the opposite end of the spectrum, some supporters reacted badly to the change, vowing to never purchase a single piece of merchandise from the club again unless they reinstated the Littlefield design.

Rovers, already expecting an ocean of varying emotions and opinions from their supporter base, pressed on with the change and in excess of 20 merchandise ranges were soon made available for purchase, all featuring the new crest. The club were rushed off their feet when it came to the changes. Less than 24 hours later, the club's July stadium audit had already started to bear fruit since Craven Park was about to host a crunch Super League tie as Rovers faced Castleford. Tony Smith and plenty of others were already sporting the new merchandise, and fans would be greeted by a winking robin eye from the stadium's big screen as they traversed through the partisan Craven Streat. The club's new crest could be seen in many areas of the stadium and the timing couldn't be better since the game was televised on *Sky Sports*.

Rovers were headstrong with their decision. Ultimately, not every single supporter understood the decision behind the move and the club would have to sacrifice goodwill with some of them in order to reach what they felt would be a positive future; filled with more commercial opportunities than ever before, increased marketability and more. Other rebrands had not gone so well due to various reasons. Whether it was Leeds United's disastrous attempt in 2018 that was scrapped within hours - or closer to home on the south bank of the River Humber, where Grimsby Town slightly adjusted their long-standing crest in order to adapt digitally, only for it to be met with widespread disapproval from their fan base since they weren't consulted beforehand. They promptly decided to rescind the crest and decided on a voting process instead.

Regardless of their feelings on the badge itself, a decent number of Rovers' fans were consulted and involved in the process. It spared Rovers from the ignominy that other sports clubs had faced. Another clear line of communication from the club was a section of their website which was dedicated to explaining their rebrand in near full detail – with the only exception being the lack of clarity over if the club had shortened their name altogether.

One prime example of Rovers' new commercial pull came in January 2022 when the club announced a partnership with New Era. At the time, New Era's reach was so vast that the likelihood of a supporter passing somebody wearing New Era merchandise on the street was very strong. Now, Rovers' supporters could wear the same headwear and represent their club while doing so.

Paul Lakin left no doubt as to how important the new crest was to closing the deal, telling the club's official website: 'New Era is a globally recognised brand that we are proud to associate our new look crest with. One of the aspirations of evolving our branding was to open new doors and opportunities for the club where the old crest simply wouldn't have been as strong. This a good example of where we have been able to forge a partnership on the back of it, and will open the club up to a potential new market'

While some fans balked at the £24.99 price point, others embraced the quality and were quick to hand Rovers their hard-earned cash in exchange for high quality headwear, the likes that the club had never seen in its entire 140-year history up until that point. Without the badge's evolution, the deal likely would have never happened.

Another upside to the club's new crest that its predecessor didn't possess was its flexibility. The old design's main feature was the three crowns and the club's hierarchy didn't feel confident that they would appeal to the younger and future generations that they were aspiring to reel in. Instead, the concept of the robin eyes and features being placed on a cap were described by Franklin as 'aspirational', especially to youngsters.

The same type of flexibility was prevalent in the NFL and it was a direct inspiration for the club. For instance, the Los Angeles Rams could feature their signature ram on one piece of merchandise and their wordmark text on another. As a result of the new crest, Rovers now had similar options.

The changing, digital world had deceived some doubters regarding its importance since some of its nuances hid in plain sight. Millions upon millions of people, ranging from young to old, would trawl through social media timelines in search of news, views, or whatever else floated their boat. For instance, if a non-fan discovered a Hull KR tweet, then they would barely be able to make out the Littlefield design in the 8mm x 8mm sized profile logo space. 75% of internet traffic was projected to be driven by mobile devices by 2025, and in anticipation, Rovers had to be ready to attract potential new fans, according to Franklin. In essence, it was another example of how the new crest's flexibility could benefit the club because the robin eyes symbol stood out as more eye-catching for possible newcomers.

A year on from the rebrand, Paul Lakin spoke about the commercial benefits that it brought: 'It's allowed us to provide a much wider range of products that could appeal to the younger market with the elements of the new crest, the robin in particular, which is a lot more appealing for merchandise. In terms of pure income sales, we've done extremely well in terms of additional sales.'

Lakin felt that there was more to come: 'It's all about developing the brand. It's only one year old and there's a lot more that we can do with the crest in terms of marketing and merchandising. And that's what we intend to do.'

When it was all said and done, 'evolution' was the prevailing word when it came to the club's new look. Whether it would stand the test of time? That remained to be seen, but if it could match or better Samuel Littlefield's design in terms of both legacy and longevity, then it would be a fine innings indeed.

A YEAR OF CHANGE

JUNE

With the English weather starting to heat up, Rovers' out-of-contract player situation followed suit. On the first day of the new month, Shaun Kenny-Dowall signed a one-year extension. With Rovers' skipper turning 35 in time for the 2023 season, the move was a gamble. Would the club be handing out a quota spot to a player that had gone on a year too long? It had to be said that Kenny-Dowall hadn't shown too many signs of letting up during 2022. Either way, the question would be answered in due course.

Aside from Willie Peters retaining one of the key moving parts that had led Rovers back up the Super League ladder, the signature also changed the overseas quota situation. Albert Vete, Brad Takairangi and Korbin Sims remained as the final three players with an uncertain future, and since Rovers' management team were already closing in on two overseas recruits, only one of the three would have a chance at landing a new deal with Hull KR.

Cornwall was said to be a lovely place to be in summertime and that's exactly where Adam Rusling would be staying until the end of the season. On 2 June, the 19-year-old had extended his deal with the side on their inaugural season. Veteran boss Neil Kelly paid tribute to the Robins for allowing the move to happen and also described the move as 'beneficial' to both Rusling and the Cornwall club itself.

A YEAR OF CHANGE

5/6/2022
Hull Kingston Rovers vs. Salford Red Devils
Betfred Super League (Round 14)

Rovers: Coote, Ryan, Crooks, Kenny-Dowall, Hall, Lewis, Milnes, Storton, Parcell, King, Johnson, Halton, Hadley
Interchanges: Vete, Litten, Minchella, Keinhorst

Salford: Brierley, Sio, Cross, Lafai, Burgess, Croft, Sneyd, Ormondroyd, Bourouh, Gerrard, Livett, Watkins, Taylor
Interchanges: Addy, Dupree, Escare, Lannon

After suffering through a four-match losing run, there was never a better time to beat Salford. The Red Devils were just two points behind the Robins at the start of the game, plus with a resurgent Leeds being just one point behind, the chasing pack were closing in on Rovers. The heat was on. All of a sudden, the lowly placing of tenth wasn't out of the question unless the results improved. If the season was to be rescued, a turnaround had to start here. The game also saw the welcomed return of Mikey Lewis, who had recovered from rupturing his ankle ligaments.

It was a cold and damp day; rather atypical of June time, even by British standards. With less than an hour until kick-off, Craven Park looked sparse, although it did later fill out more. The fans that did brave the weather had something to shout about early on thanks to a strong defensive effort from the Robins. Rovers looked like the better side in the opening exchanges and it would have been no surprise if they had opened up the scoring, but instead a cruel ricochet led to a Salford break. Facing a two-on-one situation, Ethan Ryan appeared to be helpless as the ball was switched to Ken Sio, yet Sio would be the one that ended up in the dirt as Ryan bundled him into touch in what was a magnificent effort against all odds. Belief then started to seep through the entire side; a strong defensive start laid the platform for Rovers to venture further up the field, as Lachlan Coote demonstrated his class when catching his own kick to score the first try of the game. Rovers had a break of their own minutes later, and unlike Salford, they didn't waste their opportunity. Coote was over for his second. And then a third came through Ryan Hall after an excellent long ball from Rowan Milnes.

Leading 18-0, Rovers looked like they were about to hand out a real beating. But then Salford's luck changed. After collecting a kick near his own line, Matt Parcell produced a major error by trying to offload the ball, when he should have died with it behind his own line. Salford were adjudged to have grounded the stray ball despite Lewis' best efforts. The Salford fans, who had a great view of the try, sensed that a comeback was on. After all, it wouldn't be the first time that Salford had launched a comeback at Craven Park.

The Robins didn't let the try deter them. With less than 40 seconds left on the clock, Coote slotted over a one-pointer to give Rovers a 19-6 lead heading into half-time.

The second half started just as the first had begun. Rovers were on top, and it didn't take for them long to score again. An inaccurate pass fortuitously found Shaun Kenny-Dowall, who then made a darting run at the defence, drawing the attention of five men before sending Hall in for his second. Staring defeat in the face, the away side started to become niggly. Rovers, however, showed Salford no respect. Instead, they pummelled them, and the efforts which were led by George King, received the admiration of the home faithful. Salford's off-field antics resulted in forward Tyler Dupree being sinbinned. Away from the dark arts, another stray ball was collected by Ryan who glided past the opposition to seal the game.

Rovers weren't done. Jez Litten cast about the suffering Salford line before finding Ben Crooks, who went in. Just as the Red Devils were back to a full complement of players, ex-Rovers man Harvey Livett was sinbinned. Salford did hit back on the scoreboard through a neat piece of play at the other end, only to concede again as Crooks went in for his second. Salford simply couldn't live with Rovers' pace and trickery on the day, but a late interception did see them score last to wrap up the proceedings. Just when Salford thought they had the 'last laugh', the rug was pulled from underneath them. Marc Sneyd slid after hitting his conversion, not only missing, but also abruptly landing on his backside in front of the boisterous East Stand which jeered him. In the end, Rovers were 43-16 victors.

It was moments like Ethan Ryan's exemplary piece of defending that ensured that it would always be the Robins' day. Their attitude towards defending was first-class and set them well on their way towards enjoying a comfortable afternoon. There was a number of stand-out performer. From the classy Lachlan Coote who picked up the home man-of-the-match award, to the hustle and bustle of Albert Vete, George King and Dean Hadley. So many players played their part, including Shaun Kenny-Dowall, who caused Salford endless trouble. If he could replicate that form in 2023, then he would have more than vindicated the club's decision to hand him a new contract.

But it wasn't a day about individuals when it came to the grand scheme of things. A win was an absolute must. A loss would have heaped more pressure on Tony Smith, and also accelerated the rate of what was becoming an alarming decline. As it was, praise for Smith was few and far between. The head coach was the afterthought after such an impressive win, even though the manner of Rovers' tries were very much as artistic as Smith desired them to be. Thanks to his actions in April, most of the supporters' credit for him was reserved even though it was Smith that had built this on-field project. He had made his bed and would have to lie in it, although he still had the chance to make one last golden memory with what remaining time he had left at Craven Park. The performance and result were a step in the right direction.

Full-Time Score: Hull Kingston Rovers 43-16 Salford Red Devils
Attendance: 7,023
League Position: 6th; 253 points scored; 272 points conceded; -19 points difference; 14 points

Youngster Nathan Cullen joined Cornwall on a one-month loan deal on 11 June. The 19-year-old had risen through the ranks at Cottingham Tigers to earn a deal with Rovers, although at this point he hadn't made a first-team appearance. A prop by trade, he was joining Adam Rusling at the Choughs.

He became the latest young player to head out to the lower divisions on loan. Whether he and the others would end up forging a career at Craven Park was one thing, but either way, the experience of playing first-team games enhanced their chances of gaining a contract elsewhere if opportunities didn't materialise for them during their time with the Robins.

A YEAR OF CHANGE

12/6/2022
St Helens vs. Hull Kingston Rovers
Betfred Super League (Round 15)

St Helens: Hopoate, Makinson, Hurrell, Davies, Grace, Welsby, Lomax, Walmsley, Roby, Lees, Bell, Batchelor, Knowles
Interchanges: Lussick, Paasi, Wingfield, Norman

Rovers: Coote, Ryan, Crooks, Kenny-Dowall, Hall, Lewis, Milnes, Storton, Parcell, King, Johnson, Halton, Hadley
Interchanges: Vete, Litten, Minchella, Keinhorst

Rovers' next Super League test was far greater than the last. They were playing St Helens, the side that had conquered the domestic game in 2021, and also the same team that had comprehensively beaten Rovers in the reverse fixture. If the Robins were about to pull off a surprise on Merseyside, they would have to do it without Korbin Sims, who was once again missing with no explanation.

The first ten minutes of the contest were eventful. It took the home side just a minute to take the lead when a cruel, bouncing ball deceived Ryan Hall and allowed Saints in. Then, Jack Welsby was sinbinned after a late hit on Lachlan Coote, who had just caught the ball in his own in-goal area. After two set restarts, Rovers were in Saints territory and took the lead for the first time through none other than Coote himself. However, despite being a man down, St Helens regained the lead. James Roby was celebrating his 455th Super League appearance – a competition record – and he celebrated in style by selling a dummy to multiple Rovers defenders, bagging himself a try on his special day. Saints were now cooking; they extended their lead to 16-6 after exploiting a gap that Dean Hadley had left behind.

Crucially, Rovers were the next team to score. A cut-out pass sent Hall free, bringing the Robins back into the game at 16-12. In the build-up to the match, Coote had spoken about his time at St Helens with emotion, yet he refused to be wrapped up in the home fans' boos when dispatching an excellent conversion which raised the hopes of the travelling Robins. In what was turning out to be a frenetic first half, Welsby could have counted himself fortunate to still be on the field after delivering a shoulder charge. It wasn't the only decision that went in Saints' favour, with the home side enjoying the majority of the 50/50 decisions. Even so, Rovers would have agonized over not going level or even ahead by the time the half was close to its end. They had the chances but they couldn't capitalise on them. Instead, they were having to defend as half-time beckoned. Rovers' defenders held Saints down three times which seemed like the right thing to do in that moment. But it ended up backfiring, as Matt Parcell was sinbinned for persistent holding down. Saints then kicked a conversion to take their lead up to 18-12.

Although the Robins were very much in the game, it was undeniable that the first ten minutes of the second half were crucial due to Parcell's sinbinning. If they could ride out the storm, then they had every chance.

After seven minutes of astute game management to tick away every second, and with St Helens in their own ten, everything looked rosy at the start of the second half. That was until a rampaging Konrad Hurrell flattened Albert Vete and Coote, laying the platform for a great breakaway try for the home side.

Despite the setback, Rovers kept on pushing and some slick passing seemed to undo the Saints defence, but just as Mikey Lewis was heading in for a try, the move was pulled back for a forward pass, a dubious decision in itself. Rovers appeared be in the ascendancy, but at the other end of the field, Hurrell galloped past Rowan Milnes and crashed over to extend Saints' lead further. A moment of inspiration from Shaun Kenny-Dowall which sent Coote in for his second try of the game with just minutes to spare was a little too late, although it was the least that the players deserved as they ended up losing 26-18. After Tony Smith confirmed his exit in April, one of the main questions that was asked was if the players had been distracted by the happenings away from the pitch. This performance and the Salford one answered the question a resounding 'no'. The players were committed, which was exemplified by the colossal Alex Walmsley being held up over the line in the dying moments of the game when the result was inevitable.

One major issue was the bench. It featured just one prop, albeit a sizeable one. Nevertheless, it was apparent by this point that Rovers weren't seeing value for money when it came to Korbin Sims. Allegedly one of the biggest earners at the club, as well as taking up an overseas spot, he had played on the previous day in a reserves fixture after failing to make the 21-man squad for the Saints game. The reasons as to why Sims was absent remained unclear.

To some, holding St Helens to just eight points was success. The players had done themselves justice, and if some decisions went their way and they had been a little more clinical, then they likely would've claimed a priceless win. But it wasn't to be. Instead, it was the same old story of 'so close, yet so far' when it came to matching up with the Saints. That had to change at some point.

Full-Time Score: St Helens 26-18 Hull Kingston Rovers
Attendance: 9,858
League Position: 7th; 271 points scored; 298 points conceded; -17 points difference; 14 points

In order to salvage their season, Rovers needed to reach the play-offs. With 12 fixtures remaining, just four points separated the Robins from eleventh-placed Wakefield, although only two separated them from Hull FC in fifth. A win at Toulouse meant that Castleford had replaced Rovers in sixth with everything still to play for as the season started to reach its later stages.

All but one player would be enjoying a week's break away from action as England prepared to play the Combined Nations All Stars on 18 June. The special individual that was missing out on the break was Shaun Kenny-Dowall, whom earned coach Ellery Hanley's approval by becoming the All Stars' captain for the occasion. Ryan Hall would also be involved in the game, capping off a fantastic comeback story and also illustrating how successful his Hull KR career had been up until this point.

On the flip side, 20 June brought further bad news for Luis Johnson. The 23-year-old had suffered a ruptured pectoral, ruling him out of action for 12 weeks. Unless Rovers made the play-offs and Johnson was figured into those games, his season was over. Johnson's season had never really started. He picked up a foot injury in pre-season, and after making a recovery from that, this injury had more or less finished his season. 2022 was a write-off as far as he was concerned.

The 'letting the cat out of the bag' idiom was given a whole new meaning on 23 June. It wasn't just one cat, but three, and all of them were rough and rugged. When talking to an Australian podcast entitled 'Toohey's News', incoming Rovers coach Willie Peters let it slip that the club had secured the services of three new signings for 2023: Rhys Kennedy, Sauaso "Jesse" Sue and Tom Opacic.
Kennedy and Opacic had been linked with the club for over a week, while Sue's name first came up during the podcast. Standing at 6'6" and weighing over 17 stones, Kennedy was a towering prop-forward, but had never settled in the NRL. He had played for Canberra and South Sydney but failed to nail down a first-team spot with either side. He was joining Rovers from Brisbane, where he had mainly played from off the bench. During his time back home, the 27-year-old, who would be turning 28 ahead of 2023, had balanced his rugby career with his studies. Entering the prime of his career, his studies would

switch from physiology to places such as Wigan and Warrington, as big expectations awaited him in England.

Opacic was a different story. A centre, the 27-year-old had worked tirelessly to make the centre position at Parramatta his own in 2021 and 2022. After making 21 appearances in 2021, he started 2022 as part of the Eels' NSW Cup squad, only to break back into the first-team. At the time Rovers landed his signature, Opacic was named in State of Origin selection discussion. It was regarded by some quarters as a coup, and the deal was reportedly worth $500,000 (AUD) over a three-year period, a hefty financial commitment to prise the 27-year-old away. It was another indication that Rovers were committed to Peters and his vision, as well as the goal of breaking into the elite bracket of clubs.

The signing of Sue made perfect sense. Despite being the oldest of the three at 30, Sue, just like the others, was still enjoying his prime. He was also well acquainted with Peters, having played under him at Newcastle in 2021 and 2022. Sue had made over 150 NRL appearances since 2013, and also earned international recognition with Samoa. He had versatility value, since he could play at prop, second-row and loose-forward. Despite that, it appeared that he would be played as a prop at Craven Park. When speaking to the podcast, Peters acknowledged the large amount of work that George King would go through per game, hinting that Sue would ease that workload. Above all, he was regarded as a 'hardman' down under and Rovers needed another enforcer.

The incomings were all impressive, at least on paper. All three were coming in at the peak of their careers, and all of them had good pedigree. Paul Lakin and Danny McGuire had spoken at length with Peters regarding the state of the 2022 squad. After watching every competitive game that Rovers had played throughout the year, Peters picked the troops that he would be flying over with. For his tenure's sake, they needed to be the right kind of soldier to deal with the English top-flight.

On the other side of the fence, the signings spelt the end of the line for Albert Vete, Brad Takairangi and Korbin Sims. The evidence was clear: all three of Rovers' new signings matched the aforementioned three in terms of position. Vete's stint had promised so much, but delivered little in the grand scheme of things, mainly due to injuries and suspensions hampering his two-year spell. Takairangi demonstrated his sheer class at times during 2021, but he was on a hiding to nothing after his off-field incident dominated conversations from January onwards. His season-ending injury compounded a year to forget; his Rovers career generally failed to live up to expectations. Sims was a conundrum. His form was acceptable in the previous season, but the feeling around the club was that 2022 would be a much better season for him. It didn't transpire, however, and instead Sims' appearances became fewer than ever, despite being fit to play. All three signings had to be regarded as failures when considering their import status and reputations.

From what would soon become the distant past, to a possible bright future, Will Tate signed a new two-year deal with Rovers on 24 June. He had clearly earned the approval of Willie Peters, despite failing to make a Super League appearance in 2022. Although he was still only 20, he still had more proving to do if he was to make the grade at Craven Park. Up until this point, he had only made five first-team appearances, some of which were in a disjointed side during 2020.

A YEAR OF CHANGE

26/6/2022
Hull Kingston Rovers vs. Huddersfield Giants
Betfred Super League (Round 16)

Rovers: Coote, Ryan, Crooks, Kenny-Dowall, Hall, Lewis, Milnes, King, Parcell, Storton, Halton, Hadley, Minchella
Interchanges: Vete, Litten, Keinhorst, Richards

Huddersfield: Lolohea, McGillvary, Cudjoe, Leutele, Senior, Russell, Pryce, Wilson, Levi, Lawrence, McQueen, Jones, English
Interchanges: Yates, Greenwood, Golding, Trout

Following the previous two encounters with Huddersfield, this one whet the appetite of not only fans of both clubs, but also Super League's main broadcasters: the fixture was shown live on *Sky Sports*. It was no surprise. Both clubs were trying to break out of the pack and reach the top four. If the truth be told, at this point Rovers would have been looking at the Giants with envious eyes. Even though they had a much better season than Huddersfield in 2021, year two of the Ian Watson project was much more successful than year one and the Giants were flying high in fourth place. Their results were a lot more consistent than Rovers' in 2021; and since Huddersfield barely broke a sweat in their 25-4 defeat of the Robins during the Challenge Cup semi-final, it was the Giants who were looking like the stronger side.
The roar that welcomed Rovers out onto the pitch was eclipsed by a louder one just minutes later when the side took an early lead just two minutes into the game. The fans had to wait in the sizzling heat for the game to begin and the start didn't disappoint. Rovers looked to be in again through Frankie Halton. Despite Halton appearing to ground the ball on the footage that was replayed, video referee Tom Grant controversially disallowed the score despite on-field referee Chris Kendall's original ruling of a try.
Whilst being in the midst of an arm wrestle, Rovers started to lose troops. George King had already withdrawn early on with a hamstring issue; Elliot Minchella went off for a head injury assessment; and just after the 15-minute mark, Ryan Hall was the latest casualty after suffering a rib injury. Minchella would return, although the game

looked a lot different to how it was when he went off: Huddersfield were on top. Their pressure finally paid off after grinding a tiring Rovers down through Leroy Cudjoe. His try looked less convincing than the Rovers one that was disallowed. Nevertheless, it was given and Huddersfield led for the first time. Ian Watson later admitted that one of his side's goals was to quieten down the home crowd and within half an hour, they had achieved that particular mission.

There was an air of bemusement as Jimmy Keinhorst failed to deal with a smart kick, allowing Cudjoe to score a second. The Robins' kicking game in the early stages had caused the Giants issues, but by half-time it was clear that Huddersfield were the better outfit. The injury adversity had rattled Rovers and the game was only heading one way, barring a second half revival.

Despite being just six points behind with a full half to play, Rovers opted to go short for the start of the second half. The ball ended being patted back, taking a bounce, before falling into the arms of an onrushing Luke Yates. The prop ended up storming past Coote - who was later revealed to be playing through an injury – before touching down after running 65 metres. The short kick-off had well and truly backfired. Just over a minute later, the away side caught Rovers short with some quick passing, going in for another try. Rovers' injury situation had also worsened: Mikey Lewis was playing on with a dead leg, while Coote, Minchella and Litten followed suit in terms of playing on through injury.

Cudjoe hadn't scored a try all season up until this game, but now he was a hat-trick hero as the Giants scored again. By this point, Craven Park was Huddersfield's playground and they were having a ball. Will Pryce's footwork was too much for the tired Rovers legs, resulting in another score. Some fans had already decided that enough was enough, and more streamed out after Jermaine McGillvary stormed over for another try just minutes later. In a rare instance of Rovers having a period of possession, they managed to score a late consolation after Matty Storton went in under the sticks. At full-time, it was the Huddersfield camp that were all smiles.

After the twentieth minute, the Robins were always second best. Huddersfield ran hard, finished in clinical fashion and ultimately tired Rovers out; the second half was a masterclass in punching holes through a tired defence. It was granted that Rovers had been desperately unlucky with the injuries they sustained over the game, yet that was no excuse for a poor showing, and even less excusable was the light bench that was decided before kick-off.

In another disappointing defeat, it was becoming clear that 2022 was turning into a difficult year for Rovers. The injuries were decimating the side, but by the same token, there appeared to be something not quite right with the team. Whether it was the Tony Smith bombshell or not, all was not well.

Full-Time Score: Hull Kingston Rovers 10-38 Huddersfield Giants
Attendance: 7,050
League Position: 7th; 281 points scored; 336 points conceded; -55 points difference; 14 points

After the Huddersfield game, the injury problems continued to mount. Two of Rovers' key producers in George King and Ryan Hall became the latest victims. King had a small hamstring tear, which would rule him out for around two to four weeks. Hall was suffering from a rib cartilage issue which ruled him out of the following game against Toulouse and made him a doubt for the Hull derby. King had been Rovers' most consistent prop up until this point, whereas Hall's power and size was a godsend as it related to making yardage from backfield. Both would be sorely missed ahead of a crucial run of fixtures.

A YEAR OF CHANGE

JULY

2/7/2022
Toulouse Olympique vs. Hull Kingston Rovers
Betfred Super League (Round 17)

Toulouse: Ashall-Bott, Schaumkel, Armitage, Hankinson, Macron, Norman, Gigot, Navarette, Peats, Alvaro, Bretherton, Peyroux, Paulo
Interchanges: Albert, Hansen, Belmas, Sangare

Rovers: Dagger, Ryan, Wood, Kenny-Dowall, Crooks, Milnes, Lewis, Vete, Parcell, Storton, Hadley, Halton, Minchella
Interchanges: Litten, Sims, Keinhorst, Richards

The huge month of July started with another trip France, with Rovers once again taking on the division's basement club in Toulouse. The French were desperate for a win since Wakefield had started to pull away from the trapdoor with consecutive wins - Toulouse needed three wins to catch Trinity. Meanwhile, Rovers knew what they had to do after Hull FC succumbed to a humiliating 62-16 home defeat to Leeds. The play-off door was as open as ever, but opportunity had to be seized.
Despite being hit with injuries, many would have argued that the side Rovers fielded was good enough to win in Toulouse. However, the injury issues that were now starting to decimate the squad were on show again. While two Toulouse players were involved in a head clash, Matty Storton went down inside five minutes and was forced off. His replacement, Greg Richards, then suffered problems of his own. Richards recovered, yet it was still a vivid glimpse into the Robins' injury woes which were again manifesting on the field.
After a stop-start opening 15 minutes, a pinpoint kick from Tony Gigot found Latrell Schaumkel, who scored in the corner. Minutes later, Toulouse looked like they were in again, only for a Gigot pass to be ruled forward. It was clear who was on top by this point. After some ill-discipline from Rovers, Olympique extended their lead to 8-

0 but it could have been more just five minutes later as Schaumkel somehow managed to screw up a golden opportunity. Nine times out of ten, he would have walked in for a try. The remainder of the half mostly revolved around Toulouse coming close to adding to their score, with some close shaves and excellent goal-line defence from Rovers. 8-0 was the half-time score and it flattered the away side.

Minutes into the second half, the Robins produced more fine goal-line defence, only for Toulouse to find a numerical advantage moments later. This time, a walk-in try materialised. Rovers' lack of discipline came back to haunt them again, with Toulouse taking the two points on offer to increase the score to 16-0. Tony Smith's men looked to be regressing further when Will Dagger kicked straight out onto the full after the restart, but they managed to fight for some ground. It seemed like Sam Wood was about to get Rovers on the scoreboard, before knocking on after getting over the tryline.

Chris Hankinson, who had kicked some excellent conversions on the night, wrapped up the game for Toulouse at 22-0 after the numbers game paid off yet again. Rovers did manage to score a consolation through Albert Vete, who forced himself over. But it was Toulouse who had the final say, and there was no better man to score the try than Rovers' tormentor, Olly Ashall-Bott, who capped off a great performance by scoring. Despite making a great effort to come over for the game, some travelling fans had already seen enough and left before the hooter blew. Rovers had lost again and had just won one game in eight.

The performance shared parallels with that of the Huddersfield game: Rovers were beat in every department. Worryingly, the side looked less potent in attack, with Wood's effort being one of the few notable moments in what was otherwise a forgettable 80 minutes. A rough figure of between 450-550 Rovers fans travelled to the game, a remarkable effort considering the rising costs in inflation back home. At the time, inflation had risen to 9.2 percent, which was its highest in 40 years.

Although the performances were poor, injuries were once again a factor. Lachlan Coote and Ryan Hall had failed to make it back for the game, while Matty Storton presented a fresh worry, as did Matt Parcell who was clutching his shoulder at one point during the game. Parcell did continue, although shoulder injuries were nothing new to him, having undergone surgery in the past.

The side appeared low on confidence, which was especially no good for the likes of Rowan Milnes and Mikey Lewis. The young duo were now playing behind a beaten pack. While Toulouse's forwards laid a great platform for two veterans in Norman and Gigot to play off, the situation was a polar opposite as far as Rovers were concerned. It further illustrated just how important George King was to their pack. After another disappointing defeat, calls from fans for Tony Smith to be dismissed grew louder. Some felt that the Robins' wretched form was down to Smith's shock announcement, and while the bad run did coincide with that, no side could legislate for injuries; especially in the quantity that Rovers were receiving them. Nevertheless, both Neil Hudgell and Paul Lakin were in attendance for the game and they looked far from happy with what they were seeing. The club was now well and truly showing relegation form. They had to decide whether they would stick or twist with the man that had blindsided them only months prior.

At this point, Rovers' season was firmly poised. Without a doubt, the optimism that swept through the club in pre-season had now been well and truly extinguished. After the dust had settled on Round 17, the Robins were positioned eighth; two points off the play-offs and a healthy eight points from the bottom. Castleford had suddenly hit a run of form, meaning that sixth-place stuck out as the only attainable play-off spot during this period. Hull FC, Leeds, Salford and Warrington also had a say in that, and at this juncture, a few of them looked more capable than Rovers. The Robins' next game was the old enemy – something had to give.

Full-Time Score: Toulouse Olympique 28-6 Hull Kingston Rovers
Attendance: 3,441
League Position: 8th; 287 points scored; 364 points conceded; -77 points difference; 14 points

Away from the frustrations on the field, perspective surfaced on the same night as the Toulouse game when it was revealed that former player Mick Crane had passed away at the age of 69.

Although he was mainly associated with Hull FC, Crane did have a spell at Rovers between December 1979 and December 1980. Having started his career at Hull, he rose through the ranks, and by 1977 he was the subject of a £12,000 bid from Leeds – a then record fee. Hull were strapped for cash at the time and accepted.

Crane won himself a Challenge Cup during his stay in West Yorkshire. However, the novelty of heading up and down the M62 for games and training quickly wore off, and Crane became unsettled. Roger Millward caught wind of his situation and Rovers ended up landing his services for £9,000 during the winter of 1979.

At the time, Millward had David Hall and Phil Hogan as his loose-forward options. But Hall was inexperienced in the role, while 'The Dodger' saw Hogan as more of a running second-row. As fate would have it, Len Casey became available, and Rovers wasted no time in bringing him back for what was then a world record fee of £38,000 (plus VAT). As a result, Crane's chances became very limited. Hull FC ended up making an enquiry, and after making 18 appearances and scoring four tries during his one-year spell at Rovers, Crane returned to the Boulevard in late 1980.

Despite his short stay at the Robins, Crane made an impression, just as he did for every team he played for. The news of his passing evoked memories from both sets of fans of a bygone time in the sport. In many ways, Crane was the antithesis of modern rugby league; he was a maverick who played what was in front of him, dazzling crowds in the process. On and off the field, he was known for being a character. It was also known that Crane drank, gambled and smoked. Had he remained more committed to his sporting craft, there was every chance that he could have become one of the all-time greats. Regardless, the city of Hull had lost another one of its great rugby league sons.

The sad news continued a day later when it was announced that Asuquo "Zook" Ema had died at the age of 58 following a battle with a rare form of lymphoma.

Ema carried tragedy on his back from an early age when his father was killed during the Nigerian Civil War of 1967-70. Zook was born years earlier, in 1963, after his English and Nigerian parents had met at the University of Hull. He would end up travelling to Nigeria while the conflict was ongoing, before heading back to England years later. He eventually took up rugby league, playing for Hull Boys, and would soon find his way to Hull Kingston Rovers' colts. At the time, Rovers were flying high; trophies were expected, rather than hoped for. Despite stiff competition from the side's forwards at the time, Ema began an ascension up the Craven Park ladder, and by the start of the 1983-84 campaign, he was on the fringes of the first-team. He ended up making his debut during a season in which Rovers would eventually win the Championship and Premiership double, but his fortunes changed when he suffered a serious knee injury.

Showing character and dedication, Ema came back after a year away and claimed a first-team berth throughout 1984-85 despite undergoing knee surgery a year earlier. Over the next few years, he obtained three medals and played in many finals while part of a rampaging Rovers side. But all of a sudden, everything changed.

One of the finals that Ema was involved in was the 1986 Challenge Cup final at Wembley where underdogs Castleford were the opponents. After John Dorahy missed an all-or-nothing conversion, Zook was one of the figures shown at the end of the game. He looked dejected, while Dorahy was inconsolable. For many, that game marked the start of a frighteningly quick decline for Rovers.

Ema was part of the Rovers team that succumbed to relegation in 1989, and he was also part of the one that bounced straight back up a season later. Unfortunately, things were never the same for both the club and Ema.

By 1992, Rovers were struggling to keep their heads above water, and Zook was struggling with the knee that had previously been reconstructed. He chose to retire having made 233 appearances, scoring 18 tries during that time.

Although he was a capable prop-forward and a memorable part of Rovers' mid-1980s success, Asuquo Ema's biggest impression was made away from the field. Despite facing childhood trauma that could forever haunt a human being, Ema tackled life as hard as he did his rugby opponents. He was known as an approachable man that had time for others, and those that knew him were always greeted with a healthy smile. One of his former neighbours recalled that during his playing days, Ema would bring their son a signed programme from the game that he had just played in, every single week.

In the words of Neil Hudgell, Ema was a 'champion player but much more than that, a champion man.'

On 4 July, the clock hit 11 am and it was announced that Hull Kingston Rovers had stood Tony Smith down as head coach with immediate effect. A short statement from the club read:

'The club have this morning stood Tony Smith down as head coach for the remainder of the season. Danny McGuire will take charge of all first-team matters until Willie Peters arrives in the Autumn. Danny will be assistant coach to Willie, having recently signed a three-year contract extension to stay with the Robins until the end of 2025. We would like to take the opportunity to thank Tony for all his hard work over the last three years. The club are in a much better place than when he started.'

The news wasn't totally unexpected. Rovers had won just one game in eight and that was unacceptable by any Super League club's standards, let alone one that had aspirations of competing at the top on a regular basis. However, the poor run of form had clearly shattered the hierarchy's confidence in Smith's ability to turn things around, and with the club's league season at a crossroads, it was looking like a change had to be made in order for the season to play out on a happier note.

When Smith had taken over at Rovers halfway through 2019, the club was staring down the barrel at another relegation battle. His predecessor, Tim Sheens, had rotten luck with injuries but many considered his tactics to be antiquated. Despite the magnificent achievement of coaching Rovers back into the top-flight at the first attempt in 2017, he never won the entire fanbase over. Just like other coaches, he had failed to lift Rovers from being basement dwellers.

It was a topsy-turvy end to the season, but in the end, Smith managed to keep the club in the division, aided by memorable wins over Catalans, Hull FC and Leeds. In the Leeds game, Rovers displayed an enterprising style of play which would later become the hallmark of Smith's tenure as Rovers' head coach, although at that point the priority was points over performances.

After securing another year of Super League, the recruitment for 2020 edged towards the unproven unknown, rather than the proven known.

The uncertainty over the club's league status didn't help the recruitment options, especially since the 2019 relegation battle went to the final day of the season. Still, Smith used pre-season to bed in his preferred style of play, and it already bore fruit when Rovers swept Wakefield aside in the opening round of 2020. They got edged out in the following week at Hull, yet that didn't dent many Rovers fans' pride. Despite a derby loss, 2020 felt different: Rovers looked to be playing better and they were far more adventurous. A Ben Crooks derby try that involved ten passes was proof that Rovers were looking to entertain.

Unfortunately, the wheels quickly fell off. A threadbare squad that lacked quality was quickly exposed, with injuries accelerating a hasty tumble down the table. Just as it was starting to look like Rovers would be involved in yet another battle at the bottom, the season was postponed due to the Coronavirus outbreak. Upon the seasons return, Smith had a new look. He had shaved his hair and grown a goatee. The look would end up becoming synonymous with dark times during the middle and end of 2020, with Rovers losing most of their games and the fans being left with no choice but to sit at home and stomach it. In the end, the Robins finished bottom of an 11-team division after Toronto dropped out. The only real shining light was a magnificent 34-18 victory over Wigan, a game in which Mikey Lewis bagged a brace. In hindsight, it foreshadowed what was to come in 2021.

2021 itself was a different story. The recruitment appeared to be a big step up from the previous year, with seasoned NRL imports joining the club. Yet most of the season's success was down to English players, most of which Smith coached and/or nurtured into better players. Shaun Kenny-Dowall, who was the biggest incoming of 2020, had a much-improved second season; while Kane Linnett proved to be the greatest piece of the Sheens inheritance, as well as the king of the imports.

After a disappointing home loss against Wakefield towards the end of the year, Rovers appeared to have blown their opportunity to make their first play-off appearance since 2013. In many ways, it was eerily similar to how many viewed Rovers' 2022 play-off chances at the time of Smith's departure. But instead, the team bounced back and ended up securing their top-six spot with a game to spare.

Few pundits and supporters gave the Robins a chance when they travelled to Warrington, yet they were in for a surprise. One of

A YEAR OF CHANGE

Rovers' main vulnerabilities throughout most of their time in Super League was the art of defending. Throughout 2021, Rovers had arguably defended better than they had in any other top-flight season from 2007 onwards. Away at an expensively-assembled Warrington, they showed the same defensive nous to keep the Wolves at bay, and then ended up countering them, eventually winning 19-0. It was Smith's most memorable game in charge and set up the club's first ever play-off semi-final of the modern era. On a big night in Perpignan, the journey ended when a patched-up Robins outfit went down 28-10. Old Trafford had never been so close.

Despite the disappointment of losing in France, the supporters had witnessed countless years of dross, to all of a sudden, a team on the cusp of domestic greatness. It was quite a turnaround and a large part of it was down to Smith. He had reached into the Championship, picked out a crop of players and coached many of them into top-flight talent; blooded in the likes of Mikey Lewis; gave confidence to Jordan Abdull so he could lead; and made stalwarts out of figures such as Linnett and Kenny-Dowall.

Short-term success or failure can quickly cloud a consumer's mind. Some never forgave Smith for his actions in April 2022, and that was quite understandable. He had made a decision to go into business for himself and announce his own departure. It made him and Rovers look bad. But it was Smith who bore the brunt of the criticism. Whether supporters liked to admit it or not, through his own actions, Smith had tainted his legacy at Craven Park. Still, the same supporters that criticised Smith – even upon his dismissal – were likely the same people that were fed up at seeing Rovers as a club making up the numbers, year in, year out. They were venting their frustrations at a man that had transformed Hull KR; thanks to Smith, Rovers were now an upwardly mobile club, one that was becoming attractive to much better players. If any success was about to come under Willie Peters, then Smith's paws would be imprinted into the DNA somewhere.

The biggest shame was without a doubt the note that Smith left on. When he initially was parachuted in for the 2019 rescue job, it was a three-month agreement between himself and Neil Hudgell, whom Smith had previously struck up a friendship with. It eventually became three years; a time that was met with plenty of ups and downs, joy and happiness, pride, anger, sadness and everything in-between. Above all, it was a successful period that had refocused Rovers as a club.

Tony Smith joined with something to prove and vowed to make the fans proud of the players that donned their badge, and by the end, he proved himself as one of the better coaches around, as well as having re-established a bond between the players and fans again. If matters had played out differently, Smith could have become one of Rovers' greatest coaches of all time.

Now that the Smith chapter had finished, Danny McGuire was about to start his own. Whereas Smith sounded utterly dejected for his final interview, McGuire spoke with excitement and enthusiasm for what may lie ahead, when speaking to the press for the first time since taking over. He also mentioned that he would look into promoting youngsters into first-team spots. No starting spots were guaranteed, according to McGuire.

The 39-year-old had been envisioned by many as a future head coach, although at this moment he was heading into a baptism of fire. The players were bereft of confidence and the squad was generally down on numbers after a horrendous injury list had piled up. Still, McGuire was providing a fresh voice, and with that, he had an opportunity to hand his players fresh impetus ahead of the closing months of the season. After all, it was still a salvageable campaign in terms of reaching the top-six.

McGuire's new role meant that his old one would have to be filled. A day later, it was revealed that Kevin Deighton and Stanley Gene would be sharing the responsibility of coaching the club's reserves. Gene needed no introduction and had coaching experience elsewhere, not just at Rovers. Meanwhile, Deighton was well-travelled, having had a previous stint at the club during the mid-2000s, as well as having been involved at Hull FC, England and Hull University. He was also a staunch red and white, one that had supported the club since 1973, and had been working at Craven Park since returning at the reserves and scholarship level from 2019.

A familiar face joined McGuire on 6 July. It was Brett Delaney, who had played alongside McGuire at Leeds between 2010 and 2018 and played his part in a trophy-laden era for the Rhinos. He was joining Rovers as a forwards coach on a deal that lasted until the end of 2023. The 36-year-old joined from York, where he had served as an assistant coach from the close season. Delaney had already agreed to join the Robins beforehand, as Paul Lakin recalled: 'Brett was going to be announced at the end of the season. However, when Tony departed, we took the opportunity to bring him in early so we could knit together with the coaching team and also implement his ideas early. Willie identified very early on that we needed a forwards coach and someone who was known for the defensive side of the game.'

Later that day, Hull Kingston Rovers announced the signing of Huddersfield winger Louis Senior on a two-year-contract. Senior, 22, would be joining the club immediately on loan, although the Giants did have a recall option in the event of injuries. Senior had made his first-team debut at just 17, and had gone on to make 39 appearances, scoring 22 tries. But Louis had been in and out of the Huddersfield side, just like his twin brother, Innes, who no doubt added confusion for Rovers' supporters in terms of which twin they'd signed.

The Giants had offered Senior a deal, but it proved to be not as appetising as Rovers' offer, which was believed to offer Senior more first-team opportunities. Huddersfield's fans were sad to see a youth product leave without fulfilling his destiny at the John Smith's Stadium. Plenty retained the belief that Senior could go far in the game.

Senior's signature indicated that Rovers were still going to continue the philosophy of signing young, British players. As well as that, he could have been seen as a natural replacement for ageing stars such as Ryan Hall. A succession plan was forming, although Rovers fans wouldn't have to wait until 2023 to see Senior play in their colours.

The hectic weekday continued on 7 July, when it was revealed that the club had tied Frankie Halton down to a new contract which kept him at Craven Park until 2025. The news was greeted with happiness from every corner of the supporter base. With each passing player renewal, Halton's name would always surface. Everybody wanted to see him signed up and now it had happened.

Halton had arrived at Rovers as a Super League rookie but quickly emerged as a very reliable figure following a string of excellent performances during the early part of the season. An injury in April did keep him out for a while. During his absence, the team's form suffered which highlighted how much he had been missed. Clubs in the NRL were allegedly interested in his services. While Halton's ability was never in doubt, Paul Lakin put that particular rumour to bed: 'If we would have let Frankie's contract run to one year remaining, there would have undoubtedly been a lot of interest waiting to get involved, including the NRL. He has had a great first season with ourselves and will only get better.'

For all of the negativity that surrounded the Robins after their dismal cup exit and big drop-off in the league, one thing that was still a constant was their desire to keep hold of their assets. They had already managed to renew several key players' contracts. That was in contrast to other clubs, such as Castleford and Wakefield, who were losing key players. Rovers knew about that all too well, but they were finally building something to last.

10/7/2022
Hull Kingston Rovers vs Hull FC
Betfred Super League (Round 18) – Magic Weekend

Rovers: Coote, Crooks, Wood, Kenny-Dowall, Tate, Milnes, Lewis, Vete, Parcell, Sims, Hadley, Halton, Minchella
Interchanges: Litten, Keinhorst, Maher, Fishwick

Hull: Walker, Simm, Wynne, Griffin, McIntosh, Lovodua, Gale, Satae, Houghton, Fash, Lane, Longstaff, Brown
Interchanges: Hookem, Laidlaw, Severs, Taylor

A derby always marked a 'win at all costs' situation, but none more so than Rovers' 10 July clash with Hull FC. With Rovers just two points behind Hull, and a play-off spot in the offering, the game felt like it could be season-defining for both clubs. The Black and Whites were suffering with injuries themselves but had been replenished in the form of three debuting loan players.
From the Rovers perspective, Will Tate was drafted in ahead of Ethan Ryan. The game also marked opportunities for the two outgoing props in Albert Vete and Korbin Sims. They were both starting, which would have been unthinkable during the end of Tony Smith's reign.
Most of the attention would be placed upon 17-year-old Zach Fishwick, who had made the bench. Fishwick had played for Rovers from a young age, having been signed from local amateur side Skirlaugh. A prop, his physique best matched the beastly experienced pros that he would soon be fronting up against in what was a hell of a fixture to make his debut in. Danny McGuire had spoken about giving youth an opportunity and was about to live up to it in what was his first game as a head coach.
After producing some strong opening sets, indiscipline crept into Rovers' game and Hull elected to take the two points that were on offer. Soon afterwards, there was a role reversal with the Robins receiving a penalty. An offload from Vete found Matt Parcell; Rovers' dynamic hooker outmatched the efforts of three defenders, getting the ball down for Rovers' first score.
An arm wrestle soon followed. Despite being on top, Rovers couldn't find a breakthrough. There were two instances of forward passes which ruled out two potential tries for the Robins and they were 'third

time unlucky' when another effort was chalked off due to an obstruction. Instead, FC regained the lead when Connor Wynne broke through an attempted tackle from Rowan Milnes to put his side back in front. Elsewhere, there was further bad news as *Sky*'s Jenna Brooks confirmed that Frankie Halton, who had previously withdrawn in the early stages, had fractured his collarbone. Matters worsened when a slick move saw Hull extend their lead to 14-4.

Just as Hull seemed to be taking control of the game, Rovers powered themselves back into the contest through the efforts of Sam Wood, who went in at the expense of three Hull defenders. With the hooter about to blow for half-time, Vete was stopped near the FC line. After playing the ball, the hooter sounded, although Mikey Lewis had other ideas. He kicked through for himself and scored. Surprisingly, Lachlan Coote ended a pulsating first half on a limp note when he missed what should have been a routine conversion – and it wasn't the first time. At 14-14, there was everything to play for.

Things got off to the worst possible start when FC loanee Ellis Longstaff went over in the corner just under a minute into the second half. Minutes later, Longstaff was in again after being the recipient of a clever kick through from Luke Gale. It was now 26-14. Rovers looked like they were teetering on the edge in the first half, and the same rang true for the second. Fortunately, Jimmy Keinhorst needed just two bites at the cherry to ground the ball over the line amid the attention of multiple Hull players, creating a route back into the game. After Parcell made his way back onto his feet in a world of pain following a challenge from Brad Fash, the Hull man was sinbinned for a crusher tackle. Momentum was once again back on Rovers' side. They were attacking Hull's line again; Lewis shimmied and dummied his way over, scoring another magnificent solo effort! During the celebrations, Lewis hooked his own jersey and kissed the badge that graced it. Lewis had already put in a heroic shift but it was just about to reach a new high. Running full pelt at two Hull defenders, he demonstrated strength by powering over them, leaving them in a heap as he scored his first hat-trick in a Rovers shirt. He was on fire! Coote's kicking wasn't, however, and another miss kept the score at 28-26 in favour of Hull.

There was another sting in the tail. The old enemy were now back to a full complement, unlike Rovers' right edge. The middle of the pitch was congested, allowing Hull to spread the ball over to the flank, punishing the Robins by scoring again. It was a topsy-turvy encounter at its worst and thrilling at its best, which meant that another opportunity would beckon as the game entered its final ten minutes. Elliot Minchella thought he had managed to ground the ball, giving Rovers a new lease of life. In fact, everybody thought the same, including on-field referee Chris Kendall since he sent the attempt up to the video referee, Robert Hicks, as a try. But after some deliberation, Hicks inexplicably delivered a 'no try' verdict, much to the anger and bemusement of everybody associated with KR, and to the delight and relief of those of an FC persuasion. The final points came from the boot of Gale, who knocked a penalty over to write FC into the history books as 34-28 winners.

The inquest into the Robins' defeat would be steep. Just how on earth did they lose a game in which they played the better rugby and saw the better chances against a depleted Hull side? There were a lot of factors at play. Rovers could have been more clinical. There was also little doubting that the three loan signings more than played their part in Hull's win, particularly Jack Walker and Longstaff. Coote's kicking, or lack thereof, also had played its part. Coote would later apologise to the travelling fans after the hooter was blown. Yet the biggest apology should have been made by the officials. Not only did they blow the Minchella call, they also showed their inconsistency when pulling Rovers for multiple forward passes when it appeared like Hull had done the same in at least one of their tries. Such inconsistency was harming the credibility of the game, and in this instance, it helped cost Rovers a precious two points which could have firmly placed their season back on track.

When the dust had settled, Rovers were now placed tenth; four points off the top-six, and six points away from the bottom spot. A stunning comeback from Toulouse saw them beat Wakefield on the first day of Magic Weekend, well and truly placing the cat among the pigeons at it related to the relegation battle. With Trinity coming up next at Craven Park, Rovers had to end their losing run or a relegation battle would soon become a reality during a season that had promised so much, but was starting to turn ugly with each passing game.

Full-Time Score: Hull Kingston Rovers 28-34 Hull FC
Attendance: 25,333
League Position: 10th; 315 points scored; 398 points conceded; -83 points difference; 14 points

The club received better news on 12 July when it was announced that Dean Hadley had seen a ban overturned. Just a day earlier, the RFL had announced a one-match ban for the Robins' second rower after a late hit on a kicker during the derby. With Frankie Halton looking at another lay-off after withdrawing from the Hull game early with a suspected fractured collarbone, Rovers' back row was lacking numbers. Kane Linnett had returned to training, but he was still in no condition to play.

On the topic of Hadley, he also had something to prove. He was on the verge of turning 30 and was reaching the end of his contract. Quite a few members of the team were in the same boat, and with the season heading towards its end, their chances of convincing the club to keep them on were becoming fewer and fewer with each passing week and month.

On 13 July, Rovers' second-row options were enhanced as they announced the two-week loan signing of St Helens' Sam Royle. The 22-year-old had previously captained Saints earlier on in the season when they fielded a young side at Castleford. He was highly thought of despite making just five first-team appearances after signing for the club as a teenager. Royle would quickly have to prove his worth; with the way the season was headed, Craven Park had all the makings of tough work experience.

17/7/2022
Hull Kingston Rovers vs. Wakefield Trinity
Betfred Super League (Round 19)

Rovers: Coote, Ryan, Wood, Kenny-Dowall, Hall, Dagger, Lewis, Sims, Parcell, King, Hadley, Keinhorst, Minchella
Interchanges: Litten, Maher, Fishwick, Royle

Wakefield: Jowitt, Murphy, Croft, Hall, Taufua, Lino, Miller, Batchelor, Pitts, Ashurst, Whitbread, Hood, Arona
Interchanges: Fifita, Bowes, Tanginoa, Bowden

Both sides went into this clash feeling the heat in more ways than one. Not only was the British weather about to reach its hottest since records began, but Rovers and Wakefield's seasons had reached a nadir. The losers of this game would end up in real peril; especially Trinity, who had plunged into twelfth place after Toulouse overcame Leeds on the previous night.
A groin injury prevented Albert Vete from retaining his place in the side, while Zach Fishwick kept his place on the bench. Danny McGuire's biggest call was the inclusion of Will Dagger in the halves. Rowan Milnes' form had been deteriorating for a long time and it felt like the right decision for all involved. Whether Dagger could slot in and add direction to a faltering side remained to be seen.
Chris Kendall and Robert Hicks, who would live on in infamy as the pantomime villains from the derby game, were present as touch judges. They were treated to a loud chorus of boos upon their pre-match jog by the East Stand; both men appeared to find their reception amusing. Nonetheless, the game got underway. None of the Rovers fans found it amusing when Dean Hadley and Korbin Sims appeared to be hurt in the early part of the game. For the latter, he had suffered a bee sting, but it was much worse for Hadley who slammed the ball down. He knew his time in the game was up and he would eventually be helped off the field.
The game quality wasn't good by any means. Neither side could string a good sequence of play together; especially Rovers, who kept misplacing their passes, much to the frustration of the home crowd. The groans were getting louder with each mistake. Given the high stakes and the hot temperature, mistakes were to be expected. Each

A YEAR OF CHANGE

error and contentious refereeing decision was met with vitriol; angst was aplenty.

Wakefield looked to be in with the first piece of enterprising play of the game. Lachlan Coote could only look on, until Mikey Lewis surged back and stopped the Wakefield break with a superb tackle in which he ended up stripping the ball. Just five minutes later, Trinity made another break and there was nothing Lewis could do to prevent it. Wakefield were leading and Rovers didn't look like scoring, let alone winning what had turned out to be a massive fixture. To compound the anxiety and misery, Shaun Kenny-Dowall was forced off through injury. The Robins were down to two interchanges on an unbearably hot day. Half-time came and Rovers looked nowhere near where they needed to be.

After receiving a half-time 'hairdryer treatment' from McGuire, Rovers came out a lot better in the second half and there was much relief when Jimmy Keinhorst squeezed over in the corner to make it 4-4. The groans of discontent were there to be heard again when Coote missed his conversion; a timely reminder that Rovers still had a lot of work to do.

The Robins had started to play better, and it was perhaps the luck of the green Boilermakers shirts that they were wearing for the first time, that started to sway some refereeing decisions in their favour. A soaring bomb ended up finding Ethan Ryan, who beat his opposite number in the corner by touching down to put the Robins into the lead for the first time at 8-4.

A great run from Jez Litten appeared to lay the groundwork for another try, but it was pulled back for a forward pass. Still, the supporters' nerves settled down a little more when Coote caught multiple defenders flat-footed, taking advantage of Rovers' pressure near the Trinity line. He converted his own try. Rovers' lead was tightened not long after when Dagger kicked over a drop goal with less than ten minutes to go. Rovers were on their way to a massive victory.

Just as some smiles were beginning to emerge, Wakefield had other ideas. They were fighting for their lives, just as they had done for most of their 23-year Super League run, and it was no surprise to see them kick short on the restart. Worryingly, the ball ended up back in their possession. They attacked the Robins' line and a big, looping pass ended up finding Lewis Murphy who went in with just over seven minutes remaining. With Rovers holding a slender lead at 15-10, a converted try would have surely seen them lose the game.

Pressure can make people do strange things, and to many it was a strange sight when Coote dropped a bomb that he would normally collect. The worst part of it was that the error was produced near Rovers' line. There was now five minutes left. Could the Robins hold onto a priceless win?

A desperate Trinity side threw everything they had at Rovers, who were now out on their feet thanks to each draining set. Wakefield couldn't find a breakthrough despite coming ever so close. In the end, the whistle blew, and much to the majority's relief, it was a Rovers win. Every single player had given their all for the cause and it showed at full-time; they were all breathless. Wakefield's players, on the other hand, seemed distraught at another defeat. It easily could have been Rovers in that position. The margins were too tight.

It was difficult to pick out too many stand-out performers on a boiling day that had so much riding on it. To their credit, Wakefield tackled very well for large parts of the contest, making it difficult for Rovers to get going. Lewis was one of the few sparks in the game, alongside Litten and Parcell. But it was more of a day that was based on attrition and workrate. Even though Rovers were outmatched by a bigger pack, they stuck to the task and came up with enough quality when it mattered.

Zach Fishwick showed up very well for a 17-year-old teenager. He still had a very long way to go in terms of becoming a fully-fledged Super League prop, yet his tackling skill was admirable. He was facing four experienced, sizeable pros at the other end of the field and didn't shirk the challenge. He was certainly one for the future and had already picked up invaluable experience at such a tender age.

Paul Lakin later recalled the importance of the victory: 'It clearly became a very important game, one that almost crept up on us after having a lengthy losing run. The players really dug in and fought for the badge. It was also Danny's first win as acting head coach, and therefore the importance of the result wasn't lost on anybody.'

The contest's DNA was perfect for the Boilermaker design's first outing. The players showed gallant courage to overcome the odds on such an occasion. In doing so, they took a big step towards securing top-flight rugby for 2023. For the time being, dining at the top table was the most suitable homage to the men that toiled to give Hull Kingston Rovers a footing.

Full-Time Score: Hull Kingston Rovers 15-10 Wakefield Trinity
Attendance: 7,029
League Position: 8th; 330 points scored; 408 points conceded; -78 points difference; 16 points

Rovers had a busy time away from the field during the build-up to their next game against Warrington. The club knew they would be without the likes of Albert Vete, Frankie Halton and Shaun Kenny-Dowall ahead of the game. Rovers' skipper had difficulty executing speech after copping a high shot against Wakefield, resulting in a trip to Hull Royal Infirmary. The issue wasn't expected to keep him out for too much longer. Meanwhile, Vete and Halton were suffering from a groin injury and a ruptured AC joint respectively. Both injuries took place in the derby defeat and it was expected that both would be returning in early August.

20 July saw Huddersfield recall Louis Senior from his loan at Rovers. To many, it was expected since Jermaine McGillvary picked up a knee injury in Huddersfield's most recent game. Danny McGuire expressed his disappointment given that Senior was picking up what was to be expected at Rovers in terms of style of play, yet the rug was pulled underneath him and the Robins due to circumstance.

On the following day, youngsters Bailey Dawson and Max Kirkbright headed to League 1 on loan for the rest of the season. Both aged 19, the two were aiming to pick up valuable experience in the third tier, while also making themselves available for Rovers' reserve fixtures. Dawson was joining Midland Hurricanes, while Kirkbright linked up with promotion hopefuls Swinton. Dawson would have a familiar face alongside him for his trips down the M1, since Tom Wilkinson also joined the Hurricanes on a season-long loan a few days later.

Sam Royle committed the rest of his 2022 campaign to Rovers on the same day as the Dawson and Kirkbright loan announcements. With Rovers lacking numbers due to the mounting injury list, the move made sense for all parties.

22/7/2022
Warrington Wolves vs. Hull Kingston Rovers
Betfred Super League (Round 20)

Warrington: Thewlis, Minikin, Mata'utia, Wardle, Ashton, Ratchford, Williams, Mulhern, D Clark, Harrison, Currie, Holmes, J Clark
Interchanges: Bullock, Walker, Amor, Mikaele

Rovers: Coote, Ryan, Wood, Crooks, Hall, Dagger, Lewis, King, Litten, Sims, Keinhorst, Royle, Minchella
Interchanges: Parcell, Maher, Richards, Tate

In their last visit to Warrington, Rovers made the division stand up and notice when they stunned the home side and booked themselves in their first ever Super League play-off semi-final appearance. Less than a year later, both sides were failing to meet expectations; particularly Warrington, who were sitting in tenth. Still, few Rovers fans fancied their team's chances given the relative strength of the home side, matched with the Robins' injury woes and overall poor form.

Just like in September 2021, Rovers started off with their backs against the wall as Wire quickly got on top. The Robins made life difficult for themselves by giving away a string of penalties, which would end up handing the home side a 2-0 lead. Warrington scored the first try not long after, when Jake Wardle became the beneficiary of a decisive breakaway. Wardle was in the thick of it again when he beat Lachlan Coote in the air, increasing the score to 14-0. By this point, rain was starting to pour, and boy was it pouring heavily on Rovers and their season.

During the moments they needed inspiration, the Robins got it when Ben Crooks got on the end of a kick from Ryan Hall, bringing Rovers back into the game at 14-6. The winds of change then appeared to start blowing. After the score, Warrington kicked out on the full and followed that up by giving away a penalty. They were then reduced to 12 men for ten minutes when Peter Mata'utia was sinbinned for a high shot on Coote. As blood continued to gush from Coote's nose, the rush of momentum raced through Rovers' veins. Sam Wood ended up busting his way over the Wire line, and in the absence of Coote, Will Dagger slotted the kick over to draw Rovers closer at 14-12.

Another penalty kick increased Warrington's lead by another two points as half-time beckoned. Although it was minimal damage, Rovers had cause for concern elsewhere. Hall was already struggling somewhat during the pre-match warm-ups and had started to pull up again; Greg Richards was forced off with a knee injury, while Jimmy Keinhorst wouldn't end up returning for the second half.

The final 40 minutes started just how the first 40 had begun: Warrington were dominating. The pace of the game was rather quick and Rovers were struggling in and around the ruck. It was the Robins' turn to have a 'man in the bin' when Elliot Minchella yanked Thomas Mikaele back when he was chasing a grubber. After play was resumed, Mikaele forced his way over the tryline to send the Wire into a 22-12 lead. Just as it appeared that things were once again turning in Warrington's favour, Rovers came back again. This time it was Matt Parcell, one of Rovers' driving forces in attack, who retrieved a brilliant Korbin Sims offload to touch down in style in front of the travelling fans. The optimism that the away end felt was counterpunched by the sight of a struggling Mikey Lewis. True to form, he tried his best to continue, but the damage was too great and he became the latest casualty.

The Robins had to continue without Lewis, and by this point, they were totally out of interchanges. But that didn't dissuade Rovers from taking the game to a Warrington side that had shown a soft underbelly throughout 2022. A pinpoint Jez Litten kick was met by a perfectly-timed run from Ethan Ryan, who scored in the corner after producing a stupendous take. Coote converted the difficult conversion and Rovers were in the lead for the first time! A euphoric away end roared and it wasn't too long until a loud 'Red Red Robin' was given an airing. The fans were starting to believe that they were in for a special night.

Still, Hull KR had damaged their lives from the point of view of stress, so many would still have been expecting a grandstand finish when another ball was launched high into the air. Instead, young Josh Thewlis came up with a huge error and Sam Royle was on hand to crash over to seal the deal in front of the delirious travelling faithful. The comeback was complete: Rovers were 30-22 winners on a memorable night in Cheshire.

A number of players ran their blood to water in order to get the Robins over the line, with Sims being one of them. Since being reintroduced into the team after Tony Smith's dismissal, the 30-year-old had performed very well in all three of his outings. George King was revered by many supporters as Rovers' best forward by this stage, yet it was heroic even by his standards when he shoved it to his former club by putting in an incredible 73-minute shift. It was less than a month after he had suffered a small hamstring tear.

There was no doubting that the Robins had put in a gargantuan effort to claim what was a huge win at a vital stage of the season. They were already down on numbers, and the thought of facing a menacing Warrington side – at least on paper – less than a week after a warlike contest against Wakefield felt like a bridge too far. And for the Rovers of just weeks prior, it likely would have been. But this was a new Robins outfit, reenergised by Danny McGuire with an admirable team spirit and never-say-die attitude.

Full-Time Score: Warrington Wolves 22-30 Hull Kingston Rovers
Attendance: 7,551
League Position: 7th; 360 points scored; 430 points conceded; -70 points difference; 18 points

Less than 24 hours on from that night in Warrington, it was revealed that Dean Hadley had penned a one-year extension to remain at Craven Park for 2023. The news came as a slight surprise to some given the injury issues that Hadley had not only suffered at Rovers, but throughout most of his career. It was only as recently as the Wakefield game that Hadley had gone down with a shoulder injury, and at the time of the announcement, it was unclear as to whether Hadley would require surgery or not.

Interestingly it was Willie Peters who had given the green light, keeping Hadley at Craven Park for his fourth full season following a mid-season switch from Hull FC in 2019. He was an ever-dependable, versatile player that ran his blood to water and was also tough as teak despite his injury woes. Retaining Hadley seemed the right way to go, particularly given how Rovers' injury situation had played out over 2022.

Bad news came out of the club on 25 July when it was announced that it had been fined for homophobic chanting at three home games, with the term 'rent boy' attracting the ire of the RFL. The fine was a total of £4,000, with £2,000 being suspended. This was in addition to the £2,000 fine that was previously suspended following a violent outbreak in the North Stand during the 25 February game against Castleford.

Ahead of 2023, the club would work hard to implement an improved CCTV system, as well as working with supporter groups and other initiatives to strengthen the chances of either eradicating the abuse and/or banning the culprits.

The day was made worse when Korbin Sims had received a one-match ban for dangerous contact during the Warrington game. Sims was always living dangerously due to the aggression he displayed during matches. Interestingly enough, just months prior the news would have caused a tonne of eye-rolling amongst the Rovers supporter base. But by this point, he had performed very well since being handed a first-team lifeline by Danny McGuire. In the midst of an injury crisis, an in-form Sims would be sorely missed.

A YEAR OF CHANGE

28/7/2022
Wigan Warriors vs. Hull Kingston Rovers
Betfred Super League (Round 21)

Wigan: Field, French, Halsall, Pearce-Paul, Marshall, Cust, Smith, Cooper, Powell, Byrne, Isa, Farrell, Smithies
Interchanges: Mago, Ellis, Partington, O'Neill

Rovers: Coote, Ryan, Wood, Crooks, Tate, Dagger, Milnes, Fishwick, Parcell, King, Minchella, Royle, Litten
Interchanges: Maher, Laulu-Togaga'e, Cavanaugh, Moore

By the time of their trip to Wigan, Rovers' injury problems had reached a new milestone: a total of 14 players were missing. They could only name 20 players in what was supposed to be a 21-man squad. By contrast, Wigan were in good health; not just with injuries, but in general. Under Matt Peet, they were a different proposition to the side that Rovers had beaten twice in 2021, and they were ready to exact a mean dose of revenge on the Robins.
After just over two minutes of play, the home side opened the scoring, exploiting gaps that had been left behind by the Rovers defence. To sum up Rovers' start, Will Dagger kicked straight out on the full following the try. It seemed like he and the side would be let off after Wigan threw a forward pass during the subsequent attacking set, yet Ben Crooks knocked on after a scrum and Wigan had the ball near the Rovers line again. This time they didn't pass up the opportunity. The Robins were caught short on the flanks and Wigan were in again. It became a hat-trick of tries ten minutes in when a bouncing ball made a fool of the defence, falling to Mike Cooper whose efforts were too much for two Rovers defenders.
In what was becoming a one-sided affair, Wigan's next try came through another kick: the ball was looking to be going dead, or at least that's what Lachlan Coote thought. Bevan French believed differently and went in for his second try, finishing in style. Rovers responded well given that the game seemed done and dusted so early on. Dagger made an excellent run, but the feeling of dejection grew when he went down injured after the same run. Spirits would soon lift, however, when Rovers got on the scoreboard for the first time. A cross-field

kick found Ethan Ryan, who was as reliable as ever in the air, touching down once again.

Despite improvements, the bad luck continued to haunt the Robins. This time, it was Coote who had to go off for a head injury assessment following an unpunished high tackle. He would never return, and in his place was Charlie Cavanaugh, a 20-year-old hooker who was making his first-team debut.

Rovers were 20-4 down as half-time loomed, yet they still had an opportunity to bring themselves back into the game towards the end. Regrettably, they became their own worst enemy again by throwing a forward pass after receiving a scrum near Wigan's line.

The Warriors started the second half on top. A grubber kick left the Rovers line in disarray, setting up a showdown between Ryan and Kai Pearce-Paul, with the latter winning the battle to put his side further in front. Penalties had been rolling Wigan down the field for most of the night, and the same happened again when Liam Marshall went in for his second try. The Robins' edges were vulnerable throughout the game, and after another penalty, French caught the flanks cold again to score a hat-trick.

Connor Moore, a prop that had turned professional the year prior, was brought on. He showed up well but was the latest injury casualty, being forced off with a shoulder issue.

Injuries couldn't be blamed for Wigan's next try: Patrick Mago swept through the efforts of five men to ground the ball over the whitewash. Afterwards, a far-reaching kick from Harry Smith played its part in the ball alluding Phoenix Laulu-Togaga'e. Instead, Liam Marshall was the recipient, scoring the second hat-trick of the game.

There would be one last injury on this miserable night. The *Sky* television cameras showed that young Cavanaugh had dislocated his knee. He screamed in anguish as it was put back into place. The cruel nature of Rovers' terrible run with injuries had impacted even the youngest of players. It also meant that they closed out this 46-4 reverse with 12 men.

None of Rovers' youngsters disgraced themselves with their respective outings. They all gave a good account of themselves given the environment that they had entered. The disastrous start to the game had killed any chance of them being on the winning side, although if you asked the majority of supporters, the die had already been cast before the game had begun.

A YEAR OF CHANGE

The club dropped to ninth when Round 21 was all said and done. With six games remaining, they were two points off the top-six and eight clear of the bottom. Realistically, just one win would eliminate any lingering fears of relegation. The side would have to get patched up and ready for the following Thursday, because it was time for Toulouse Olympique to visit Craven Park.

Full-Time Score: Wigan Warriors 46-4 Hull Kingston Rovers
Attendance: 11,032
League Position: 9th; 364 points scored; 476 points conceded; -112 points difference; 18 points

DAN CROWTHER

A YEAR OF CHANGE

AUGUST

Now that the dust had settled on the whirlwind month of July, August arrived and it had all the makings of 'make or break' as it pertained to Rovers' hopes of beating the odds and landing a place in the top-six. Five games awaited after injuries had already decimated the side over the previous months. Even Albert Vete's predicament had worsened; his groin injury had developed into an abscess issue.

The injury situation left Paul Lakin puzzled: 'Our current injury list is astonishing and stretching us to the limit. We will definitely look into if there are any reasons why we are suffering so badly and Willie may well have a view going into the 2023 pre-season.' But Lakin was quick to see the positives amid an injury malaise, adding: 'It is fantastic to see some of our academy lads make their debut for the club, we are very proud of our young players coming through to challenge for first-team places. That, as most people are aware, is an important part of our strategy.'

Earlier on in the year, a state of war broke out between Russia and Ukraine on 24 February. Although a quick end was typically predicted, it hadn't come to pass and instead the war was still ongoing. Ukraine's vicissitude of fortunes had seen every-day streets turned into a dystopian graveyard, with innocent people's lives being traumatised – or destroyed completely – in the process. As of August, a staggering 6.3 million Ukrainians had fled the country.

A sizeable amount of them turned to England for a new life, and Rovers would play a part in acclimatising a small number of them to their new surroundings. The Hull KR Foundation announced that a 'Ukrainian Fun Day' would be taking place at Craven Park on 15 August, allowing around 100 refugees to get a chance to meet the club's players and staff, as well as to develop a basic understanding of rugby league. They would also be recipients of a stadium tour.

It was a nice idea. In some ways, if a positive outcome was attained and the Ukrainian newcomers became hooked on the club, then it would provoke historical tie-ins of the late 19th century when Rovers first moved into the East Hull area. Its inhabitants quickly became enamoured with the club, giving them something to look forward to and smile about. While the Russian state continued to be unrepentant about the destruction it had caused in Ukraine, the refugees that were to be part of the event could at least be safe in the knowledge that they had a new helping hand that cared.

On 2 August, it was announced by St Helens that they would be recalling Sam Royle from his loan spell at Craven Park due to 'a number of injuries and suspensions'. As it happened, Royle played no part in Saints' next game – he wasn't even named on the bench. Nonetheless, Rovers had to contend with further issues when it came to fielding a team.

Just a day before the team's game with Toulouse, Rovers fans discovered that the side would be without Will Dagger for the rest of the campaign. He became the latest injury casualty, suffering a ruptured Achilles in the defeat at Wigan. Charlie Cavanaugh was also out for the remainder of the season, having dislocated his patella during his first-team debut.

4/8/2022
Hull Kingston Rovers vs. Toulouse Olympique
Betfred Super League (Round 22)

Rovers: Laulu-Togaga'e, Ryan, Wood, Kenny-Dowall, Tate, Litten, Milnes, Sims, Parcell, King, Keinhorst, Halton, Minchella
Interchanges: Crooks, Storton, Maher, Fishwick

Toulouse: Ashall-Bott, Schaumkel, Jussaume, Hankinson, Russell, Norman, Albert, Navarrete, Peats, Alvaro, Peyroux, Bretherton, Marion
Interchanges: Pelissier, Belmas, Hansen, Sangare

The *Sky* cameras were dissecting Rovers' every move again as Toulouse rolled into town, fighting for their Super League lives.
The Robins welcomed back Shaun Kenny-Dowall, Korbin Sims, Jimmy Keinhorst and Frankie Halton for the clash. Jez Litten would be starring in the halves due to the injury crisis, while Phoenix Laulu-Togaga'e was making his first top-division starting appearance at full-back.
Even though it would have taken an unlikely turn of events to drag Rovers back into a relegation fight, apprehension still existed among some quarters of the fanbase. It was probably the by-product of not only the club's 2016 relegation and its circumstances, but also seeing the Robins as basement dwellers for the middle and latter part of the 2010s. So, to dispel any concerns and also keep their hopes of a top-six finish alive, only a win would suffice.
A strong opening ten minutes almost saw Rovers in front, until a Kenny-Dowall effort was ruled as a double movement. Just minutes later, the Robins were knocking at Toulouse's door again; this time, Halton fired a pinpoint pass to Elliot Minchella, who took the ball over the line to open up the scoring. Kenny-Dowall had started very well, not only causing Toulouse all kinds of problems with the ball, but also in defence, shutting down a play after shooting out of his own line. For all of his efforts, Toulouse would score on the same set, throwing the ball out wide with Matty Russell going over in the corner. The game was tied up at 6-6.

Some edge was added to the contest. Corey Norman kicked straight out onto the full and did not like the attention he received from Sam Wood, a moment which almost instigated a fight. It certainly got the fans further invested into the game. Norman was not only a great pantomime villain, but a good player too, and he was starting to exert his influence on the contest. Once George King and Korbin Sims withdrew for their well-earned rest, Toulouse started to dominate.

The next score was truly a freak try. A Lucas Albert grubber ricocheted off the boot of Will Tate. PLT was quick with his reflexes, but he couldn't retrieve the ball and instead he looked on in horror as it fell to Daniel Alvaro, who touched down to send Toulouse into the lead for the first time. In truth, half-time couldn't come quick enough for Rovers who went into the interval 12-6 down.

The second half started even worse. Rovers had to defend four sets near their line before Toulouse's pressure finally told through Latrell Schmaukel. When the away side started to take control in the first half, the ground was stunned into silence. But now boos rang around as Toulouse – who hadn't won an away game all year – were now in control at 16-6.

Rovers were lacking quality on the night, whereas Toulouse benefitted from the quality of Norman. However, they didn't lack application and endeavour, and the fans knew that, and decided to get behind their side who had been doing it tough for long periods of the game. The supporters started to find their voice and Albert kicking straight out onto the full helped increase the volume. Rowan Milnes had attracted some of the crowd's moans and groans throughout the night, yet he entered the good books when his grubber kick was collected by Ethan Ryan who scored.

The try was followed up by an arm-wrestle on the field and the crowd's atmosphere darkened down with it. With ten minutes remaining, the Robins were losing by the scoreline of 16-10 with Toulouse desperately grinding them down with each passing set. Just when Danny McGuire's tiring troops needed a moment of inspiration, they got it. Kenny-Dowall made a huge play to take Rovers near Toulouse's line, and his good work was continued by Minchella, who managed to keep the ball alive, passing it to Parcell, who managed to offload to Kenny-Dowall, who aptly rounded off a determined passage of play by offloading to Halton who went over! There was something in the air; that tangible feeling that something special was about to happen, especially when Milnes converted the try.

The energy from the terraces spilled over onto the pitch. Suddenly, tired bodies found an extra spring in their step as they charged towards Toulouse's end. The belief intensified when Rovers were awarded a scrum in enemy territory following a knock-on. Rovers spread the ball wide and found a gap, and it was none other than Milnes who exploited it, racing through to put Rovers back into the lead with less than five minutes to go. An outburst of relief swept through the terraces; particularly the notorious East Stand, which was bouncing at the sight of what only five or so minutes earlier seemed like an unlikely comeback.

Milnes converted his own try which received another loud roar. Olympique received the ball back from a short kick-off, but they couldn't muster up enough energy to march down the other end and rob Rovers of a special night. The Robins were 22-16 victors.

At full-time, Kenny-Dowall hugged Halton in delight. Rovers' skipper had been awesome on his return, leading from the front with both his offensive and defensive play. He had staked a big claim to become Rovers' best import of the Super League era and it was nights like this which made it hard for people to say otherwise.

There were some other injury concerns. PLT had been forced off at half-time, being replaced by Ben Crooks. Meanwhile, Wood picked up a shoulder injury halfway through the game. Although he was given the green light to continue, the nature of Rovers' bad luck suggested that the injury may have had longer-term complications.

It was a game in which Rovers couldn't afford 'to lose'. Indeed, it was a time for jokes, laughter and smiles because as far as the threat of the drop was concerned, the Robins were well and truly out of it. Milnes' game-winning try was not only celebrated in East Hull, but around houses and pubs in Wakefield, too.

The situation in Super League had changed again. Rovers were positioned ninth; a point away from sixth place and just two away from fifth. Leeds were occupying the sixth spot, making the Robins' game against them in the following week bigger than ever. But for now, it was time to reflect on another memorable comeback that had been produced under McGuire.

On a night of defiance, Rovers had edged out a very determined and desperate team, one that were fighting for their contracts, and in some cases, livelihoods. Despite showing a paucity of skill, the Robins displayed an enormous amount of courage and determination, and in the end it was enough. Whether it would be enough to make the play-off grade remained unclear, but for now it was another enjoyable comeback, and certainly a good omen for 2023.

Full-Time Score: Hull Kingston Rovers 22-16 Toulouse
Attendance: 6,763
League Position: 9th; 386 points scored; 492 points conceded; -106 points difference; 20 points

Just when Rovers thought that they had the services of Korbin Sims for their game against Leeds, they had to think again. On 9 August, it was announced by the RFL that Sims had been handed a two-match ban for 'Other Contrary Behaviour' in the match against Toulouse. Everybody connected with the club knew that he had always lived dangerously as it related to his rough tackling style. But in this instance, it appeared as though Sims had been banned for a push on a Toulouse player who was blocking Sims' way when he was returning to his own line.

11 August saw the club announce that Scholarship head coach Pete Grayburn had decided to leave the club after almost ten years in the role. 'He proved a really vital link between players and the community,' said Paul Lakin. 'He is a good coach and has been an integral part of the club.' Stanley Gene would be replacing Grayburn in the role.

A YEAR OF CHANGE

12/8/2022
Hull Kingston Rovers vs. Leeds Rhinos
Betfred Super League (Round 23)

Rovers: Ryan, Crooks, Wood, Kenny-Dowall, Hall, Litten, Minchella, Storton, Parcell, King, Halton, Linnett, Keinhorst
Interchanges: Maher, Richards, Tate, Laulu-Togaga'e

Leeds: Hardaker, Tindall, Newman, Sutcliffe, Handley, Smith, Myler, O'Connor, Thompson, Gannon, Tetevano, Dwyer, Oledzki
Interchanges: Mustapha, Austin, Walters, Johnson

Rovers' weighty injury problems brought a new issue to the fore: Danny McGuire was unable to name a recognised half for this crunch tie against his ex-side after Rowan Milnes had gone down with a rib cartilage injury during training. There was some good news, since the Robins welcomed back Kane Linnett, Matty Storton and Ryan Hall. Former Rovers favourite Scott Murrell, who had recently announced his retirement for the end of 2022, was brought out onto the pitch to be honoured by the fans before kick-off. It was a pity that he was still contracted to Keighley, otherwise he could have pulled on a shirt given the state of play.

The Robins got off to an excellent start, taking the lead just over two minutes in as Matt Parcell beat the efforts of multiple defenders to score. Much to the home fans' surprise, Sam Wood was the one who converted the try. The game was less than ten minutes old and Rovers were in again, this time through Hall who got on the end of an excellent kick through from Litten. At this point, Rovers were an uncontrollable beast that had sprung from their Craven Park lair; they were causing the Rhinos all kinds of problems. Leeds were gasping for water, not just due to the warm weather, but also because Rovers had starved them of the ball for over ten minutes.

Confidence grew amongst the home fans. Each tackle was met with a build-up that led to a cheer. Unfortunately, one of the tackles led to a penalty. In the resulting set, the away side profited from missed tackles and got themselves on the scoreboard through what was their first attack of the game. Another blow took place, with Shaun Kenny-Dowall withdrawing due to a knee injury.

Despite the absence of their leader, Rovers were back into attack and extended their lead through the returning Linnett, who was another recipient of a kick through from Litten. *Sky* cameras were present again, and the video referee's overly long look at the try drew frustration and boos from the Rovers supporters. The frustration grew deeper after Richie Myler scored Leeds' next try, throwing a dummy and bringing the score ever-closer at 14-12. Despite being the better of the two sides, Rovers led by just two points. The Rhinos looked far more clinical.

Leeds finally took the lead through Myler. Their unlikely tries, mixed with some penalties, had given the away side confidence and it was now them who led by the scoreline of 18-14, much to the bemusement of the home fans who had seen their side's super start to the game fade away at an alarming rate. There were more injury problems too, with Greg Richards being the latest to be forced off.

A reckless shot from Blake Austin caught Litten around the shoulder area after the half-time hooter sounded, provoking an irate response from Litten's teammates. It almost led to a full-scale brawl between the two sets of players, but the situation was defused.

Leeds built on their lead, with Morgan Gannon getting on the end of a decent move. The away outfit were now 22-14 up and despite not looking too impressive in the first half, it was the Rhinos that were now looking better with ball in hand. Meanwhile, Rovers were starting to look like they were out of ideas. The penalty count was mounting up against them.

The loudest cheer of the night came when referee Jack Smith penalised Leeds for a blatant forward pass. Rovers' fans clearly felt that Smith was out to get their side. After this point, the East Stand did their best to rouse the tiring players.

It helped recharge the Rovers men, who were now deep in Leeds' half. After a number of set restarts, Mikolaj Oledski was sinbinned. Craven Park had witnessed a comeback just a week earlier… was the same about to happen again?

From the fans' vantage point, Elliot Minchella was over for a try, only to be marked short. Rovers then went route one unsuccessfully. At this stage, Leeds had an answer for everything that the Robins threw at them. Frustratingly, the Rhinos dragged Rovers into an arm-wrestle by producing astute game management. To compound matters, Litten's kicks weren't as rewarding as they previously had been. The

Robins' lack of natural halves was coming back to bite; while Myler and Austin consistently found touch in good areas, Rovers lacked similar direction at a critical point in the contest.

A handling error from Wood was scooped up by Gannon, who sped past tiring Rovers legs to score an all-important try for the side with 12 men. Although if you asked many Rovers fans on the night, Leeds were merely down to 13 at that stage. Wood atoned for his error by going in for a try, sparking hopes of a late comeback. But it never materialised, and instead Rovers were beaten 28-20 in a game that they couldn't afford to lose.

The players' efforts couldn't be questioned on the night. They had played their hearts out for the cause. Unfortunately, it just wasn't enough as Leeds' proficiency in key moments, as well as their advantage of being able to field at least one half, proved to edge the contest in their favour.

Jack Smith's refereeing performance was the focal point of the Rovers supporters' inquests. Although Smith's decisions were inconsistent and he did lose control of the game at times, he wasn't at fault for the individual mistakes and missed tackles that Rovers produced.

Even with that in mind, the players themselves couldn't be faulted too much. Their resources had been stretched to the limit; they were down to two interchanges as early as the latter stages of the first half. The fans stuck by them throughout the game. If anything, Danny McGuire's stint as interim head coach had reinvigorated the relationship between the players and the supporters.

After the match, McGuire told the press that Kenny-Dowall had torn his MCL and that Richards' hamstring had also been torn. Their seasons were effectively over. The loss of Kenny-Dowall in particular was a hammer blow; his leadership and performances had guided Rovers over the line many times.

The Robins' situation was so desperate that McGuire also mentioned that he was contemplating a playing return if the rules allowed it. However, this was said in jest.

Elsewhere, wins for Castleford and Salford placed great doubt upon the chances of Rovers reaching the top-six. A heavy loss for Hull FC moved the Robins up a place the league table, but they were now three points adrift of the six with four games remaining and had a negative points difference compared to those within reach. Barring a rich vein of form, the hunt for the play-offs appeared to be over.

Full-Time Score: Hull Kingston Rovers 20-28 Leeds Rhinos
Attendance: 8,028
League Position: 8th; 406 points scored; 520 points conceded; -114 points difference; 20 points

Rovers received another blow during the build-up to their away game at St Helens. On 15 August, Ethan Ryan and Matt Parcell were both ruled out of the game, having been charged for incidents that occurred during the Leeds match. Ryan was receiving a 'Grade B' offence, which was for a use of his knees, while Parcell was given a 'Grade A' for dangerous contact.

Two days later, Rovers announced that Zach Fishwick had signed a new four-year deal with the club. Fishwick had only turned 17 in March, but for anyone who watched him at academy level, he was always one to look out for due to possessing a manly look and physique at such a tender age. He became the first homegrown derby debutant for Rovers since 31 March 1972, when Ray Cardy made his bow.

It was in games like the Hull derby in July, and crucial fixtures at home against Wakefield and Toulouse, that Fishwick showed maturity to compete at the highest level from the bench. He still had a long way to go, however there was no denying that the potential was there.

19/8/2022
St Helens vs. Hull Kingston Rovers
Betfred Super League (Round 24)

St Helens: Hopoate, Makinson, Hurrell, Davies, Bennison, Welsby, Lomax, Walmsley, Roby, Lees, Bell, Batchelor, Wingfield
Interchanges: Lussick, McCarthy-Scarsbrook, Paasi, Royle

Rovers: Coote, Barley, Keinhorst, Tate, Hall, Lewis, Milnes, Storton, Litten, King, Halton, Linnett, Minchella
Interchanges: Vete, Maher, Laulu-Togaga'e, Fishwick

17-year-old Connor Barley, the nephew of former Rovers star Paul Cooke, was making his debut on the wing. Barley was a teammate of Zach Fishwick's during their time at Skirlaugh Bulls and was the latest youngster to be handed an opportunity in trying circumstances.
It didn't get any harder than St Helens away. The Saints had become the preeminent side of the late 2010s and early 2020s and the steam train was showing little signs of slowing down. They needed just a few more wins to wrap up yet another League Leaders' Shield. With Rovers coming to town all bruised and patched up, the signs weren't good.
The game got off to the worst possible start when George King lost the ball after the first tackle. The Robins gave away a penalty not long after which compelled Saints to take an early penalty kick. In truth, St Helens didn't need to. They were well on top despite some promising early moments from Rovers. Tommy Makinson made their pressure tell with a fine finish and it marked a period of dominance for the home side.
After more pressure, Makinson was in again and Rovers were soon 20-0 down after just 30 minutes of play, and that was the scoreline as half-time approached. The side had shown flashes of promise, and were almost in for a try but for a forward pass. Still, there was no question that Saints were much the better outfit. St Helens' fans had grown accustomed to success so much so that after their team's second try was scored, an air of calm emanated around the home terraces. In a sense, it was comparable to Ancient Rome when herds of wild beasts would tear the human challengers apart. After a while, it 'gets old'.

A YEAR OF CHANGE

It felt like nothing would change when Joey Lussick went in during the early stages of the second half. But things changed; Rovers did improve. One of their rare breakthroughs finally came off when Albert Vete unselfishly put Kane Linnett over for a try. But then it was back to business as usual when Saints, through Jon Bennison, extended their advantage.

Rovers got another try through Will Tate, who had capitalised on a rare mistake from Makinson. But what was to come had Paul Cooke dancing around his living room.

A pinpoint kick from Jez Litten found its target, before the ball was passed over to Barley who handed off Bennison to crash over in the corner. It was an unbelievable moment for young Barley, who had already looked dangerous during moments in the game.

Saints had the final say with a try from Ben Davies, finishing the contest at 38-12 in favour of the home side. 'They came, they saw, they conquered'.

The reality of Rovers' injury and suspension situation had made defeat almost a foregone conclusion. When the Robins were healthier in June, they pulled Saints very close, but this outing was always going to be an uphill task. To their credit, the players did put in a big effort which was no surprise since it had been the DNA of Danny McGuire's spell in charge.

One of the shining lights of this match was the involvement of the likes of Barley and Fishwick. If either of them went on to make it in the game, then the invaluable experiences they were having during 2022 would stand them in good stead for the rest of their careers. It was unfortunate that Daniel Okoro had suffered a mid-season injury, otherwise he could have tasted top-flight rugby too.

With three games remaining and the Robins now two wins away from becoming level on points with the sides occupying the play-off spots, any hopes of a miracle were surely about to be extinguished in the coming weeks…

Full-Time: St Helens 38-12 Hull Kingston Rovers
Attendance: 10,048
League Position: 8th; 418 points scored; 558 points conceded; -140 points difference; 20 points

On the following day, Rovers announced the capture of Wakefield second rower James Batchelor on a two-year deal. The rumour was set all the way back in May, when *Sky Sports'* Jenna Brooks had proposed that the 24-year-old was on his way to Craven Park.

The news followed Wakefield's 26-18 win at Hull FC, which had occurred on the same night Rovers lost at St Helens. The result all but sealed another year of Super League for Trinity, which likely led to the announcement.

Batchelor was another exciting addition to the Craven Park ranks. Another domestic recruitment, he fit the bill in terms of age and reputation. He was adored by Wakefield's supporters, the same fans that heralded him as one of – if not the – best performer throughout what was another difficult year for them.

By this point, Batchelor, Louis Senior, Rhys Kennedy, Jesse Sue and Tom Opacic had all been officially confirmed as Hull KR players for 2023 and beyond. Although 2022 still had potential for a few more memories, the following year was about to start dominating the minds of those that followed the club.

Lachlan Coote became the latest player to have his season cut short. On 22 August, the club announced that Coote had suffered his third concussion of the campaign, ending his season immediately. The 32-year-old had a mixed first season. At times, his class was a cut above, inspiring the side to many victories, while at other times he was disappointing amid rumours that he was playing through injuries.

He arrived at Rovers with a big reputation, having been a vital cog in the wheel for St Helens. The Robins weren't at Saints' level, which would lead to Coote being exposed far more than he ever was when at Saints. He was turning 33 in the following April. Due to his mixed fortunes, 2023 would likely determine how much of a success the Australian had been.

The topic of concussion was back on the agenda just two days later, when it was announced that the club had released Tom Garratt from the remainder of his two-year contract. The news came as a big disappointment, although it was expected by quite a few fans due to Garratt's lengthy absence from the team. At the time of the announcement, the news felt like a world away from 1 April, which was the date of his last game.

Rovers had just dismantled Warrington and Garratt had gotten into the flow of being a professional player. He was very much becoming part of Tony Smith's successful Championship acquisitions list. And then all of a sudden, concussion symptoms brought his Hull KR career to a swift and brutal end.

During his absence, it was described that Garratt had been suffering from concussion-like symptoms. However, upon leaving the club, he took it upon himself to visit a different doctor and an osteopathic specialist who confirmed to him that he didn't have concussion and likely never did. According to them, after Garratt had been impacted by a jaw injury, cervical instability caused damage to the autonomic nerves and circulation in his neck, which created the concussion-like symptoms. He confirmed that it was a very complex issue, hence his endless absence from April until his release.

Now feeling 100 percent, Garratt vowed to play on. He described a potential return to playing for Rovers as 'proper closure' following his release. As well as that, he thanked the supporters that supported him during his time on the pitch, as well as those that kept in touch after his issues started.

He would undoubtedly receive offers from elsewhere. Whether Rovers would be one of the clubs interested in his services remained to be seen, but there was an appetite for it as far as the fans were concerned. They had caught a glimpse into Garratt's potential and wanted to see more.

25/8/2022
Wakefield Trinity vs. Hull Kingston Rovers
Betfred Super League (Round 25)

Wakefield: Jowitt, Murphy, Gaskell, Croft, Kershaw, Miller, Lino, Aydin, Ashurst, Hall, Arona, Crowther, Bowden
Interchanges: Fifita, Kay, Shaw, Butler

Rovers: Lewis, Ryan, Keinhorst, Tate, Hall, Litten, Milnes, Storton, Parcell, King, Halton, Linnett, Minchella
Interchanges: Vete, Sims, Maher, Wood

Belle Vue was not only finally being redeveloped; it also had the potential to be the site where Rovers' 2022 dreams would be crushed once and for all. Wakefield could have claimed league survival with a victory, although defeat elsewhere for Toulouse would've deliver the same outcome.
Mikey Lewis had played full-back during multiple loan spells with York and he was back in that position for this game since McGuire wanted to start all of his creative players.
The opening portion of the game was very much an arm-wrestle, one that Rovers were winning. The Robins would have been in front if not for a lack of execution and individual mistakes. After trying different ways to breach the Trinity guard, they found a way through Albert Vete. It was the simplest way; he bullied his way over, route-one style. As the first half was coming to its end, the home side piled on the pressure, yet failed to convert it into points. Rovers went into half-time with a 6-0 lead.
The immediate concern of the second half centered around Lewis, who came off for a head injury assessment. It became clear that he failed his HIA when he was later seen in his club tracksuit. While he looked on, Rovers were starting to feel the heat of Wakefield's pressure. Trinity finally scored through Lee Kershaw, who navigated his way through the defensive efforts of Ethan Ryan and Will Tate.
Wakefield's try injected a healthy dose of momentum through their veins - it was now them that were the ones in the ascendency. Although both sides lacked execution over the course of the game, Trinity came up with a moment of quality again. This time, two of their brightest attacking stars aligned; Mason Lino managed to switch

the ball to Lewis Murphy, who crossed over in trademark acrobatic fashion.

Murphy was at the centre of Wakefield's third and final try. A lovely grubber kick bounced perfectly for Max Jowitt, who crossed over with ease to seal the game in Trinity's favour and end Rovers' play-off hopes. David Fifita, a huge prop that had served Wakefield with great distinction for seven years, put the icing on the cake in his Belle Vue farewell by slotting over the two-pointer. The final score was 18-6.

It was a bitter affair, one that was fuelled by the man in the middle. Marcus Griffiths had missed multiple instances of Lino tackling players in the air. As well as ignoring the laws, Griffiths was also accused of handing the majority of the 50/50s in Wakefield's favour. McGuire described the officiating as 'terrible'. Away from the refereeing performance, Rovers put in a great deal of effort but failed to execute in important moments and it came back to bite them.

The post-match scenery for the two camps was noticeably different. Wakefield and their supporters were ecstatic. A handful of Trinity's fan favourites basked in the glory of a successful home swansong and doubtlessly celebrated long into the night. Meanwhile, the Rovers camp trudged off the pitch, downbeat in the knowledge that their season was over. The travelling supporters headed back to East Yorkshire dreaming of a better 2023, for any hope of success in 2022 was done and dusted.

Full-Time: Wakefield Trinity 18-6 Hull Kingston Rovers
Attendance: 4,653
League Position: 8th; 424 points scored; 576 points conceded; -152 points difference; 20 points

A day on from the Wakefield defeat, Rovers announced their newest addition ahead of 2023: Trinity's own, Yusuf Aydin. The Turkish international prop was about to turn 22, having already played 11 Super League games in 2022, which included a brief loan spell at Leeds. Willie Peters was pleased to land his man, praising Aydin's 'high' work rate. He fit the club's portfolio of young and hungry players with plenty of upside. Peters was reshaping the squad in his own image and Aydin had all the makings of becoming a positive acquisition.

On the same day, Jez Litten and Jimmy Keinhorst received bans for an accidental trip and a dangerous throw respectively. Keinhorst was just a one-game ban, while Litten was banned for two which would end his campaign barring a successful appeal.

Mikey Lewis' season was done after failing his head injury assessment during the clash at Belle Vue. The new protocol for concussions was 11 days, meaning that it came too late for Lewis since Rovers were playing Wigan on 29 August and Hull FC on 3 September. It was a great shame all round. Lewis had provided Rovers with X factor, but for he and many other players, it was time to rest up and look ahead to 2023.

A day later, the Robins announced that a further ten players would be following Tom Garratt out of the exit door. The list included Adam Rusling, Albert Vete, Bailey Dawson, Ben Crooks, Brad Takairangi, Charlie Cavanaugh, Korbin Sims, Nathan Cullen, Tom Wilkinson and Will Maher.

The departure of Crooks would give the likes of Will Tate, who was starting to show improvements towards the end of the season, better opportunities of playing first-team rugby in 2023. The decision to let Maher go would place pressure on the club in terms of their new props working out. Danny McGuire paid tribute to Maher, describing him as an 'unbelievable' signing for Rovers and alluded to him being lower down the Craven Park pay scale. Both players would be leaving the Robins with their best wishes. But if Rovers were to move further up the ladder, they needed to evolve their squad.

One name that was absent during the releases was Greg Richards. There was a lot of uncertainty as to his situation. He hadn't set the world on fire during his first season at the club, and having signed just a one-year deal albeit with an extension clause, the writing appeared to be on the wall. It also further confused some supporters when Richards wasn't included on the annual Super League 'out of contract' list mid-year. Unbeknownst to many, Richards had triggered an extension in his contract after reaching 15 appearances following the defeat to Leeds on 12 August. The fact that the clause was included in his contract made him exempt from the list. At times, Richards had showed himself to be a useful squad member, but he had a lot more to prove in 2023 if he wished to avoid falling under the same category as Crooks and Maher.

29/8/2022
Hull Kingston Rovers vs. Wigan Warriors
Betfred Super League (Round 26)

Rovers: Laulu-Togaga'e, Ryan, Wood, Tate, Hall, Minchella, Milnes, Maher, Parcell, King, Sims, Linnett, Storton
Interchanges: Vete, Moore, Fishwick, Barley

Wigan: Hanley, Miski, Jake Bibby, Sutton, O'Keefe, Halsall, Astley, Havard, Shorrocks, Mago, Nsemba, McDonnell, Partington
Interchanges: Hill, Jack Bibby, Forber, Eckersley

There was a collective sigh of relief from Rovers' supporters when Wigan named a squad which featured eight academy players who were yet to make their first-team debut. Despite a marked improvement under Matt Peet in 2022, the Warriors had already conceded the top spot to St Helens before their game at Craven Park. As for Rovers, their injury crisis had resorted them to putting square pegs in round holes again, with Elliot Minchella starring in the halves. Albert Vete was joined on the bench by three young teenagers who themselves were more or less guaranteed a spot in the 17 for the forthcoming week at Hull given the state of play with injuries.
Although it was the last game at Craven Park for many, many months, the occasion of playing a youthful side with little to play for subdued the atmosphere. The fans had something to cheer in the early goings, however, when Ryan Hall attracted four defenders and managed to get an offload away to Will Tate who did the honours. Offloading was crucial to the Robins' next score, with Hall getting on the end of a move which increased Rovers' lead to 8-0.
On his home farewell, Korbin Sims managed to get on the end of a well-executed Rowan Milnes grubber kick – it was his first try for the club. At the other end of the pitch, Wigan's supporters had travelled in good numbers for a Bank Holiday game with little riding on it, and they were out of their seats when their youthful side struck back after catching Rovers' defenders wrong-footed.
Back at the other end, there was more slack defending, this time from Wigan. Matty Storton, who was enjoying a fine game, managed to ground the ball despite three defenders trying to stop him. It was

Rovers who led 20-6 as the half-time hooter sounded. They appeared to be well in control.

A well-timed pass from Vete sent Zach Fishwick in for his first-ever Rovers try; Vete looked happier than Fishwick, jumping on his shoulders during the happy celebration scenes. The Robins were attacking again, this time slick hands brought about an Ethan Ryan try, extending Rovers' lead to 32-6.

Wigan's Ben O'Keefe marked his debut with a try, rounding a group of Rovers players to go over. In a try-friendly contest, it was the Robins' turn to go over again. A cut-out pass found Hall, who attracted a big group of defenders and offloaded to Ryan who scored his second, this time from the other side of the pitch. Ryan was everywhere!

Rovers always looked in control of the game, but that was because of their clinical attack, as opposed to their defence. They closed the game out by shipping three unanswered tries, taking the score from 38-12 by the time of Ryan's second try, to 38-28 come full-time. The defending was sloppy, although it was easy to sympathise with the players following their rigorous schedule and lack of luck on the injury front.

On the topic of injuries, Matt Parcell was the latest. He had suffered with his knee and was forced off midway through the game. It was said that he had an outside chance of returning for the final game at Hull FC.

Matty Storton was handed the home man-of-the-match award. Although it wasn't a surprise, there were many good performers on the day, including Rowan Milnes. After suffering a mid-season collapse in form, Milnes had recovered well following a brief time on the sidelines and helped lead Rovers around the field in this instance. The end to the game wasn't ideal, nor was Rovers' situation. Even so, they had sent their supporters away with a victory on Craven Park's last outing of what had been a challenging season. In order for 2022 to end on a truly happy note, the team needed to eke out one last big effort to win the bragging rights decider at the MKM Stadium. The short countdown to the derby had already begun…

Full-Time Score: Hull Kingston Rovers 38-28 Wigan Warriors
Attendance: 7,315
League Position: 8th; 462 points scored; 604 points conceded; -142 points difference; 22 points

A day after the Wigan result, Korbin Sims announced his retirement from rugby league at the age of 30. He had made his decision months prior and envisioned the 3 September Hull derby as his last ever game as a professional. Just hours later, the rug was cruelly pulled from underneath Sims by the RFL's Match Review Panel, who handed him a three-match ban after he allegedly made Grade C contact with referee Chris Kendall during the Wigan game.
Replays showed that the collision with Kendall was minimal at best. For somebody that had given great service to the sport from a young age, the ending to his professional career was nothing short of sad.

The month ended with further bad news, as Jez Litten's ban for the Hull FC game was upheld. Litten had been a live wire and despite the side regressing in terms of league position, Litten's form was good during a challenging year. He certainly had the backing of Danny McGuire, who was confident that the 24-year-old would one day represent England. With Matt Parcell's involvement doubtful, and Charlie Cavanaugh already ruled out for the rest of the campaign, the Robins were without a recognised hooker ahead of the final game of the season at Hull FC.

DAN CROWTHER

A YEAR OF CHANGE

SEPTEMBER

The start of September saw Rovers' injury crisis reach its peak: for the final game of the season, Danny McGuire could only name a 16-man squad. It meant that only three players would make the bench. They were already a busted side. It would take something truly special for Rovers to walk out of the MKM Stadium with a win, especially since Hull FC looked comparatively healthier. It had been four years since Rovers last tasted victory on the Black and Whites' home turf.

On the same day, the club recalled Max Kirkbright from his loan spell at Swinton. It fuelled conversation that Kirkbright may have been about to be called up to the first-team for Rovers' final game of the season. It was certainly interesting timing, since Swinton's final game of the season fell on the same day as the Hull derby; as well as the fact that the Lions had made the League 1 play-offs, meaning that their season continued into the weekend after.

3/9/2022
Hull FC vs. Hull Kingston Rovers
Betfred Super League (Round 27)

Hull: Connor, McIntosh, Scott, Vulikijapani, Barron, Smith, Gale, Sao, Johnstone, Taylor, Lane, Longstaff, Gardiner
Interchanges: Laidlaw, Litten, Houghton, Satae

Rovers: Ryan, Tate, Keinhorst, Wood, Hall, Milnes, Laulu-Togaga'e, Vete, Minchella, King, Halton, Linnett, Storton
Interchanges: Moore, Fishwick, Barley

For the final game of 2022, Danny McGuire was unable to name a full set of recognisable pivots as Phoenix Laulu-Togaga'e started in the halves, while Elliot Minchella deputised as the hooker in the absence of Matt Parcell. The youthful trio of Barley, Fishwick and Moore made up the three-man bench. Hull FC were the favourites with the bookies. The 16 men of Hull KR had it all on if they wanted to upset the odds.

The injuries and lack of play-off place for either side failed to dissuade both sets of supporters from generating a great atmosphere at the start of the game. It was the FC fans who were the happier bunch when Sam Wood produced an incorrect play-the-ball in Rovers' opening set. Just as Hull appeared to be in for the first score, they came up with a mistake of their own. A pattern of both sides making errors had emerged. That was until Rovers finally got a grip of the proceedings. This time, it was the Robins' turn to threaten near the line and they made it count. A cross-field kick found Jimmy Keinhorst. The ball was then back to Will Tate, who scored the first try of the game in front of the travelling supporters.

It didn't take long for the home side to strike back. Luke Gale, on his FC swansong, pulled the Black and Whites back into the game by finishing off a good team move. However, FC were short on the flanks for Rovers' next try, with Ryan Hall benefitting from the weak numbers out wide. The Robins were leading 12-4 and Hall would have been in again, if not for Miteli Vulikijapani. Either way, Rovers were looking like the better of the two injury-stricken sides.

Young Hull winger Harvey Barron was starting to be targeted in the air, and this time Rovers were in the money: Barron came up with a howler, spilling the ball behind his own tryline. Rowan Milnes got on the end of it and Rovers looked well on their way to victory. By this point, they were strangling Hull in terms of field position. An off-the-ball incident near Hull's sticks gifted Rovers a penalty, and FC's lack of composure and discipline was compounded when Gale was sinbinned for dissent.

Rovers' 16 men had undoubtedly forged a strong spirit ahead of the game, and with FC now the side at a disadvantage, they looked to exhibit a similar vibe. Hull were suddenly fired up for the following defensive set, as they pushed the Robins back towards their own line. But it was a false dawn; Hull couldn't find their attacking prowess and it was becoming a familiar theme throughout the game.

Albert Vete was having a stormer on his final appearance and his performance was rewarded with a try after charging over the line from dummy half. The scoreline was now 24-4. The last act of the first half consisted of Hull finding the advertising board after an attempted pass. Rovers were the ones in control and the result was looking ominous.

The second half had started just like the first, with FC making the majority of the errors. Rovers scored again. This time, Ethan Ryan got on the end of a fine passage of play to score the game-sealing try. The players celebrated in front of the deflated Hull fans. Their team went into the game the favourites, but now they were watching their beloved Airlie Birds sink without a trace. Instead, 'Red Red Robin' was the song that was echoing around the ground.

Scott Taylor appeared fortunate to avoid the sinbin after an altercation with Vete, but it didn't matter since Taylor and his side weren't even close to laying a glove on the Robins.

Minchella was the one who ended up completing the rout, with the try originating from dummy half, just like Vete's. The score ended at 36-4. It was the 16 men of Hull Kingston Rovers that had conquered their nearest and dearest rivals, meaning that the Robins had defeated Hull twice in three attempts over the course of 2022 and had finished above them for two consecutive seasons.

After the full-time whistle, Vete was the recipient of a well-earned beer, courtesy of a Rovers fan. He downed the majority of it and poured whatever remained over his head. He had finished his time at the club in style, with the performance itself being a reminder of what he was capable of when fully fit and fired up.

'16 men and we're taking the piss' had been one of the chants from the away end. The Rovers supporters had gone into 2022 expecting another good season and in many ways, it hadn't materialised due to injury issues. It was the same injury problems which had made this result remarkable. It took a herculean effort to eke out the effort levels required to dismantle Hull on their own patch. According to McGuire, the performance was for the fans. In the most unlikely of circumstances, Rovers had signed off the season in style.

Full-Time: Hull FC 4-36 Hull Kingston Rovers
Attendance: 16,999
League Position: 8th; 498 points scored; 608 points conceded; -110 points difference; 24 points

Less than 24 hours after Rovers' cruising victory, Shaun Kenny-Dowall was named as part of the 2022 Super League Dream Team. The centre had been a colossal figure on the field, making the accolade a well-deserved one. The fact that he was the only player in the line-up that didn't come from a side that finished in the top-six further illustrated his achievement. The news also marked the second consecutive season that a Hull KR player had been named as part of the illustrious 13; the last time that happened was between the years of 2009 and 2010.

September 2022 was a shortened month for the club as far as playing went. In the previous year, the side had stretched their September out all the way until the very end of the month when they travelled to a partisan Perpignan to attempt to book themselves in what would have been the club's first ever Super League Grand Final appearance. On the bright side, this season did end on a happier note, even if the occasion of a dead rubber paled in comparison to a semi-final. There was nothing more than a lot of Rovers fans loved than rubbing Hull's noses in it, especially from a disadvantaged position.

Elsewhere, there was some better news for Korbin Sims, who was named in Fiji's star-studded 25-man squad for the World Cup. Perhaps Sims would finally be afforded the chance to play out the remainder of his playing career on his own terms.

But for Rovers, it was time for reflection on another season that had passed…

A YEAR OF CHANGE

EPILOGUE

It would have been foolish to classify the 2022 season as a success on the field given that the playing side dropped down two positions in the league table and missed out on the play-offs. By the same token, it wasn't without its circumstance, and Rovers' horrific run with injuries was the worse that Paul Lakin had ever known in all of his near-two decades of working in professional sport: 'I've never been in a club where we've got to a position where we can't field a full allocation of players. Many, many times this season, by half-time we'd be down to 15 players. It's been unprecedented in that respect.'

Willie Peters had been well-aware of the injury situation and discussions with the existing backroom staff had already taken place in terms of how to improve the situation for 2023. 'With injuries, there is an element of bad luck but it can't all be bad luck and we do need to look at the reasons behind them and improve the likelihood of less injuries.' Lakin said.

While winter would be a time where some Rovers supporters would be twiddling their thumbs in the absence of their team, it was a period in which many of the players would be recovering and refuelling.

On the field, the players rarely, if ever, disgraced themselves. The most concerning points, aside from the big drop-off towards the end of Tony Smith's tenure, was the defeats against the likes of Huddersfield, St Helens and Wigan. In particular, the losses to Huddersfield were the most disappointing. Ian Watson's side had unsuccessfully fought for a play-off spot in the previous season, with the Robins beating them to it. This time around, Huddersfield had beaten Rovers in all three of their competitive meetings. Not only that, but they looked far more convincing and launched themselves into third position come the season's end. Whereas against the top clubs, Rovers were outmatched at home against the full-strength sides of St Helens and Wigan. One of Peters' immediate tasks would be to bridge that gap.

As far as the existing squad went, Mikey Lewis continued on his path to playing maturity with a good season. It was becoming clear by the end of the campaign that he was well and truly a commodity that the club couldn't afford to lose; be it short, medium, or long-term. At 21 years of age, albeit with work still to do, his potential remained sky high.

George King had more than a few doubters when he switched from Belle Vue to Craven Park at the back end of 2020. In the end, he proved to be an instrumental signing and was associated with helping Rovers' pack become a more formidable unit than it had been in the previous years. An incredible 73-minute stint at Warrington amid Rovers' injury crisis was one of King's best contributions of the season and it was made more special by the fact that he had suffered a small tear to his hamstring less than a month beforehand. That kind of contribution isn't forgotten. In general, he was one of the side's strongest performers of the year and it was no surprise that he would end up picking up the club's Player of the Year award, even pipping Dream Team member Shaun Kenny-Dowall.

One of the few concerns that surrounded King was the enormous workload that he would go through over a season. While it aided the cause, sooner or later it would prove detrimental to his physical health. There was also a noticeable drop-off when he would depart the field, and the same happened during 2021 but hadn't been rectified. Simply put, Rovers needed to reduce his workload and secure a prop that would lead the pack in a similar vein. Willie Peters had already identified the need to do so, and more interestingly, he had talked up the incoming Jesse Sue as the man that would help King 'a lot'.

Under the reign of Tony Smith, the club had cast their scouting net into the Championship, drawing a number of handy players. Ethan Ryan, who had only played 11 games in two years prior to the season's start, had proven himself to be a Super League standard performer after relaunching his Rovers career in style during the Good Friday clash with Hull. He was also a blossoming fan favourite in part thanks to his uncanny ability to leap and catch contested balls on his way over the whitewash. His Spider-Man like grip was there to be seen in early 2021, when he produced a game-winning take to secure a vital win over Huddersfield. The leap and catch that he made in the late July comeback against Warrington was arguably the most memorable, however. The result itself was also one of the main highlights of a topsy-turvy year.

Frankie Halton was the latest addition to the successful bunch, with the club yielding an incredible return from their investment in terms of performances. Such was Halton's rise that just several months into his top-flight career, he had already been linked with big opportunities which came as no surprise to those watching him week in, week out.

He was one of the best finds of the year and had already signed an extension which kept him at Craven Park until 2025. The importance of tying down key talent was not lost on Lakin: 'I think it's really important that we do sign them up. This club hadn't been able to do it three or four years prior and even further back than that. It's been a clear goal of ours in the last couple of years. It's also important because they form the backbone of the squad going forwards, almost like a band of brothers growing up together,'

Lakin continued: 'You also have to strike the right balance between experience and youth, and always try to make sure whichever players coming in are better than the players going out. By and large, we've got it right more often than not and hopefully that will be the same for next year.'

Experience was a pertinent discussion when it came to the side, as was its overseas contingent. Albert Vete, Brad Takairangi and Korbin Sims had arrived with big reputations but failed to deliver over the course of their time at the club. In terms of performances, they varied from mediocre to outstanding; especially Vete, who showed the supporters what they had been anticipating since he joined, when he created a gigantic hole in the Hull FC players' defence and pride on the final game. Likewise, Sims had been one of Rovers' better players when reintroduced back into the side, but his chances were too limited beforehand which was incredulous given his overall status.

All three men simply hadn't made it to the field enough times to warrant an extension. Although the club's incoming overseas trio would have to perform well if the Robins were to push on, if they made it to the field most weeks, then that would be an improvement compared to Rovers' lack of return on the outgoing three.

Another aspect of Rovers' situation with their experienced group of players was some of the ages. At the start of 2023, Ryan Hall and Shaun Kenny-Dowall would both be 35 and Kane Linnett was turning

34. With those three names, you had the bulk of the core behind Rovers' improvements at the start of the decade. Sooner or later, their bodies would start to break down and they would need replacing. Therein lied one of the toughest decisions that the club would have to make from the point of view of replacing them. Aside from the excellent Matt Parcell and the new recruits, the overseas quota landscape would likely change in the next year or so.

Off the field, it was a mostly positive year. Right at the start, the Robins broke a new matchday sales record during their season opener against Wigan. Paul Lakin also mentioned that the club was enjoying stronger sponsorship income. The Boilermakers shirt, which proved lucky since Rovers won both of the games it was played in, became the club's fastest selling shirt in history. In general, the line-up of replica shirts proved to be collectively popular, since they became the biggest combined kit sales since the 2017 season.

Craven Streat, which had cost Rovers a hefty five-figure fee, continued to be a popular jaunt for fans of all ages. Its apex in 2022 came during the 15 April victory against Hull FC; it was busy even hours before kick-off and was the location for many celebrations come the game's end.

For all of the positives, the club still wasn't breaking even and that would remain one of the greatest challenges.

The attendances over the course of the season remained in the low 7,000s, which was a disappointment considering that Rovers had attracted bigger gates during the most recent non-COVID season – 2019 - as well as the fact they were seeking to redevelop the stadium which would likely include an extension to its capacity. It was easy to sympathise with the absent fans, however. Aside from the natural drop-off due not being as successful as the previous year, inflation continued to rise and was hurting attendances figures across the game. For many, their main priority was making ends meet in the face of soaring bills.

Still, Lakin didn't allow any of the setbacks on or off the field to lower his enthusiasm on the club's future: 'We've made a lot of progress but there's a long way to go and a lot more bigger things to happen, hopefully around the land development and infrastructure around the stadium. There's lots of plans and lots of opportunity. We've only just begun, really. On the pitch, we've achieved nothing yet but we're heading in the right direction. Off the field, there's lots of exciting projects that I see now and in the medium term, to grow the club and we fully intend to do so.'

For chief executives at any club, it always took many years to truly reshape an organisation from the point of view of overall infrastructure, and it would be no different for Lakin and Rovers. One noticeable difference between his new stint and what came before was that there was an increase in professionalism. Whether it be the players, or the ladies working at the stadium's bars, they were dressed with the club's new emblem present. Lakin explained the thought behind it: 'First impressions are important. We are all as one. No matter where you work or what your role is, we all represent the club and the crest. A more professional outlook was something that I was definitely looking for.'

Rovers had to look the part on the field as well as off it. In 2022, they fell short of the standards that they had previously set but it didn't deter Lakin: 'We had a coach parting that brought a lack of stability, then we had an injury crisis that I've never seen before. In that respect, I'm quite pleased with our finish. Under the surface, I think that we are progressing really strongly as a club. The building blocks are already in place for next year.'

Tony Smith was one of the focal points of 2022, for better or for worse. His name wasn't going away, either. In fact, things were set to become more interesting. Just days after the Robins' 36-4 defeat of Hull FC, the Black and Whites dispensed with the services of coach Brett Hodgson. Smith then crossed the city divide to take over the reins at Hull. He became the third coach in history to cross it; Johnny Whiteley did the same in 1970 but the other way round. Steve Crooks reached the end of his tether mid-way through 1997. He resigned from the club and joined Hull, staying there for over a decade which included two caretaker spells. By far the most memorable switch in colours was when Arthur Bunting, a long-serving player at Rovers as well as a former coach, joined Hull during the late '70s and transformed their fortunes, becoming a legend at the Boulevard.

Smith had been a divisive figure. Some fans immediately began to dislike him after the way Rovers' season capitulated under his watch, while others still respected the man that was one of the main driving forces behind the Robins' upturn in fortunes. Either way, he was now a sworn enemy. The historic rivalry between the Hull clubs was about to embrace a new chapter.

For some time, 2023 had been the focus of many after it became clear that the 2022 season would end with no play-off tie. There was no reason that the next season couldn't be a big improvement and a year in which Rovers could banish the disappointing aspects of 2022 deep into the annals of history.

Despite the new campaign being several months away, Paul Lakin was already looking forward to it: 'I'm excited. The next couple of months will be more about other areas of the club that we can work on. It's not a downtime period, in fact it's an extremely busy time now - especially when you aren't in the play-offs,'
He reflected on Rovers' ability to conduct their business early: 'I do feel that the early business we did in late spring will benefit us greatly going forwards because it's not a big pond that we fish in. There's not been too many names that have come up since we've made our signings that have made me think others would have been a possibility. Being able to recruit early is a definite advantage.'

Lakin also felt that the situation of the incoming head coach being based overseas prior to his arrival benefitted the recruitment cycle: 'Willie has been in Australia, day in, day out and knows all the players over there and had the ability of being able to convince the likes of Jesse, Tom and Rhys face-to-face.'
The domestic-based recruits didn't go unnoticed either: 'The likes of Louis Senior, James Batchelor and Yusuf Aydin. They're all of that age group that particularly appeals to us, young and hungry with a lot of potential to develop going forwards. They've all had good seasons. Particularly James, whose had a great season.'
The Robins' new additions had to come in and hit the ground running in order for the whole operation to continue to move forward. Although they appeared to be good additions on paper, nothing was ever set in stone, and the club knew that better than most.

Likewise, Willie Peters would need to enjoy a good first season in charge. He was coming into the club as a rookie, given that it was his first gig as a head coach. He already had a great knowledge base from working under the likes of Adam O'Brien, Trent Barrett, Wayne Bennett and others. Even though he had already mentioned that he wouldn't be rocking the boat, Rovers did need some changes, particularly in their defence which was something he was already aware of. Aside from the back end of his tenure, Smith was one of the few coaches throughout the Super League era that managed to improve the side's ability to defend. Peters needed to follow suit if he was to make a success of his time coaching in England. Rovers couldn't endure another season of being outside of the top-six if they were to continue their rise on the pitch and away from it.

When it was all said and done, 2023 was a story for another year. Rovers had genuine reasons to be optimistic both on and off the field, but that work was to be carried out in the future. For now, 2022 was a year of ups and downs; one that was filled with the ecstasy of courageous victories, upsetting defeats, unexpected controversies, a historic stadium purchase and everything in between. It was, most certainly, *a year of change…*

2022 Player Statistics

Name	Starts	Ints	Apps	Goals	D/goals	Tries	Points
Abdull, Jordan	12	1	13	13	0	2	34
Barley, Connor	1	2	3	0	0	1	4
Cavanaugh, Charlie	0	1	1	0	0	0	0
Coote, Lachlan	17	0	17	32	1	9	101
Crooks, Ben	15	1	16	0	0	4	16
Dagger, Will	12	1	13	9	1	0	19
Fishwick, Zach	1	6	7	0	0	1	4
Garratt, Tom	4	2	6	0	0	0	0
Hadley, Dean	14	1	15	0	0	0	0
Hall, Ryan	25	0	25	0	0	15	60
Halton, Frankie	19	2	21	0	0	4	16
Johnson, Luis	4	0	4	0	0	0	0
Keinhorst, Jimmy	13	13	26	0	0	3	12
Kenny-Dowall, Shaun	23	0	23	0	0	4	16
King, George	28	0	28	0	0	1	4
Laulu-Togaga'e, Phoenix	3	4	7	0	0	0	0
Lewis, Mikey	18	0	18	0	0	9	36
Linnett, Kane	15	0	15	0	0	4	16

DAN CROWTHER

Name	Starts	Ints	Apps	Goals	D/goals	Tries	Points
Litten, Jez	12	14	26	0	0	1	4
Maher, Will	5	11	16	0	0	0	0
Milnes, Rowan	20	1	21	15	0	3	42
Minchella, Elliot	25	2	27	0	0	5	20
Morore, Connor	0	3	3	0	0	0	0
Parcell, Matt	21	4	25	0	0	7	28
Richards, Greg	0	15	15	0	0	0	0
Royle, Sam	2	1	3	0	0	1	4
Ryan, Ethan	19	0	19	0	0	10	40
Sims, Korbin	7	11	18	0	0	1	4
Storton, Matty	16	9	25	0	0	5	20
Takairangi, Brad	5	0	5	0	0	2	8
Tate, Will	7	2	9	0	0	3	12
Vete, Albert	6	10	16	0	0	3	12
Wood, Sam	21	1	22	2	0	6	28

A YEAR OF CHANGE

Award Winners of 2022

Hull Kingston Rovers (Event held at the Hilton Hotel, 1 September)

Roger Millward Player of the Season: **George King**
RFS Player of the Year: **Shaun Kenny-Dowall**
INFOJAM Members' Player of the Season: **Jez Litten**
OXEN Sports Young Player of the Year: **Zach Fishwick**
Hull KR Foundation Women's Player of the Season: **Abbie Kudla**
DNS Academy Player of the Season: **Louix Gorman**
Green & Green Tackle of the Season: **Ethan Ryan** (vs. Leeds Rhinos, 29 April)
HireBase Try of the Season: **Lachlan Coote** (vs. Hull FC, 15 April)

Rovers Supporters Group (Event held at the Legends Bar, Craven Park, 8 August)

Colin McNicol RSG Player of the Year*: **Mikey Lewis**
hullkrfans.co.uk Player of the Year: **Matt Parcell**
Chris Fallowfield Award (Outstanding Contribution): **Pete Lancaster** and **Sue Thompson**
Trevor Bailey Young Player of the Year: **Mikey Lewis**
Funniest Teammate of the Year: **Will Maher**

*This award was voted for by RSG members and non-members

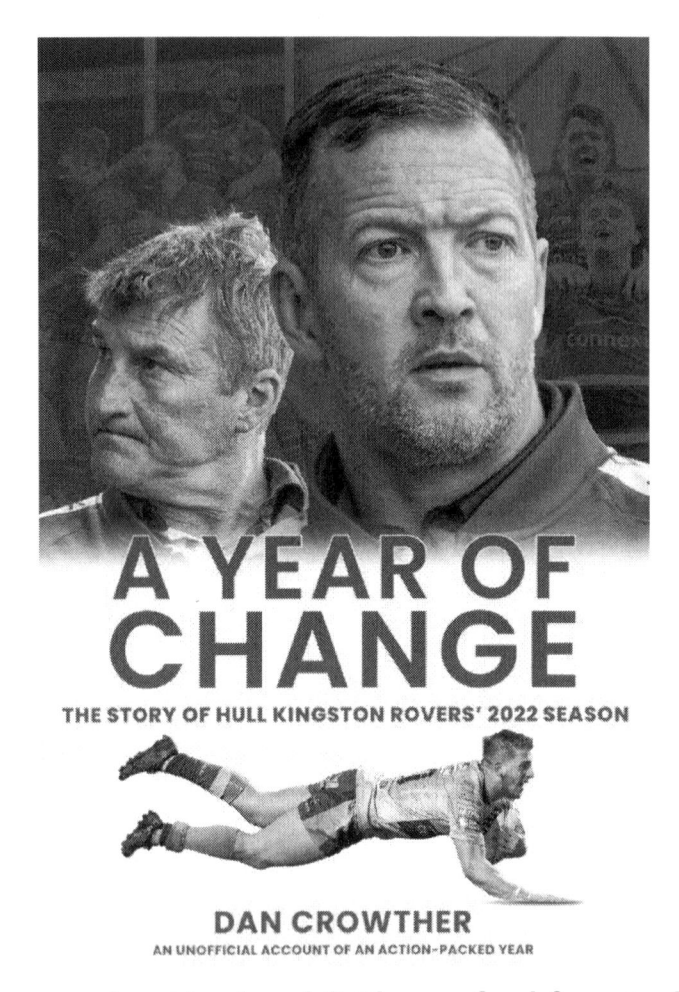

Did you enjoy the book? Please feel free to leave a review on Amazon. Every review helps.

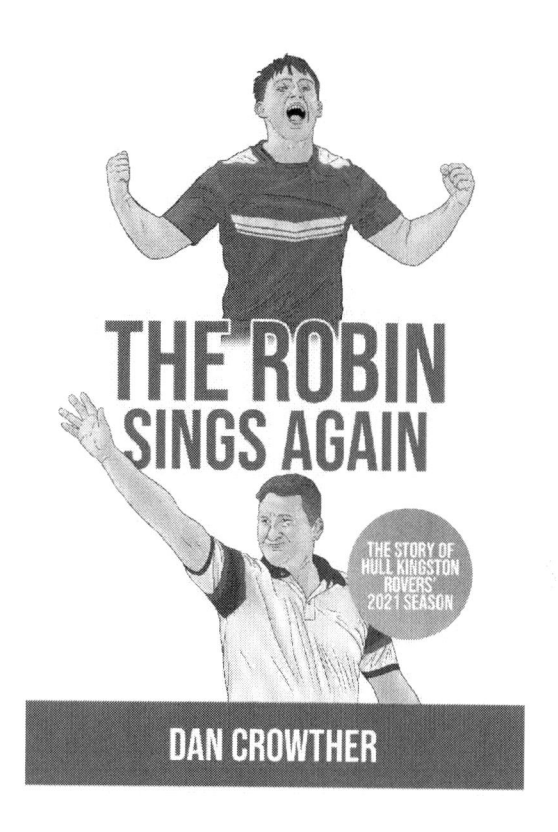

"Essential reading for everyone from the red side of Hull" – author and historian Professor Tony Collins

"A historical reference point for years to come", "A must buy for any Rovers fans", "Fantastic", "Great present", "Couldn't put it down!"

References

Pugh, R. (2016) The Robins: An Official History of Hull Kingston Rovers. Scratching Shed Publishing Ltd

Collins, T. (2020) An extract from 'Rugby League: A People's History': https://www.rugby-league.com/article/57046/womens-long-history-in-rugby-league

ABOUT THE AUTHOR
Dan Crowther

Born and raised in Hull, Dan Crowther was born into a family that had split loyalties between the two distinguished Hull clubs. Out of good judgment, or perhaps for his sins, he chose to follow the Robins.

He has always maintained a passion for sport and writing, which led to him penning his first book, *The Robin Sings Again*. In the past, his work has featured in fanzine and magazine publications.

Printed in Great Britain
by Amazon